OCS Study
MMS 2001-050

Coastal Marine Institute

Improved Geohazards and Benthic Habitat Evaluations: Digital Acoustic Data with Ground Truth Calibrations

Final Report

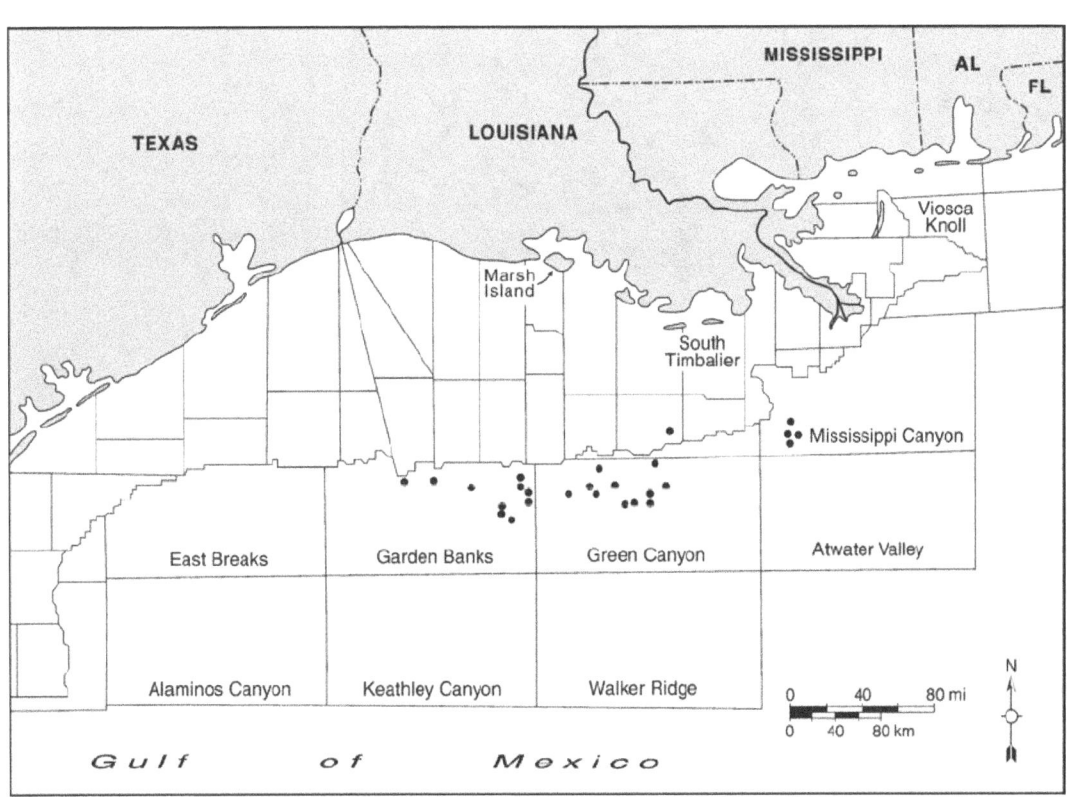

U.S. Department of the Interior
Minerals Management Service
Gulf of Mexico OCS Region

Cooperative Agreement
Coastal Marine Institute
Louisiana State University

OCS Study
MMS 2001-050

Coastal Marine Institute

Improved Geohazards and Benthic Habitat Evaluations: Digital Acoustic Data with Ground Truth Calibrations

Final Report

Author

Harry H. Roberts

July 2001

Prepared under MMS Contract
14-35-0001-30660-19910
by
Coastal Studies Institute
Louisiana State University
Baton Rouge, Louisiana 70801

Published by

U.S. Department of the Interior
Minerals Management Service
Gulf of Mexico OCS Region

Cooperative Agreement
Coastal Marine Institute
Louisiana State University

Disclaimer

This report was prepared under contract between the Minerals Management Service (MMS) and Coastal Studies Institute, Louisiana State University. This report has been technically reviewed by the MMS and approved for publication. Approval does not signify that the contents necessarily reflect the views and policies of the Service, nor does mention of trade names or commercial products constitute endorsement or recommendation for use. It is, however , exempt from review and compliance with MMS editorial standards.

Report Availability

Extra copies of the report may be obtained from the Public Information Office (Mail Stop 5034) at the following address:

U.S. Department of the Interior
Minerals Management Service
Gulf of Mexico OCS Region
Public Information Office (MS 5034)
1201 Elmwood Park Boulevard
New Orleans, Louisiana 70123-2394

Telephone Number: (504) 736-2519
or   1-800-200 GULF

Citation

Suggested citation:

Roberts, H.H. 2001. Improved geohazards and benthic habitat evaluations: digital acoustic data with ground truth calibrations. OCS Study MMS 2001-050. U.S. Dept. of the Interior, Minerals Mgmt. Service, Gulf of Mexico OCS Region, New Orleans, La. 116 pp + appendices.

iii

Preface

The Digital High Resolution Acoustic Data for Improved Benthic Habitat/Geohazards Evaluation study is focused on developing a better understanding of seafloor geology of the Gulf of Mexico continental slope in order to increase our predictability of geohazards and chemosynthetic communities, particularly in areas of hydrocarbon seepage-venting. Those are the areas that are commonly accompanied by acoustic wipe-out zones in high resolution acoustic data sets. This report is a summary of research sponsored by the U.S. Department of Interior Minerals Management Service (MMS), Gulf of Mexico Region OCS through the Coastal Marine Institute at Louisiana State University (Contract no. 30660/19910).

This study was conducted by the PI as both a field and a laboratory investigation. Field data sets consist of high resolution seismic profiles and side-scan sonar data collected by instrumentation assembled by the Marine Geology subprogram at Coastal Studies Institute at Louisiana State University with technical support from the Coastal Studies Institute Field Support Group. Supporting high resolution acoustic data sets and 3D-seismic profiles and surface amplitude extraction data have been contributed by numerous major companies in the petroleum industry. In addition, very important seafloor verification data acquired by a manned submersible have been primarily supported by NOAA's National Underseas Research Center at the University of North Carolina (Wilmington), as well as dives supported by the Louisiana Quality Education Fund (LEQSF). This combined research has led to talks at regional, national, and international professional meetings and peer-reviewed scientific publications (listed separately in the Technical Summary accompanying this report). This report describes the rationale for the study, techniques applied, data sources, results of two successful field data collection cruises, sites analyzed and used in the evaluation, data gaps, results, interpretation, and recommendations.

The study was undertaken with the intent of producing a practical guide for interpreting geohazards, particularly those associated with hydrocarbon seepage and venting, and the presence or absence of associated chemosynthetic communities. In the course of conducting this investigation, fundamental knowledge about the linkage between slope geology, seepage rate, and biologic response has emerged. This new appraisal of the impacts of hydrocarbon seepage and venting on slope geology and biology is discussed in the summary sections of this report. In addition, the strong influence of high quality 3D-seismic data on geohazards evaluations is discussed along with the variability of seafloor types that produce a common response as acoustic wipe-out zones on high resolution seismic profiles. Interpretation criteria are still evolving, but the most rigorous interpretation scheme is available in this final report.

In keeping with MMS guidelines, this report has been written for an audience of knowledgeable lay-people. The report is accompanied by an extensive list of scientific publications that can function as sources for specific scientific information and a glossary of terms used in geohazards and hydrocarbon seep/vent research.

Acknowledgments

This research would not have been possible without the cooperative input of ideas and data from many petroleum companies working on the Gulf of Mexico continental slope. These companies willingly shared high resolution acoustic data taken in support of geohazard surveys and engineering projects. In addition, many companies shared 3D-seismic surface attribute data for specific sites being addressed by this investigation sponsored by the Minerals Management Service through a Cooperative Agreement (Contract No. 14-35-0001-30660) with the Coastal Marine Institute at Louisiana State University. Companies that deserve special recognition for their help in this study are Amerada Hess, BHP, BP, Chevron, Conoco, Mobil, Shell,and Texaco. Personnel in these companies who have helped the author assemble data for the examples included in this study, and also for areas not used, are too numerous to list. The author wishes to thank these people for their helpful cooperation. In addition, it is important to call attention to other funded research projects that produced data directly used in this study. The Louisiana Education Quality Support Fund (Contact No. LEQSF 1994-1997- RD-B-12) provided six days of submersible dive time on sites used in this MMS-CMI study. These direct observations have been valuable "calibration points" for linking acoustic data to real seafloor conditions. Regarding the seafloor verification part of the study, the author is especially appreciative of the valuable submersible funding that has been supplied by the NOAA National Underseas Research Center, University of North Carolina at Wilmington (Grants NA 80AA-8-00081, NA88 AA-D-UR004 and NA36 RU0060). The submersible work and the support ship of Harbor Branch Oceanographic Institution are acknowledged for their excellent cooperation in meeting the objectives of our dive programs. Finally, the author would like to thank his scientific colleagues both at Louisiana State University and Texas A&M University for the exchange of ideas and scientific products relating to hydrocarbon seep research.

Table of Contents

List of Figures

List of Tables

I. Introduction

Oil and gas exploration and production in deep water (beyond the shelf break) of the northern and northwestern Gulf of Mexico are currently being carried out on a much greater scale than in any equivalent setting in today's oceans. New evaluation techniques based on improved acquisition and processing of 3D-seismic data suggest that 2.33 billion barrels of liquid hydrocarbons and about 27.5 trillion cubic feet of gas exist in "proved reserves" in 754 active fields in the Gulf of Mexico OCS region. Within the U.S. Exclusive Economic Zone these resources from the Gulf of Mexico are by far the most important from a strategic and economic point of view. With growing world populations that need hydrocarbons and the potential for political instability in the Middle East and other important oil-producing areas, it is in the best interest of the United States to reduce dependency on foreign oil reserves by developing our own resources. The most promising hydrocarbon frontier in America is off Louisiana and Texas in water depths ranging from 300-2500 m.

Renewed interest in deep water exploration in the Gulf of Mexico has stimulated economic growth in oil-related industries and presented scientists and engineers with a new set of challenges uniquely associated with little known areas of the deep slope environment. In 1996 an exploratory well was drilled on top of a mammoth structural feature at the base of the slope in over 2500 m of water (Alaminos Canyon). At the time, this drilling project represented a glimpse of the future for the Gulf's northern continental slope. The 1995 Minerals Management Service offshore lease sale (OCS Sale 161) resulted in leasing over 3 million acres to 62 different companies. Follow-up drilling of prospects acquired during this sale has led to to significant discoveries in the deep-water province of the Gulf of Mexico. In July of 1999 BP Amoco announced four major oil discoveries, including the largest made to date by any company. The largest of these discoveries is the "Crazy House" prospect, located in a water depth of 1830 m in Mississippi Canyon Blocks 776,777, and 778. This field alone is estimated to contain over a billion barrels of recoverable oil. The other three discoveries range in depth from 1220 m to 1980 m. For BP Amoco these three discoveries add about 600 million barrels of recoverable oil to their reserves in the southern Green Canyon area. The total Gulf of Mexico reserves for BP Amoco alone is about 3 billion barrels. Although there are many technological challenges associated with working in ultra deep water of the Gulf, most major petroleum companies are actively exploring these areas.

Hydrocarbon exploration and production activities are taking place in a dynamic and complex geologic framework for the northern Gulf of Mexico continental slope, which is inherited from the interplay of massive sediment input since Cretaceous times and the compensating movement of allochthonous Jurassic salt. The end product is perhaps the most geologically and ecologically complex continental slope setting in today's oceans (Figure 1). Therefore, it becomes important for basic science, applied science, and regulatory reasons to develop a better understanding of slope processes and seabed characteristics in this province where "ground truth" data are scattered and have been collected primarily for site-specific reasons.

1

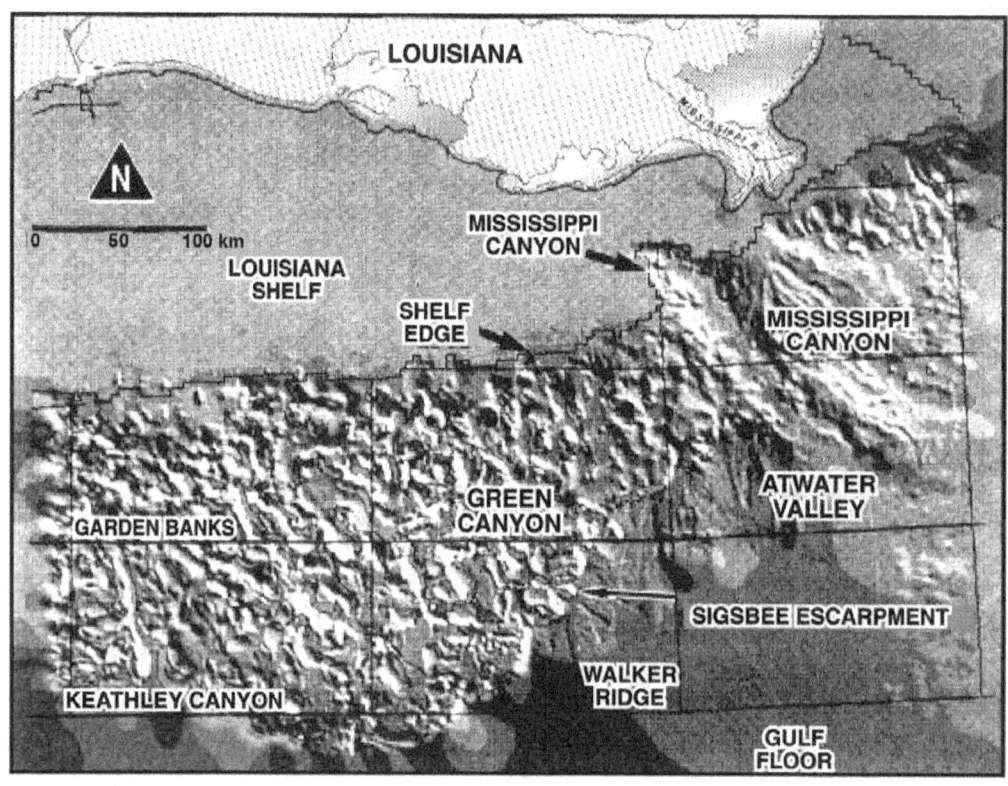

Figure 1. Complexity of the Louisiana-Texas continental slope are revealed in high resolution and computer enhanced Seabeam bathymetry. The dome and basin topography is related to the interplay between the input of massive volumes of sediment and the deformationof underlying salt.

The petroleum industry and the Minerals Management Service (MMS) are both mandated to understand the physical-biological-geological complexities of the outer continental shelf and upper continental slope region (OCS) of the northern Gulf of Mexico because of the combined demands for resource utilization and management. Within simple geologic frameworks the tasks of both resource extraction-utilization and rational environmental management of these efforts are reasonably well understood. However, in extremely complex settings like the northern Gulf of Mexico OCS, MMS must anticipate environmental management problems in a geographic region that has received minimal financial support to determine physical-biological-geological characteristics and spatial-temporal variability of these properties. With continuing interest in oil and gas exploration in deeper and deeper areas beyond the continental shelf edge, industry has met the challenge with innovative engineering concepts and designs for drilling, production facilities, and resource transport systems. In order to effectively manage OCS activities, MMS must incorporate the best possible information from industry and academia to develop new concepts and technologies for environmental assessment. It is in this spirit that this study was undertaken in order to provide criteria and concepts for improved interpretation of sea floor geology and habitats of sensitive benthic communities.

The intent of this program is to use both digital and analog high resolution acoustic data sets (geohazards data) as the primary data sources with digital 3D-seismic surface attribute data as an added source of interpretive information and direct observation-sampling by research submersible for sea floor verification. As this program has progressed, it has become absolutely clear that the sea floor verification step is necessary on multiple examples within each feature category before reliable interpretation criteria can be developed. In addition, sea floor attribute mapping (Hill 1996; Roberts et al. 1996) from 3D-seismic data has added a new dimension which provides a means of mapping gas in surface sediments and the presence of hard mineralized bottoms. Combined with high resolution acoustic data sets and sea floor verification data, the surficial information provided by 3D-seismic makes a powerful combination for interpreting sea floor geology and thereby benthic habitats.

Operational, engineering, and regulatory guidelines require industry to evaluate potential drilling areas, platform sites, and pipeline routes for the purpose of both identifying potential geohazards and the presence of federally protected biologic communities (particularly chemosynthetic communities). On the regulatory side, MMS strives to formulate environmental management guidelines in the general framework of rapidly expanding resource development. Both industry and MMS need the best available data sets to meet their objectives. Our understanding of the sea floor at continental slope depths in the Gulf of Mexico is based primarily on scattered site-specific data sets acquired with a variety of instrumentation types. Many sea floor features such as faults and submarine landslides plus other forms of mass movement are relatively easy to identify even on mediocre acoustic data sets. There are however, many sea floor features that morphologically range from mounds to depressions that represent themselves on high resolution seismic profiles as acoustic wipe-out zones or zones of no organized subsurface reflection horizons. These features present a particularly difficult problem for those tasked with interpreting sea floor geology from remotely sensed high and medium resolution acoustic data. Most interpreters consider acoustic wipe-out zones to be the product of bubble phase gas in surface and shallow subsurface sediments (Bryant 1981; Hovland and Judd 1988). Previous studies, which have incorporated ground-truth verification of zones of no acoustic return through cores and direct observations using an ROV or manned submersible, demonstrate that acoustic wipe-out zones can be associated with many different types of features and sea floor types. They range from mud volcanoes (Neurauter and Bryant 1990; Neurauter and Roberts 1994) to mud mounds containing gas hydrates (Brooks et al. 1985) to areas of lithified sea floor (Roberts and Aharon 1994) and extinct expulsion sites (Roberts et al 1998). Through manned submersible inspection of these sea floor types and features which have acoustically turbid interiors, it has been determined that most of them are the products of fluid and gas expulsion. Liquid and gaseous hydrocarbons are commonly found associated with acoustic wipe-out zones, and the presence of chemosynthetic organisms is common but not absolute. So, the challenge becomes one of definitive identification of various types of sea floor features that have a common general response on high resolution seismic data sets. Therefore, the overall objective of this study is to apply state-of-the-art digital acoustic data, both high resolution seismic and lower resolution, but deeper penetrating 3D-seismic as well as side-scan sonar data, for developing a conceptual framework and reliable criteria for identification of sea floor features and areas that are the products of hydrocarbon venting-seepage. Within this overall aim of the study a parallel purpose is to better understand how to interpret the presence or absence of chemosynthetic communities from standard high resolution acoustic data collected for geohazards evaluation and 3D-seismic surface amplitude data. The establishment of reliable interpretation criteria coupled to digitally acquired data has the potential to greatly increase the reliability of geohazards evaluations suitable for compliance with MMS regulations for chemosynthetic communities without the added expense of bottom video and/or photographic survey.

This study differs from other attempts to classify sea floor types in the northern-northwestern Gulf of Mexico (e.g. McDonald et al. 1996) in that four separate data sources are focused on identification of a spectrum of different feature types that possess the common acoustic response that has been linked to hydrocarbon seepage venting and presence of chemosynthetic communities, acoustic wipe-out zones. The data sources are: (1) standard high resolution geohazards acoustic data sets (surface tow and deep tow), (2) project-acquired surface-tow high resolution acoustic data, (3) 3D-seismic surface amplitude extraction data, and (4) sea floor verification of sites using a manned submersible. Concurrent research projects sponsored by NOAA, the petroleum industry, and Louisiana Quality Education Fund have provided data sets necessary to make a regional comparison of areas displaying acoustic wipe-out characteristics. The variability of acoustic response within and between areas provides the key information on which a meaningful conceptual framework and interpretation criteria can be formulated. Systematic analysis of this variability in acoustic response as correlated to real characteristics of the sea floor makes this investigation different from previous research.

The hypothesis to be tested by this study is: Systematic analysis of digital high resolution acoustic data and 3D-seismic coupled with sea floor verification provided by manned submersible observations over a wide variety of sea floor features exhibiting acoustic wipe-outs will produce a set of interpretation criteria that will significantly improve our ability to predict the character of the modern OCS sea floor and the occurrence of chemosynthetic communities. The presence or absence of chemosynthetic communities is directly dependent on delivery of hydrocarbons to the sea floor. This delivery system is a product of the continental slope's geologic framework. Therefore, understanding the geology of hydrocarbon seep-venting sites is viewed in this study as fundamental to being able to predict general sea floor geologic and biologic responses.

A. Geologic Framework

In order to understand the geologic framework and stratigraphic architecture of the northern Gulf continental slope, an appreciation of the evolution of allochthonous salt, associated faults, and intraslope sedimentary basins is essential. Seismic profiles and well data (various types of well logs and associated micropaleontological data) provide the main elements for evaluating the evolving depositional environments, sedimentary facies, and salt characteristics. Some authors have produced sequential structural restorations from these types of data sets (Worrall and Snelson 1989; Diegel et al. 1995; Peel et al. 1995; Rowan 1995; and McBride 1995). Such reconstructions help explain the evolution of salt structures coincident with sedimentation. This new understanding of the dynamic changes that have taken place through time to give us the present slope configuration is possible because of improved seismic imaging technology (Ratcliff 1993), better physical modeling of salt-sediment systems (Vendeville and Jackson 1992), and the application of sequential restorations (McBride 1996). Such innovative new work on the slope has shown us that tabular allochthonous salt sheets and nappes are not new to the slope, but have occurred previously and have undergone various stages of deformation and evacuation (Diegel and Cook 1990). The emplacement and eventual evacuation of allochthonous salt appears to vary spatially and temporally throughout the northern Gulf of Mexico basin. No single model for salt movement can explain the array of salt geometries presently imaged in the subsurface. However, it is clear that original salt geometries and the manner in which they interact dictate the positions of later minibasins, remnant salt diapirs, extensional growth faults, contractional structures, and strike-slip deformation (McBride 1996). In addition, it is clear that this framework provided by salt deformation and sediment loading is the template for understanding the complexities of the modern sea floor.

Salt deformation and ultimately slope configuration is largely linked to the ways sediments are input to deep water. As is now widely recognized by the geologic community, sediment input to the outer shelf and continental slope is strongly modulated by sea level changes (Suter and Berryhill 1985). During periods of sea level lows, fluvial systems entrench themselves as they prograded across the shelf to eventually deposit their sediments in thick and discrete shelf-edge deltas (Suter and Berryhill 1985; Roberts et al. 1991; Sydow and Roberts 1994; Anderson et al. 1996). In addition, these rapidly deposited deltas load the shelf margin, an inherently unstable area, frequently causing shelf-edge failures that contributed large volumes of sediment to downslope depositional sites (Coleman et al. 1983). The interplay between intense periods of sedimentation, largely at low sea levels, and compensating salt tectonics has resulted in a present-day slope configuration that is characterized regionally by numerous domes and basins (Martin 1980) as can be seen in Figure 1. As a product of the processes outlined above, the interdome basins are filled with thick sedimentary sequences composed of sand-rich slope fans and turbidities as well as thick clay-rich units. Because of sea level forcing of fluvial-deltaic sediment input to the continental slope, during periods of high sea level, fine-grained hemipelagic sediments with a high pelagic foraminiferal content drape the slope topography, except on topographic highs in outer shelf and upper slope settings, where physical processes may remove much or all of this deposit. These sediments vary in thickness but are typically 3-5 m thick on the mid-to upper-slope.

B. Seafloor Geology

Faulting is a process that occurs on many scales within the continental slope setting, from major growth faults that cut thousands of meters of sedimentary section to much smaller compensating faults related primarily to salt movement in the shallow subsurface. In addition to off-setting the sea floor and creating local topography with oversteepened slopes that lead to various forms of mass movement, faults are responsible for numerous constructional sea floor features related to the vertical flux of fluids and gases and expulsion of these products at the ocean bottom. At one end of the feature spectrum are large mud volcanoes (Neurauter and Bryant, 1990; Neurauter and Roberts, 1994) formed by fine-grained sediment forced up faults. Hedberg (1974) identifies the process of sediment flux by gas-filled formation fluids up faults as being responsible for creating mud diapirs as well as mud volcanoes. At the other end of the spectrum, vertical flux of gases and fluids may be very slow. Microbial degradation of both hydrocarbon gases and crude oil associated with this process can catalyze by-products such as calcium-magnesium carbonates that create a variety of sea floor features including hard grounds and mound-like structures of various dimensions (Roberts et al 1992 a,b). This process has been described from other settings, such as accretionary prisms, where salt tectonics is not a factor and only biogenic methane is the hydrocarbon source (Ritger et al., 1987; Paull et al., 1992). The following discussion highlights important small-to-mesoscale features on Louisiana's continental slope that make the surficial geology of this province very complex.

1. Dome-Top Mounds

Common features on the sea floor over shallow subsurface salt diapirs are carbonate mounds having various dimensions and frequencies of occurrence. Although almost every upper slope diapir crest thus far investigated in this study has carbonate mounds of some description, one of the best examples of a wide-spread mound complex occurs in the Green Canyon Area, Block 140. Each one of these mounds is the site of slow seepage of both hydrocarbon gases and crude oil. The mounds have developed from deposition of both calcium- and magnesium-rich carbonates, a by-product of microbial activity at the seep sites. Carbonates derived from this process have been described in detail from other localities by Ritger et al. (1987) and Paull et al. (1992). This process produces carbonate that is ^{13}C depleted and at this site δ^{13}C values of -48 to -55 are common. Most samples analyzed thus far have been composed of Mg-calcite, although dolomite comprises up to 40% of some samples (Roberts et al. 1992b). The average relief of these mounds (Figure 2) is about 10 m with some greater than 20 m. Details of the mound-forming process are currently being interpreted from submersible-derived data sets. At this location, the mounds have developed during several late Pleistocene cycles of sea level change (Roberts and Aharon 1994) and display coarse sediment lags which seem to be evidence of considerable dome-top erosion. On surface amplitude data derived from 3D seismic (Roberts et al. 1992a), this site displays a "bright" high amplitude response related to a hard, reflective bottom, but no indication of gas in near surface sediments. This response is consistent with a reflective, irregular, carbonate interface where seepage is a very slow process. On the upper slope near the shelf edge, seep-related mounds with similar amplitude signatures are veneered with biogenic carbonates developed primarily during periods of Late Pleistocene lowered sea level when the photic zone coincided with mound depths.

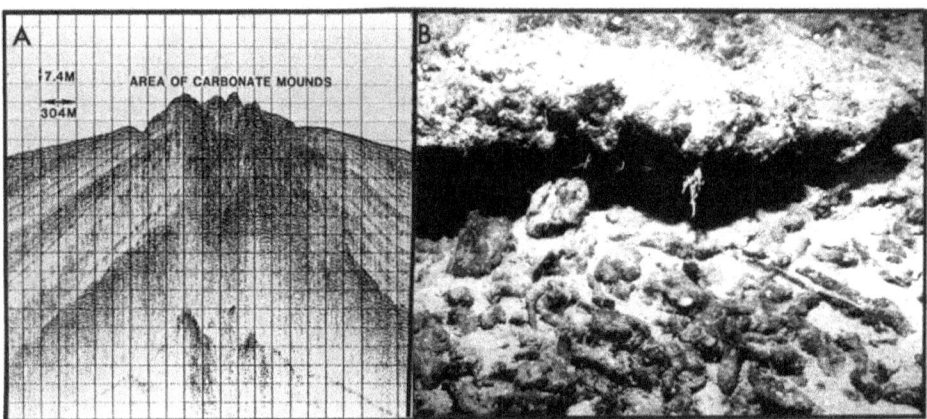

Figure 2. (a) High resolution sparker profile across a dome top illustrating the mounded seafloor, acoustic wipe-out zones beneath these mounds, and truncated bedding on the dome flanks. (b) Large clasts of authigenic carbonate are common constituents of the sediments on the dome top and around the mounded carbonates.

2. Dome-Top Erosional Features

Studies of currents active on the upper continental slope (e.g. Hamilton, 1990) indicate that intrusions of the Loop Current and its westward-moving eddies have associated currents at upper slope depths sufficient to transport sand-sized sediments. Regional relief features, specifically dome tops, represent zones where much of this energy is naturally focused. Certainly, the coarse sediment lags, as described above in associations with carbonate mounds, and the commonly occurring truncated beds associated with the dome-top settings reflect the existence of persistent and on-going erosive forces. In isolated cases, coarse sediments, largely composed of biogenic grains (shell hash) and nodules/clasts of diagenetic origin, are organized into migratory bed forms (Roberts 1995). This association is direct evidence of strong bottom currents on the upper slope and helps explain truncation of bedding and missing sedimentary sections associated with the sea floor over salt structures.

3. Gas Hydrate Outcrops and Associated Mounds

Because of the strong fault-related vertical flux of both gas and water to the sea floor, as described above, gas hydrates are able to exist at or near the sea floor in water depths greater than about 500 m (Figure 3). Gas hydrates are ice-like substances composed of rigid cages of water molecules that enclose molecules of hydrocarbon gases, primarily methane.

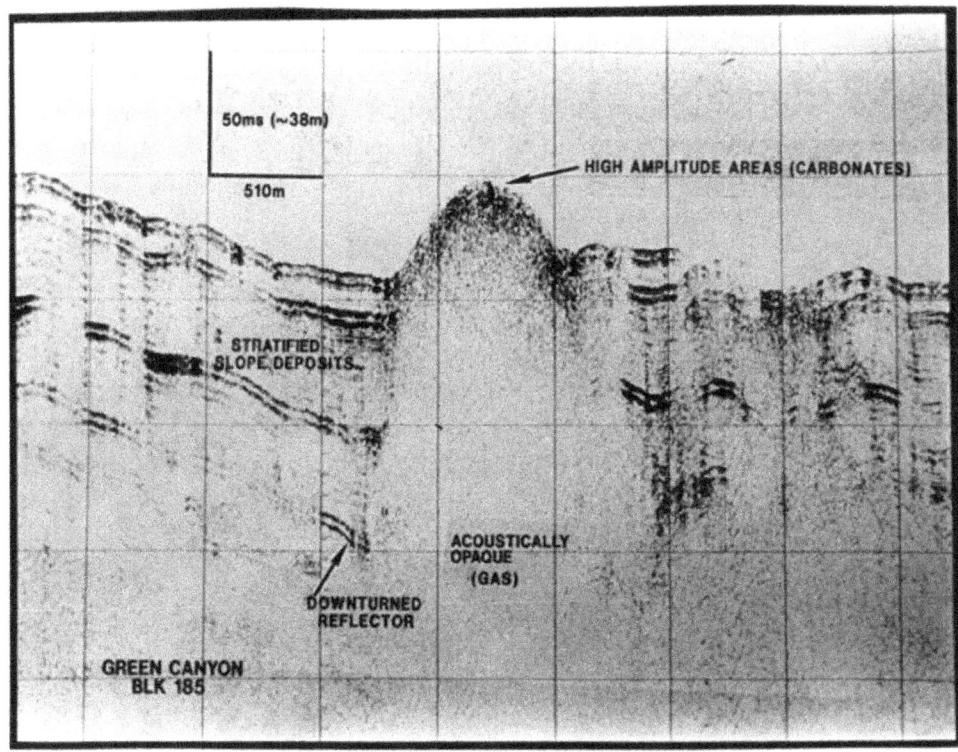

Figure 3. A high resolution seismic profile (15-in³ water gun) across a known gas hydrate complex in Green Canyon Block 185. Note the acoustic turbidity or acoustic wipe-out zone associated with the feature and its mound-like shape.

They occur under special conditions of temperature and pressure where the supply of hydrocarbon gas is sufficient to stabilize the molecular architecture of the hydrate. Abundant deep-seated hydrocarbons, numerous and complex fault systems that function as transport pathways, nearly continuous fault adjustments related to salt tectonics, and a myriad of surface hydrocarbon seeps, makes the Louisiana continental slope an ideal setting for hydrate accumulation. Recently, they have been observed as "outcrops" on the sea floor by the author and others (McDonald et al. 1994). In most cases, however, hydrates occur below the surface with an overlying and insulating layer of fine-grained sediment. Collectively, the process of vertical flux of water and gas up faults results in mound-like accumulations. These features characteristically display acoustic "wipe out" zones beneath their surfaces on high resolution seismic profiles. In addition to affecting local topography/geology, gas hydrates associated with larger mound-like buildups function as a rather constant trophic resource for chemosynthetic communities. Also, as interpreted from piston cores and direct submersible sampling, they are intermeshed with authigenic carbonates. These carbonates frequently take the form of small nodular masses to ledge-like outcrops. Both types are usually very ^{13}C-depleted, but may have varied carbonate mineralogies.

4. Mud Vents and Mud Volcanoes

When the transport of fluids, gases, and fine-grained sediment up-fault planes is rapid, cone-shaped accumulations of mud often develop. As Neurauter and Bryant (1990) and Kohl and Roberts (1995) point out in studies on the northern Gulf of Mexico continental slope, these features are not only common in this setting, but they have been described from many submarine environments throughout the world oceans (Hovland and Judd, 1988). From submersible observations, Neurauter and Roberts (1992) noted that active mud volcanoes have caldera-like depressions that contain fluid mud bubbling with gas that is frequently mixed with globules of crude oil. As the pool of fluid mud upwells over the lip of the crater, sheets of sediment-rich fluid flow down slope, add a new accretion unit to the cone's flank, and extend the diameter of the mud volcano's base. Features of this description occur on a variety of scales from small cones less than 1 m (Figure 4a) diameter to large features with over 30 m relief and bases of over 1 km in width (Figure 4b). Kohl and Roberts (1994) demonstrate that the process of fluid mud extrusion results in displaced microfaunas and inversion of biostratigraphic marker horizons in slope sediments. For example, they show that surface sediments at four vent sites contained microfossils yielding age dates of Pleistocene to early Miocene. In some cases, fluid mud extrusion takes place without the formation of a cone-shaped vent. For example, small-scale sheets of mud are extruded on the surfaces of gas hydrate mounds, perhaps an expulsion product during the hydrate-forming process. In other cases, thick sheets of mud flow kilometers down slope from extrusion sites such as those in the Garden Banks, Block 338 area, a case study discussed later in this report.

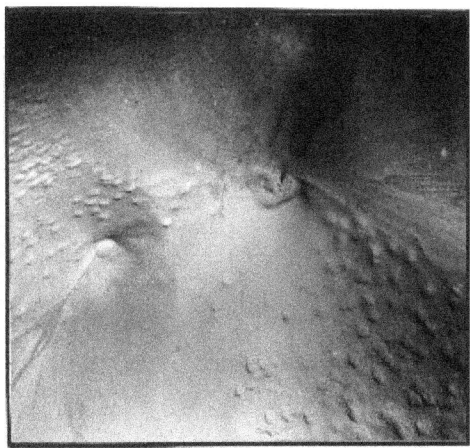
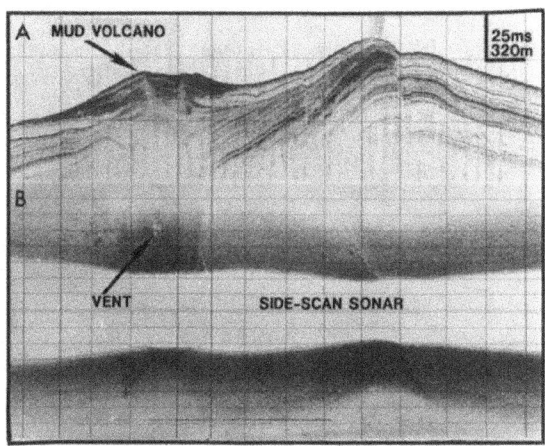

a   b

Figure 4. (a) A small mud volcano from Green Canyon Block 272 shows all the features typical of larger forms that reach heights of over 30 m above the surrounding seafloor. The field of view in this photograph has a width of approximately 5 m. Note the gas-induced micro-pockmarks around the mud volcanoes. (b) This high resolution seismic profile of a mud volcano with two distinct vents is located in Green Canyon Block 97. Note the stratified units that form the core flank and the concentric form on the underlying side-scan sonar record.

5. Slope Instability Features

Rapid deposition of sediment at the shelf edge, faulting, and vertical migration of shallow salt create instabilities primarily by over-steepening of slopes. A wide range of failure features results, from massive shelf edge evacuation features (Winker and Edwards 1983) to small-scale slumps along fault faces and on the sides of diapirs (Figure 5). Depending on scale, massive volumes of sediment can be transported downslope in association with subaqueous mass movement processes (Coleman et al. 1986). These processes currently pose a considerable risk to man's activities on the northern Gulf's continental slope. Even thin deposits of hemipelagic highstand sediments that drape topography of the slope display a tendency to fail (Doyle et al. 1992). Sediments displaced by slumps, submarine landslides, and other mass movement processes tend to have chaotic-to-acoustically opaque internal reflectors on high resolution seismic data and commonly produce small-scale irregular surface topography. Some intraslope basins contain fill-sequences of repeated and stacked chaotic units that are interpreted as the products of massive failures. These deposits likely originated at or near the shelf edge during periods of lowered sea level and failed during the sediment loading process. Vertical movement of salt is also very important in creating oversteepened slopes that lead to slope failures. The rugged surfaces of these deposits and chaotic internal reflectors mimic similar slumped units currently found at the sea floor in many places on the present continental slope.

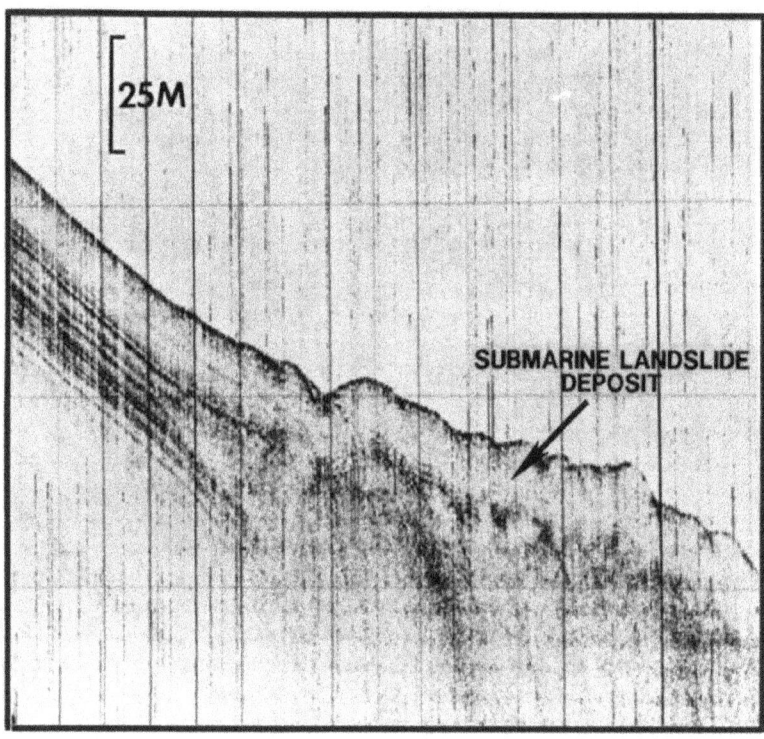

Figure 5. This picture shows submarine slump deposits that have originated from the flank of an adjacent salt diapir in East Breaks Area, Block 211. Note the acoustically opaque nature of the displaced material and the irregular surface profile evident on this 3.5 kHz record.

C. Data Base

Our present understanding of the surficial geology of the Gulf's northern continental slope has resulted primarily from the interpretation of geohazards data sets acquired in support of petroleum company activities. Early data sets consisted of high resolution seismic profiles from a variety of acoustic sources (sparkers, minisleeve exploders, small air guns, etc.) deployed in surface tow mode. These initial data sets were also collected as analog records which meant that the operator played a large part in record quality and there was no chance of post data collection processing. In addition to seismic and echo sounder profiles, most geohazards surveys had side-scan sonar data, also initially in analog format. After the mid-1980s most side-scan data were digital and corrected for slant range and boat speed. From these data sets it was discovered that the sea floor at slope depths in the Gulf was covered with mounds, pinnacles, depressions, and other sea floor features of unknown origin. Many of these features were accompanied by zones of "acoustic wipeout" or "acoustic turbidity" where no internal reflection events were visible beneath the surface reflector on high resolution seismic records. Reflective gas plumes in the overlying water column were also found to be common to some of these areas. As interest in deeper and deeper parts of the slope increased as the search for hydrocarbons moved toward the middle and lower slope, deep-tow instrumentation was developed to compensate for the lack of resolution of data collected in surface-tow mode. Deep-tow data collection systems became

10

generally available in the mid-to-late 1980s, but are still not universally used for geohazards surveys primarily because of cost. These systems typically contain a conventional 100 kHz side-scan sonar and 3.5 kHz sub-bottom profiler. They produce excellent data collected at a constant height above the bottom. Now, autonomous underwater data collection vehicles (AUVs) are replacing the deep-tow system.

In most geohazards surveys, if ground truth is provided it is by piston or gravity cores. However, since the mid-1980s a variety of research submersibles have been used to improve the "calibration" between acoustic data and actual conditions at the sea floor (Kennicutt et al. 1985; Roberts et al. 1989; Doyle et al. 1992; McDonald et al. 1994; Roberts and Aharon 1994).

This project has utilized geohazards data sets collected for the petroleum industry of many different vintages and acquisition modes (Appendix A). In addition, high resolution acoustic data, primarily seismic profiles with some supporting side-scan data have been collected for this project using state-of-the-art seismic sources and digital acquisition and processing software (DELPH 2). The seismic sources include a Geopulse Boomer, Seismic Systems S-15 (15 in^3) water gun, and a Seismic Systems GI (50 in^3) air gun. The water gun and air gun are supported by a Hamworthy 50 cfm seismic compressor (see Appendix 2 for equipment details). The advantage of collecting seismic data in a digital format for the project is that data processing can be accomplished both during and after acquisition. This option, not available with analog data, provides a method for improving image quality in a post-cruise laboratory setting through applying deconvolution, stacking, a swell filter, and other routines.

A relatively new and important source of data for application to practical engineering problems on the slope sea floor as well as for meeting regulatory requirements is 3D-seismic data. This new trend of utilizing 3D-data for engineering and regulatory applications is being driven by the widespread coverage of the continental slope as a product of industry's accelerated pace for development of deepwater exploration and production projects. Although resolution at the sea floor and in the shallow subsurface is not equivalent to high resolution seismic used for standard geohazards surveys, there are some clear advantages. For example, 3D-data once loaded on a workstation, provide a rapid and accurate method for linking subsurface geology to sea floor configuration. In addition, the mapping of surface attribute data in conjunction with phase data can quickly identify areas with hard, reflective surfaces from those where surface and near-surface sediments are charged with gas. The main limitation of 3D-data is reduced definition when compared to good quality high resolution geohazards survey data. Utilization of 3D-seismic data on this project, specifically surface amplitude maps, has provided a separate and important line of evidence for making the best possible interpretation of sea floor geology and, indirectly, biology.

Perhaps the most important data for this project have been the sea floor observations made from research submersibles. These data in conjunction with results of analyses on samples collected have been used to calibrate remotely sensed acoustic data to real world surficial conditions on the continental slope. The PI as well as colleagues from other institutions have been collecting data (personal observations, video, 35mm photos, cores, and grab samples) for over a decade in an effort to develop a better understanding of surficial geology and biology of the continental slope, particularly in conjunction with those features linked to hydrocarbon seepage or venting. The Johnson Sea-Link from Harbor Branch Oceanographic Institute in Fort Pierce, Florida has been the vehicle of choice and the one most used. This vehicle is limited to a diving depth of 1000 m. Therefore, all examples selected for presentation in this report occur in water depths shallower than 1000 m.

In order to build the best possible understanding of sea floor features that display acoustic wipeout zones on high resolution seismic records and may or may not have associated chemosynthetic communities, four quite different data sets were utilized: (1) standard high resolution geohazards data (surface-tow and/or deep-tow), (2) digital acoustic data (acquired as part of this project) showing the same feature in different perspectives, (3) 3D-surface attribute data, and (4) direct observation or sea floor verification using a research submersible. Sites for study were selected only if these four data sets were available or could be made available within the time-frame of the study. All data sets reviewed for the study are listed in Appendix 1. Sites identified for study are listed in Table 1 and Figure 6. Survey tracks over critical features indicating data collected by the PI in support of this project are given in Appendix B.

Table 1. Sites and features that were the focal point for data collection in support of this study.

Area and Block	Feature	Area and Block	Feature
Ship Shoal 286	Mud Mound	Garden Banks 189	Diapiric Mound
Green Canyon 18	Large Buildup	Garden Banks 201	Mounded Seafloor
Green Canyon 53	Mud Volcano	Garden Banks 215	Gas-prone
Green Canyon 53	Collapse Depression	Garden Banks 260	Mounded Carbonates
Green Canyon 53	Mounded Carbonates	Garden Banks 304	Mud Vent
Green Canyon 140	Mounded Carbonates	Garden Banks 304	Gas Vent
Green Canyon 143	Mud Volcano	Garden Banks 304	Mounded Carbonates
Green Canyon 152	Fluid Expulsion	Garden Banks 338	Expulsion Center
Green Canyon 180	Mounded Seafloor	Garden Banks 382	Expulsion Center
Green Canyon 185	Hydrate Complex	Garden Banks 427	Diapiric Hill
Green Canyon 193	Hydrate Mounds	Mississippi Canyon 709	Hydrates
Green Canyon 232	Hydrate Mounds	Mississippi Canyon 843	Hydrates
Green Canyon 234	Hydrate	Mississippi Canyon 885	Grassy Sediments
Green Canyon 237	Brine/Hydrate	Mississippi Canyon 929	Mineralized Cones
Garden Banks 171	Mounded Carbonates		

The criteria for evaluting the acoustic properties of specific sea floor features, field of features, and sedimentary units flanking features/areas of interest are listed in three tables: (1) side-scan sonar image characteristics, (2) seismic facies, and (3) surface reflection characteristics. The criteria for determining the characteristics of side-scan sonar records and the character of surface reflections on seismic records are straight forward and deal with simple geometries or qualitative measures of reflection signal strength. No detailed explanation of the terms used in these tables was considered necessary for this report. However, terms used to describe the subsurface (seismic facies) are defined in the following section of the report. Following these definitions are seven cases studies of sites that are critical to the overall conclusions drawn from this investigation. Each case study is represented by excellent data sets that present some important variations on the theme of acoustic wipe-out zones and sea floor response to hydrocarbon venting/seepage.

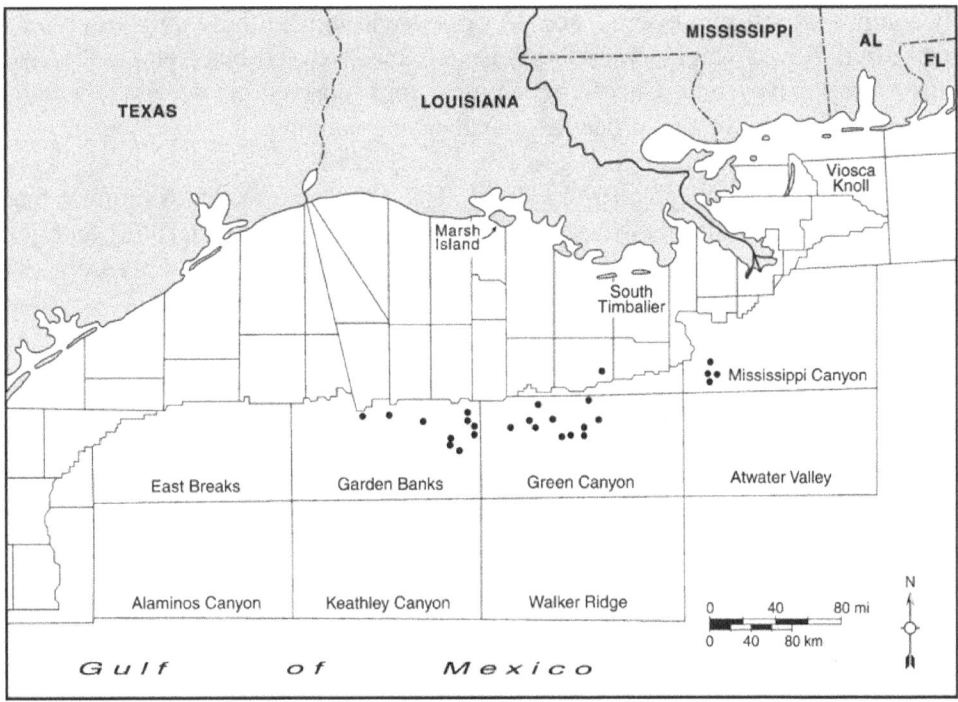

Figure 6. Map of the Louisiana Texas continental slope, deep water leasing areas, and the locations of case history sites.

1. Seismic Facies

a. <u>Gently Divergent and Parallel Layered</u> This reflection pattern is very common on the continental slope and the seismic expression is a series of even-layered, parallel, or gently divergent reflections. These reflection horizons tend to be rather continuous and show little amplitude variations laterally. The uniformity of these reflections suggests deposition in uniform layers over large areas. When data sets permit, these parallel or slightly divergent reflectors are usually stacked and can be traced over distances of many kilometers. Units are measured in meters to 10s of meters. This facies is common in areas of low relief.

b. <u>Strongly Divergent</u> This reflection pattern is common on the flanks of diapiric structures where sediments have obviously been eroded from the regional topographic high and deposited on the diapir flanks. Although the reflection horizons tend to be rather continuous, they clearly diverge downslope over distances of a few kilometers and sometimes are accompanied by distinct amplitude changes over short lateral and vertical intervals. These types of reflection horizons tend to occur in stacked groups, each group having an upper truncation surface. This seismic facies is usually found on the flanks of regional diapiric structures.

13

c. <u>Onlapping</u> Onlapping facies represent sedimentary units that fill a depression, such as a small basin or trough, and reflectors of the fill truncate against the reflector that defines the geometry of the depression or basin of deposition. Onlapping units are generally parallel and relatively continuous reflector events. For the slope environment, these units can typically be the products of turbid flows. Not all onlapping seismic facies are well-behaved parallel and continuous reflection horizons. Chaotic reflection events representing debris flow and other deposits created by mass wasting processes can also be onlapping.

d. <u>Layered or Acoustically Turbid Drape</u> The drape facies forms a uniform blanket of parallel reflections or an acoustically turbid unit that conforms to an underlying topography. There is little evidence of thinning over topographic highs except on the upper slope (<1000 m). There also is very little evidence of onlapping in this type of seismic facies. The modern condensed section or hemipelagic blanket that occurs at the surface is 3-7 m thick, covers most topography on the modern slope, and constitutes a drape seismic facies. This deposit has been the product of a relatively slow and carbonate-rich hemipelagic rain of suspended sediments (pelagic clays and calcareous foraminifera tests primarily) since the retreat of fluvial systems from the shelf edge following the last glacial maximum (~ 18 kyr BP). Thicker drape deposits are common deeper in the sedimentary section and are frequently observed on high resolution seismic records.

e. <u>Sigmoid-Progradational</u> This seismic facies has a sigmoid configuration in dip sections and represents progadation, both on the shelf and slope. In a strike direction this pattern can appear either roughly parallel or divergent. This type of seismic facies pattern is clearly progradational when viewed in dip orientation. Downlap is common at the base of these reflection events. Amplitudes may vary in the basal areas and sometimes these sigmoid reflectors interface with chaotic units.

f. <u>Oblique-Progradational</u> The oblique-progradational seismic facies also denote outbuilding, usually at or near the shelf edge. Both oblique-progradational and sigmoid-progradational seismic facies are common in shelf edge deltas that form sediment sources for slope deposition during periods of lowered sea level. Downlap occurs at the base of these reflection events and chaotic reflections of limited extent occur at the bases of oblique-progradation reflection events.

g. <u>Chaotic</u> This seismic facies occurs on a variety of scales in high resolution seismic facies. Wavy-discontiuous reflection events between boundaries defined by rather continuous reflectors are typical of this facies. Reflection amplitudes also vary considerably within the unit of discontinuous reflectors. This seismic facies generally defines units that have been deposited by gravity-driven density flows and mass movement events. These units can display erosion at their base, but evidence of erosion is not always present. They commonly have irregular upper surfaces.

h. <u>Contorted-Discordant</u> Mounded remnants of bedding interfingered with contorted units, wavy-discordant reflectors, and hummocky reflector events, particularly at the upper surface of the entire unit, are typical of this seismic facies. Mass transport processes are probably responsible for most units that fit this description. The mounded components with internal bedding probably represent large blocks of sediment that have failed from oversteepened slopes and did not completely degrade during the transport process.

i. <u>Acoustically Turbid</u> A lack of clear reflection horizons is common to the subsurface of many features on the continental slope. This response is most commonly associated with bubble-phase gas in the near surface sediments resulting in an acoustic wipe-out zone. However, some areas of acoustic turbidity appear to be stacked and separated by well-defined reflectors. Others contain discontinuous reflectors, some of which may be parallel and reflect bedded sediments, while others are more chaotic with overlapping parabolic reflectors. Still, in other cases, parallel and parabolic reflectors are mixed in a matrix of acoustically turbid seismic facies.

II. Case Studies

The body of this report consists of individual case studies of features or groups of features that were selected for study based on their characteristics on high resolution acoustic data, as well as accessibility of data to the project. As stated in the introductory parts of this report, the focus of this research effort is to develop criteria for better assessment of geohazards, particularly those associated with fluid and gas seepage/venting, and habitats for protected chemosynthetic communities. Features characterized by acoustic wipe-out zones have presented considerable problems regarding definitive interpretations. The task of interpreting highly complex sea floor types, particularly those that incorporate acoustic wipe-out zones, is truly a difficult one and is the reason no widely-used interpreatation schemes are available at present. One of the problems has been the availability of actual ground tuth data to verify remotely sensed approximations of seafloor characteristics. Echo sounder traces, seismic profiles, 3D-seismic attribute data, and swaths of side-scan sonar data are only proxies of real conditions at the seafloor. For the first time, this study attempts to use both high resolution acoustic data (seismic and side-scan sonar data) with exploraiton scale 3D-seismic data (primarily surface amplitude and phase data) in conjunction with direct sea floor observation-sampling to assess sea floor and shallow subsurface characteristics. The ultimate goal is not an improved description of specific sea floor characteristics but to develop a better understanding of sea floor feature evolution, the fundamental processes responsible for feature development, and an improved method for evaluating these features from remotely sensed acoustic data.

The following section of this report presents selected case studies of a wide variety of different sea floor types and features. After reviewing many data sets, these case studies were selected from a group of 29 features (Table 1) on which industry had already acquired high quality acoustic data sets and field verification data had been or could be collected as a part of this project. All the sites are located on the upper continental slope in water depths less than 1000 m. This depth-restricted zone is necessary because of the depth limitation of manned submersibles readily available to the Gulf of Mexico for scientific work.

A. Case Study: Large Complex Mound, Garden Bank Block 161

1. Introduction

In 1985 a high resolution geophysical survey was conducted in GB161 for the purpose of evaluating the block for geohazards and a prospective drilling site (Figure 7). Most of this block is occupied by a large, complex mound (location 27°49.83'N; 92°30.24'W) the base of which extends to the south to neighboring GB205. The geomorphology of this mound is one of a large positive feature comprised of numerous smaller mounds giving the mound surface a "lumpy" appearance on seismic and bathymetric profiles. The crest of the mound reaches a water depth of approximately 200 m while the mound base in GB205 is in approximately 380 m of water (Figure 8).

In October-November of 1997 Fugro-McClelland Marine Geosciences, Inc. was contracted to conduct a geotechnical site investigation. This investigation consisted of a primary soil boring that was completed in two stages because of weather. The final penetration depth

17

was 128 m. The first portion of the boring penetrated to 16.5 m. Core sampling and piezocone penetrometer testing was conducted in the first portion and core sampling was continued to the final depth. Water depths at the soil boring locations were 297.5 m and 298.5 m respectively. Extensive laboratory testing was conducted on the samples from these borings.

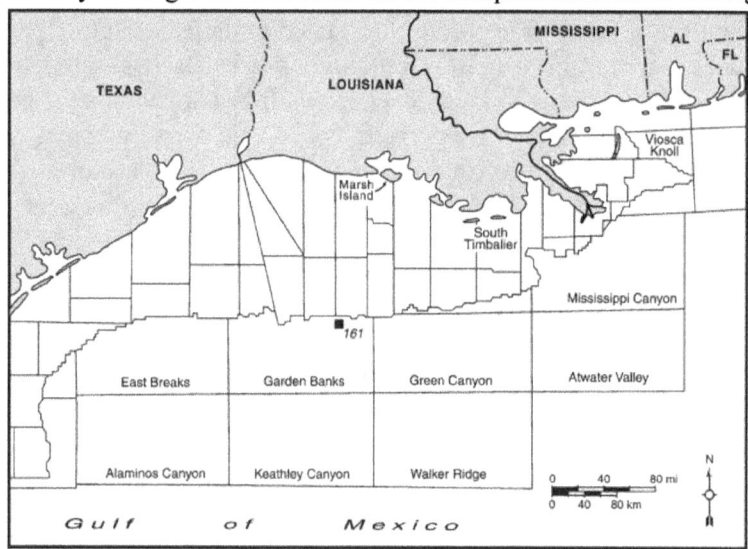

Figure 7. Map showing the location of Garden Banks Block 161.

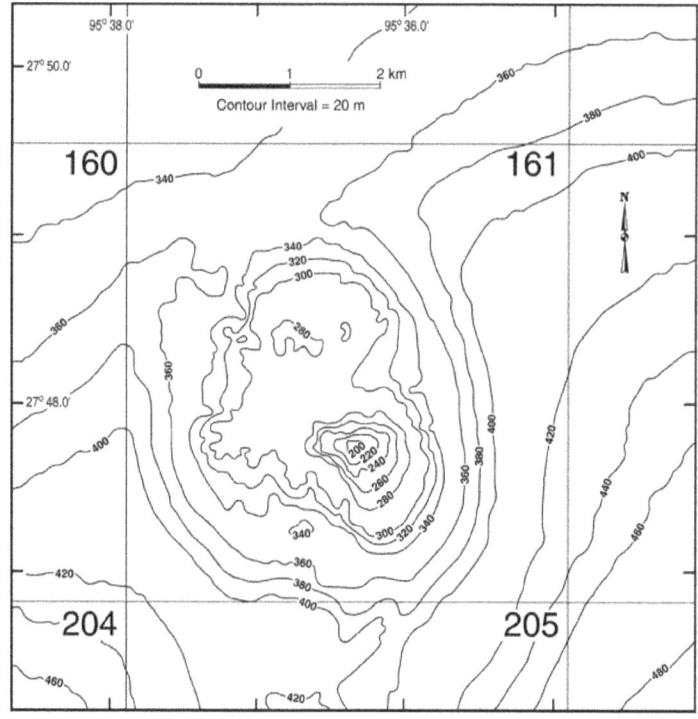

Figure 8. Bathymetric map illustrating the large mound-like feature that nearly occupies the entire GB161 Lease block.

18

The GB161 data set from this geotechnical investigation is interesting and unusual because it affords a rare opportunity to probe the interior of a feature represented both on high resolution and 3D-seismic records as an acoustic wipe-out zone. Generally, industry avoids features represented as acoustic wipe-out zones, so little in the way of subsurface sampling has been carried out on this class of features. Therefore, the GB161 mound was selected as a case study for this report because it provided insight into the subsurface character of a mounded sea floor area that is acoustically opaque in seismic data.

2. Geologic Setting

The study site is at the transition between the continental shelf and continental slope south of the eastern chenier plain of western Louisiana. According to Berryhill et al. (1987), GB161 is located in an area of late Wisconsinan deltaic deposition at the shelf edge and on the upper continental slope. In the south additions of the East Cameron, Vermillion, and western South Marsh Island lease block areas, the shelf is entrenched with complex channel networks that point to or attach themselves to an irregular and elongate shelf edge depocenter. Zones of diapiric uplift surround this shelf edge delta complex and appear to have responded to the rapid sediment loading during and after the relatively short period of deposition. Deltaic deposits in the shelf edge depocenter are well over 100 m thick on sparker lines used to map the shelf-slope transition. Shelf edge deltaic deposition and diapirism (salt and shale diapirs) are penecontemporaneous and interacting processes as demonstrated by the mapping of deformed late Wisconsinan deposits by Berryhill et al. (1987). Their maps of the principal area of late Wisconsinan deltaic deposition for the Garden Banks region shows a deltaic lobe extending into the lease block to the north of GC161 and that GC161 fits into a region of diapiric uplift. When one studies the rounded plan-view shape of this feature which has a diameter of over 5 km, the presence of an acoustic wipe-out zone that extends deep into the subsurface, upturned stratigraphy along the feature flanks, and a concentric structure on 3D-seismic surface amplitude data these characteristics are compatible with the interpretation of perhaps a salt-cored diapir. The sediments from the geotechnical boring, however, suggest another origin.

3. Available Data

In 1985 COMAP Geosurveys Inc. was commissioned by Pennzoil Exploration and Production Company to conduct a standard geohazards survey of GB161. The geophysical systems used to collect high resolution acoustic data from this block were (a) precision hydrographic echosounder, Raytheon DSF-6000 dual frequency (24 kHz and 200 kHz) digital survey fathometer, (b) a side-scan sonar and subbottom profiler, Edo Western integrated 4055 deep-tow system for simultaneous acquisition of high resolution surface and shallow subsurface data, and (c) a multichannel Seismic System (EG&G model 402-7 nine-electrode sparker). The combined 100 kHz side-scan and subbottom profiler system was found to produce the best subbottom data at the elected frequency of 3.5 kHz. The subbottom profiler data as well as the side-scan data were displayed on an EDO Model 706 mapping recorder. The sparker (8 kilojoules) data were recorded with a Texas Instruments DFS V recorder system. This system recorded 24 channels of data in SEG B format. Survey positioning was accomplished using the SYLEDIS BETA System, a short-to-medium range radio positioning system using frequencies in the 420-450 MHz band.

Additionally, in 1997, Fugro-McClelland Marine Geosciences, Inc. was engaged to conduct a seismic and geotechnical field investigation involving the acquisition of a boring (total length 128 m) as well as in situ and laboratory testing. Field and laboratory tests, including classification and strength tests, were performed on the sediment samples to evaluate pertinent index and engineering properties of the sediments encountered. An advanced laboratory testing program was conducted to evaluate sediment stress history and normalized strength behavior using samples still in their shelby core tubes. Due to unusual sediment characteristics additional chemical and geological testing was performed on selected samples. As part of the Fugro-McClelland geotechnical evaluation of the site John Chance and Associates collected a coarse grid (300 m line spacing) of additional high resolution multichannel seismic data which also confirmed the lack of organized reflectors from the mound interior. Finally, 15 in³ water gun profiles were digitally acquired as part of this study to further investigate the seismic characteristics of the GB161 mound.

4.   Feature Characteristics

Figure 8 illustrates that the study area is characterized by a local topography feature with considerable positive relief above the surrounding sea floor. As was clearly demonstrated in the original 1985 COMAP Geosurveys sparker data, the mound-like feature has an acoustically opaque interior. The 3.5 kHz subbottom profiler data displayed little penetration and the side-scan sonar images of the mound surface lacked sufficient crispness and feature difinition to add to a reasonable interpretation of the mound and its possible origin. Figure 9 illustrates the most recent attempt to image this feature with a high resolution acoustic source. Note the sharp truncation of bedded sedimentary units against the interior of this feature, its acoustically opaque interior, and the multimound character of its surface and near-surface morphology.

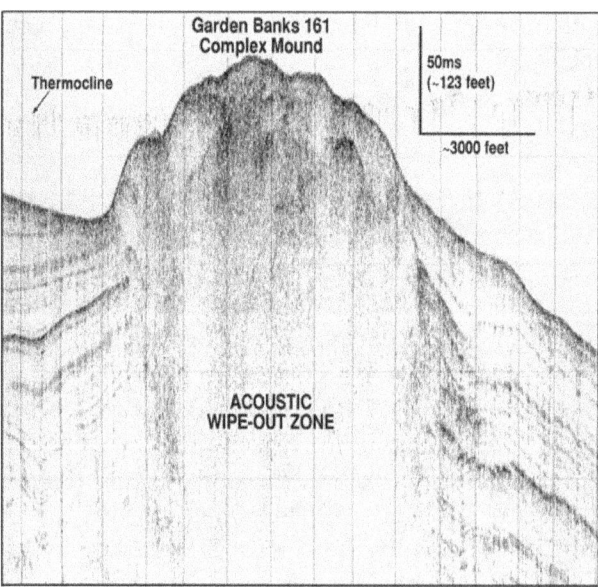

Figure 9. An E-W profile of the GB161 mound digitally acquired as part of this investigation using a Seismic Systems S-15 water gun as an acoustic source.

Analysis of 3D-seismic surface amplitude data over this feature and at depth (Figure 10) illustrates that sea floor amplitudes are in the same range as the surrounding "background" areas. Furthermore, amplitude slices through the mound into the subsurface indicate that the circular shape is maintained and that minor reflectors above background within this feature describe a concentric pattern. However, there is little amplitude signature within this feature even at considerable subsurface depths.

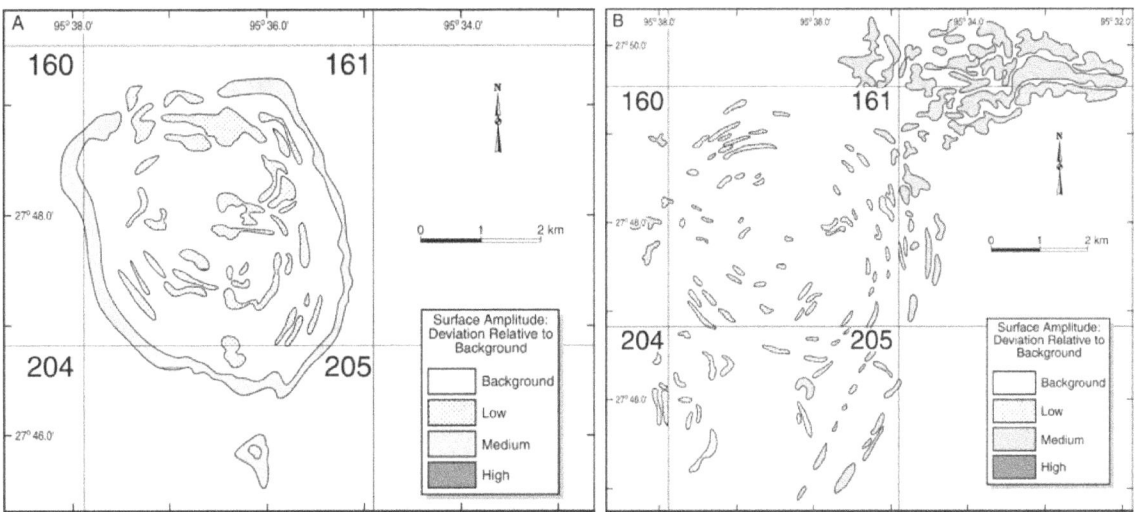

Figure 10. (a) A map of 3D-seismic surface amplitude data from the GB161 mound area. Note the lack of amplitude expression over the mound. Slightly higher amplitudes on the mound flanks are not considered real since these zones do not translate into the subsurface. (b) An amplitude slice made through the subsurface extension of the feature at the 1 sec (TWTT) horizon.

Observation and sampling (short cores) transects made across the GC161 mound in 1998 using a manned submersible (Johnson Sea-Link, JSL-1, Dive 4064) confirmed the rather smooth and nondescript nature of the sea floor. During this dive no rock outcrops or white bacterial mats (*Beggiatoa* sp.) were found during the dive which lasted nearly 3 hours. The surface sediments, upon later analysis, turned out to be largely of hemipelagic origin. However, mixed microfossil assembledges were encountered suggesting mixing with older sediment.

The boring taken at the apex of the mound provided critical data for a confident interpretation of the origin and formational conditions associated with this feature (Roberts et al., 1999). The results of the geotechnical testing program revealed unusual soil characteristics at the site. With exception of approximately 5 m of soft clay at the top of the boring the remainder of the sedimentary section (to a depth of 128 m) provided contradictory results. Undisturbed shear strength values indicated that the sediment was overconsolidated while effective vertical stress measurements suggested that the sedimentary sequence is underconsolidated below a subsurface depth of about 23 m (Roberts et al., 1999). The reason for these differences was that test results were affected by the inclusion of shale clasts and chemical cementation of the clay matrix (Figure 11). Cementation was the result of chemical precipitation in the presence of the high concentrations of salt and other chemical compounds present within the sediments (Roberts et al., 1999).

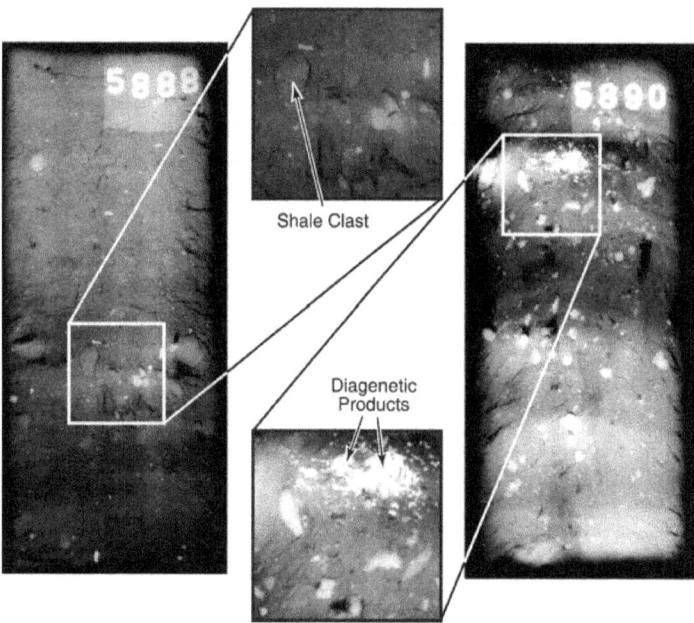

Figure 11. X-ray radiographs of two cores from Boring 1 (exposure 5888 from 16.7 m and exposure 5890 from 66.9 m) illustrate (a) a massive nonstratified structure and (b) suites of unusual coarse-grained components in a fine-grained matrix. The coarse components include shale clasts, calcite rhombs, and odd-shaped nodular diagenetic masses (modified from Roberts et al., 1999).

Measurements of the pore fluids extracted from selected sediment samples, revealed a salt content level at least eight times greater than normally found in marine soils. The pore fluid salt concentration level for the Boring 1 profile is shown in Table 2. High pore fluid salt concentration levels influence basic soil index properties like water content and unit weight measurements. Measured water content values for Boring 1 appear up to 70% lower and effective unit weight values as much as 20% greater than corrected values based on corrections suggested by Norrany (1984). These high salt concentration levels approach or may have exceeded a supersaturated level.

Table 2. Pore fluid salt concentration for Boring 1, Garden Banks Block 161.

Sample No.	Depth (m)	Mg (ppm)	Ca (ppm)	Na (ppm)
S-37	16.6	1,138	1,867	90,052
S-65	45.6	869	1,991	110,798
S-84	66.9	887	1,830	110,350
S-111	95.5	1,149	2,760	116,476
S-127	115.8	1,033	1,714	108,664
Avg. Sea Water		1,290	411	10,760

The pore water analysis clearly indicates that sodium and calcium levels in the porewater of these samples are considerably elevated above those levels expected in normal seawater. Magnesium levels, in contrast, appear to be near normal seawater levels or below. The calcium concentrations are 4 to 5 times higher than one would expect if the pores of these sediments were filled with deep marine water. Sodium level are even higher. They range from 9 to 11 times higher than values for normal seawater, suggesting perhaps that interstitial fluids may have derived from dissolution of salt.

Analysis of selected samples from Boring 1 by X-ray radiography revealed an unusual suite of sedimentary particles comprising the sediment column represented by this boring. Figure 11 illustrates two X-ray radiographs from Boring 1 that display the salient characteristics of sediments analyzed from eleven samples representing the stratigraphic interval 7.5 - 125.0 m (Roberts et al., 1998). All samples analyzed by this technique were characterized by a lack of stratification and an abundance of shale clasts as well as diagenetic inclusions in the form of nodular masses, replaced burrows, altered shell material, and cement-filled microfossil tests. On a freshly cut core, to the unaided eye, very few of these inclusions are visible. However, using the X-ray radiography technique enhances density contrasts between inclusions and the matrix which makes the two distinguishable, one from the other. For example, the sample acquired at a subsurface depth of 57.2 m contains an abundance of diagenetic material from gravel-to-silt size. These inclusions, and others like them in the remaining core samples, were found to be composed of mostly Mg-calcite and pyrite as determined from both X-ray diffraction and microscopic examination. Close inspection of all X-ray radiographs indicates the presence of rhombic grains in the coarse sand to fine gravel size ranges. Analysis of the rhombs indicates that they are composed of calcite.

Inclusions that produce more subtle images on X-ray radiographs are scattered throughout every sample analyzed. These particles are rounded-to-subrounded, occur in the course sand-to-gravel size range, tend to be composed of fine-grained sediment, and have a density that is slightly higher than the surrounding clay-rich matrix. Close inspection of these inclusion types under the binocular microscope indicates that they are "shale clasts" that appears to have been transported from deeper subsurface horizons and partially rounded before deposition. Analysis of the shale clasts for microfossils yielded fauna from late Pleistocene to Eocene, indicating that many of the shale clasts originated deep within the sedimentary basin beneath the GC161 mound.

5.   Feature Synopsis and Interpretation

The GB161 mound has the same apparent attributes as many mounds of the upper continental slope which are built of low strength gas-charged sediments derived from considerable depths in the subsurface. A cone-shaped exterior and an interior characterized by an acoustic wipe-out zone supports this interpretation. However, when all data sets are collectively analyzed, including those generated from a 128 m boring into the center of the mound, it is clear that this feature has unusual characteristics. The 3D-seismic surface amplitude map (Figure 10) illustrates an interesting and unexpected characteristic of this feature, it has no surface amplitude expression that deviates from background. Considering the multiple vent-like topography of the mound top and acoustically opaque interior, one would expect that venting gas and perhaps fluid mud would be present at the surface and perhaps chemosynthetic communities and authigenic carbonate outcrops. None of these sea floor conditions and features were observed during site verification data collection using a manned submersible. Direct observations made during the field verification phase were further supported by the lack of hard targets on side-scan data and by the persistent reflection strength of high resolution seismic surface reflectors. However, profiles and amplitude slices through this feature using 3D-seismic data indicate a rather chaotic pathway from deep within the subsurface to the mounded sea floor feature. Close inspection of the amplitude slices indicates that there are slight variations in amplitudes that describe a concentric pattern within the general subsurface extension of the surface mound which is an acoustic wipe-out zone in profile view (Figure 12).

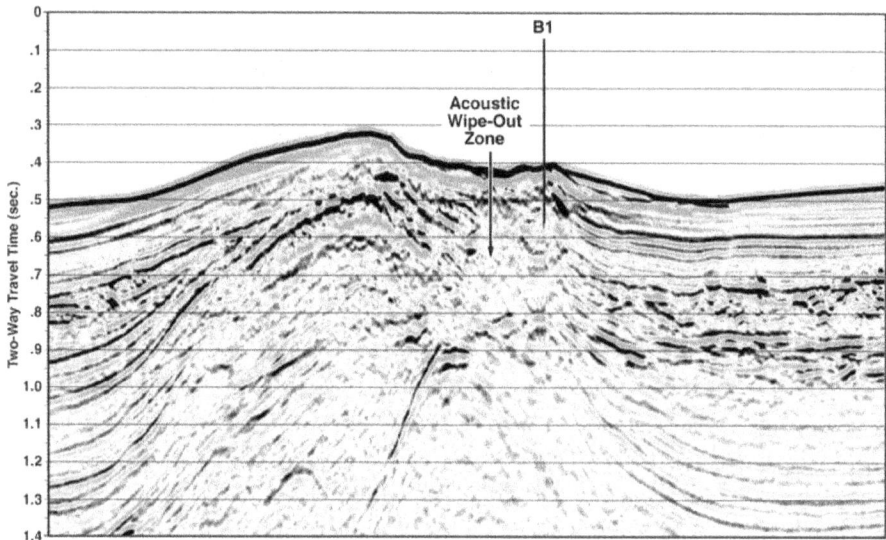

Figure 12. This 3D-seismic profile of the GB161 mound illustrates the complex subsurface configuration, the chaotic and acoustically turbid zone beneath the mound, and the position of Boring 1.

Data acquired from analysis of samples from Boring 1 help finalize an interpretation of this feature. Geotechnical data were confusing and appeared rather contradictory. That is, shear strength measurements suggested the sediments were overconsolidated while sensitivity test results indicated sensitivity lower than most marine clays in the Gulf of Mexico. A sedimentological evaluation of selected cores from Boring 1 helped explain these and other unusual properties of sediments beneath the GB161 mound. Numerous diagenetic products (e.g. pyrite, halite, calcite, gypsum) were found in sediments throughout Boring 1 (Figure 11). In addition, pore waters throughout the boring were 10 X normal marine salinity. In association with the diagenetic inclusions were well-defined, semi-lithified shale clasts that displayed rounding, presumably from vertical transport. Careful analysis of these shale clasts indicated that they contained microfossils ranging in age as far back as Eocene. Therefore, when taken as a whole, the data assembled on the GB161 mound suggest that this feature was constructed by fluidized sediment expulsion originating from deep within the subsurface. The fact that (a) the present sea floor feature has no surface amplitude expression that is different from the regional background, (b) transported and displaced shale clasts as well as a diverse group of diagenetic products are part of the sediment suite, and (c) that hemipelagic sediments cover the mound surface suggests an extinct sediment extrusion feature and supports the interpretation of a dormant expulsion feature. No chemosynthetic communities were found in association with this feature even though it is a classic mound-like buildup with an acoustic wipe-out zone beneath it, like "Bush Hill" (GC185). Acoustic characteristics of the GB161 mound are tabulated in Tables 3 to 5.

Table 3. Side-scan sonar image characteristics for GB161 case study.

	Feature	Feature Field	Flanking Areas
Acoustic Backscatter			
Strong			
Moderate			
Weak	X		X
Mixed			
Target Shapes			
Bumps			
Cones			
Mounds			
Pinnacles			
Depressions			
Irregular			
Target Surface			
Smooth	X		X
Irregular			
Variable	X		
Feature Occurrence			
Isolated			
Asymmetric Groups			
Linear			
Circular			
Elliptical			
Polygonal			

Table 4. Seismic facies for GB161 case study.

Seismic Facies	Feature	Feature Field	Flanking Units
Gently Divergent-Parallel			X
Strongly Divergent			
Onlapping			
Downlapping			
Drape			X
a. Layered			
b. Acoustically Turbid			
Sigmoid Progradational			
Chaotic			
Contorted-Discordant			
Acoustically Turbid	X		
a. Complete	X		
b. Stacked Zones			
c. Chaotic Discontinuous Reflectors			
(1) Parallel			
(2) Parabolic			
(3) Mixed			

Table 5. Surface reflection characteristics for GB161 case study. F = feature; FF = feature field; FA = feature adjacent field.

	3.5 kH Pinger			Intermediate Source			3D Seismic		
	F	FF	FA	F	FF	FA	F	FF	FA
Surface Reflection Strength									
Strong									
Moderate	X			X			X		X
Weak			X			X			
Variable									
Width of Surface Reflectors (MS)									
0-2	X		X						
2-5				X		X			
>5							X		
Variable									X
Reflector Characteristics									
Simple Doublet						X			X
Stratified	X		X						
Prolonged	X			X			X		
Chaotic									
Windowed									
Bright Spots									
Surface Reflection Geometries									
Planar			X			X			X
Wavy									
Mounded	X			X			X		
Scarped									
Isolated Pinnacle/s									
Isolated Depression/s									
Parabolics									
Isolated									
Multiple									
Overlapping									
Phase Inversion									

25

B. Case Study: Mound, Garden Banks Block 189

1. Introduction

While conducting a high resolution geophysical survey of Garden Banks Block 189 in preparation for construction of an oil and gas production platform for Texaco USA, a large mound of unknown origin became important because of its proximity to the proposed platform site. The location of this mound (27°46.48'N; 93°17.74'W) is approximately 225 km south of the town of Cameron, along Louisiana's western coast (Figure 13). The lease block containing this feature (GB189) spans water depths ranging from 165 m to 256 m and is located just below the shelf edge on the upper continental slope. This part of the continental slope displays complex bathymetry resulting from a long geologic history of sedimentary loading and salt tectonics.

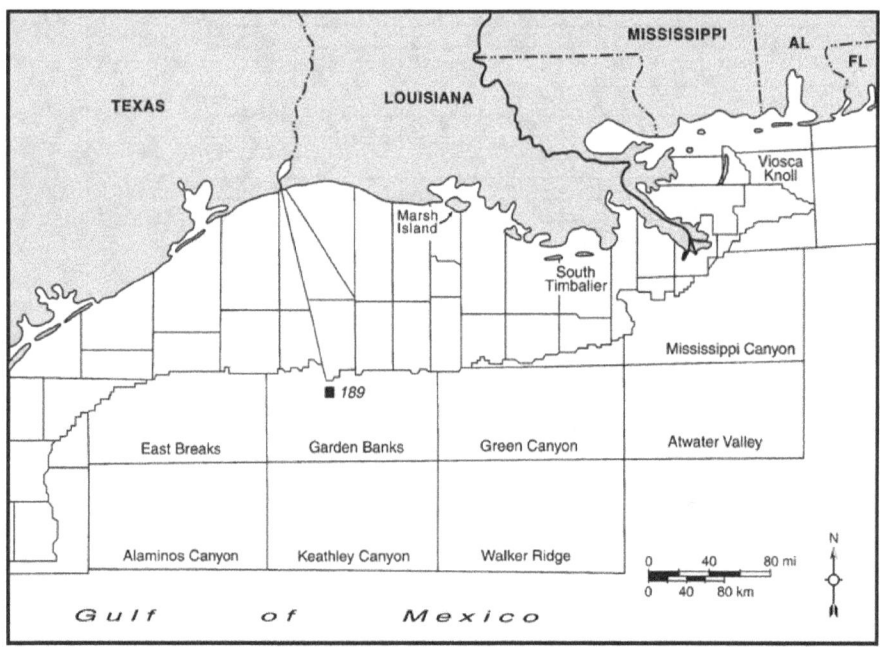

Figure 13. Location map for GB189.

2. Geologic Setting

It is now generally known and accepted by geoscientists that the delivery of sediments to present deep water areas of the Louisiana-Texas continental slope has been closely tied to frequent sea level changes, particularly during the Plio-Pleistocene time interval (Poag 1973). It is also accepted that sea level fell to approximately 120 m during the last glacial maximum, approximately 18 kyr BP (Aharon and Chappell 1986). Since the top of the GB189 mound is currently at 182 m water depth, this feature would have been in slightly over 60 m of water at the latest maximum lowstand of sea level.

The upper slope region near GB189 is characterized by the occurrence of salt masses in the shallow subsurface. Berryhill et al. (1986), through the mapping of shelf-edge and upper

26

slope depositional sequences as revealed on high resolution seismic profiles, discovered that diapiric structures just south of GB189 were actively moving during the late Pleistocene and have remained active into the Holocene. As Berryhill et al. (1986), Sydow and Roberts (1994), Roberts (1995), and others have stated in slope-related research, the movement of salt on short geologic time scales is probably related to the rapid introduction of large volumes of sediment during periods of falling-to-low sea level. At these times, fluvial systems entrench themselves as they migrate across the shelf. They build depocenters at the edge of the shelf where sediments are introduced directly to the slope or are transported downslope as the product of mass wasting processes.

Shelf edge deltas that formed during the Pleistocene have been mapped by Berryhill et al. (1986), Sydow and Roberts (1994), Anderson et al. (1996) and Winker (1996). According to the work of Berryhill et al (1986), the nearest area of major deltaic deposition during the late Pleistocene was about 19 km upslope and to the northwest of GB189, which was probably in the downslope sediment pathway of this depocenter. Piston cores from GB189 analyzed by the author revealed sands around the base of the mound as well as on the mound flanks. Since the sand is currently exposed at the modern sea floor, it is reasonable to assume that its input to the slope occurred during the latest Pleistocene sea level lowstand period.

3.   Available Data

Original geohazards data sets were acquired by John Chance and Associates, Inc. of Lafayette, Louisiana. A narrow beam EDO Western 24 kHz bathymetric profiling system was used to establish water depth charges and sea floor topography within GC189. Shallow sub-bottom data were obtained with an ORE 3.5 kHz pinger profiler. This acoustic source acquired usable information to subsurface depths of approximately 75 ms (~50-60 m). Intermediate penetration was accomplished with a high resolution sparker system. The sparker system was used to fill the data gap between sub-bottom profilers, like the 3.5 kHz O.R.E profiler used in this survey, and low frequency exploration-scale seismic sources. Subbottom penetration of the sparker used on the GB189 survey was over 1000 m with a bed resolution of about 2 m. The frequency range of this sparker was 25-2000 Hz with an adjustable energy range from 100-24,000 joules. Sparker data were collected in single channel as well as multi-channel modes. All geophysical survey data collected by John Chance and Associates, Inc. were spatially controlled by STARFIX navigation system and collected in a surface-tow configuration. Additional high resolution data were collected as part of this project. Seismic profiles across the mound were acquired using a Seismic Systems (model S-15)15 in^3 water gun supported by 50 cfm Hamworthy seismic compressor. This acoustic source produces useful data to a subsurface depth of over 200 ms (~ 180 m) with a bed resolution of less than 2 m. An EG&G Model 260 digital side-scan system was used to study surficial features. These acoustic instruments were used in a surface-tow configuration with GPS-based navigation. TEXACO made available 3D-seismic surface amplitude data to the project for comparison with other data sets. Research submersible Johnson Sea-Link, JSL-1, Dive 3306, provided ground truth observations for calibration of acoustic data to sea floor conditions.

4.   Feature Characteristics

Bathymetric data (Figure 14) show that the GB189 mound is circular in plan-view, has a diameter of ~ 760 m and maximum relief above the surrounding sea floor of approximately 60 m. On low power pinger data the mound appears acoustically opaque (Figure 15).

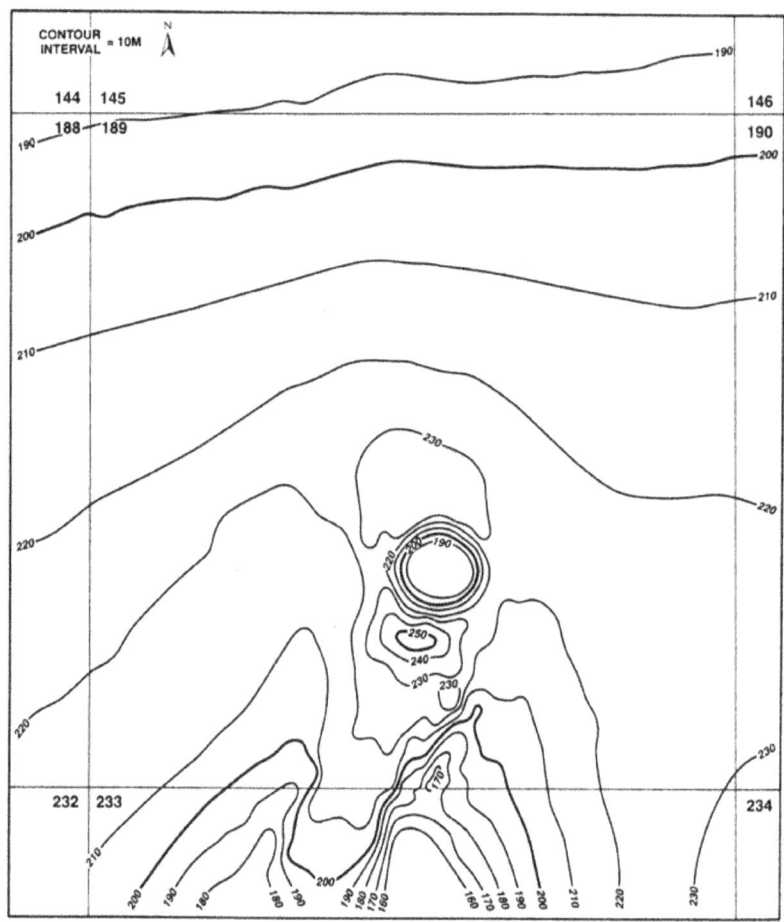

Figure 14. Bathymetric map of the GB189 area showing the symmetrical mound in the south-central part of the block and the graben-like trough that trends to the south away from the mound.

However, both water gun (Figure 16) and sparker data (Figure 17) show that the mound interior is characterized by a single prominent internal reflection horizon in addition to being otherwise acoustically opaque. The opaque internal nature of the mound was originally interpreted to be the product of bubble-phase gas in the sediment (Fugro-McCelland, Marine Geoscience Inc, personal communication). Whelan (1977) demonstrated that even very low gas concentrations could attenuate seismic energy resulting in an acoustically turbid signature or acoustic wipe-out zones.

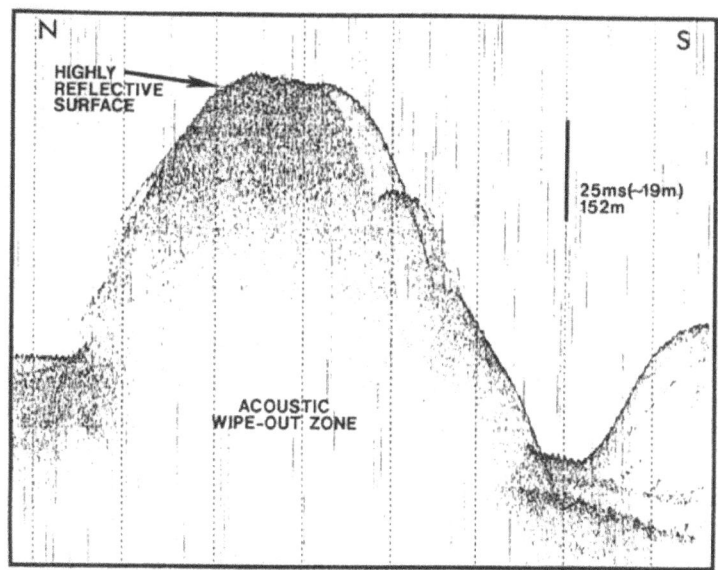

Figure 15. A 3.5 kHz profile oriented north-south across the feature. Note the distinct mound-like profile, the highly reflective top surface, and acoustically opaque interior.

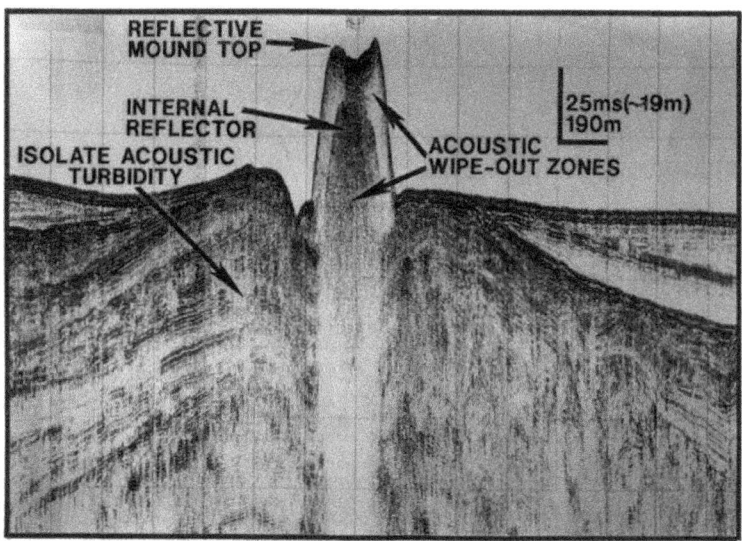

Figure 16. This north-south oriented 15 in³ water gun profile reveals important characteristics about the GB189. Note elevated rims of the feature, the extremely reflective upper surface, and the distinct reflector below an acoustically opaque upper interior of the feature. Also note the domes adjacent beds, onlap on the youngest sedimentary units and the patchy acoustic wipe-out zones in the shallow subsurface.

The mound is situated at the northern end of a north-south trending graben defined by bathymetry (Figure 14) and bound by well-developed faults. Side-scan sonar records indicate that the flanks of the mound are relatively smooth, but clusters of low-relief hard targets surround a central depression on the mount top. This depression is clearly visible on the water gun profile (Figure 16). Sediments of the top also exhibit a strong backscattering of acoustic energy, suggesting that they have different characteristics from those of the flanks.

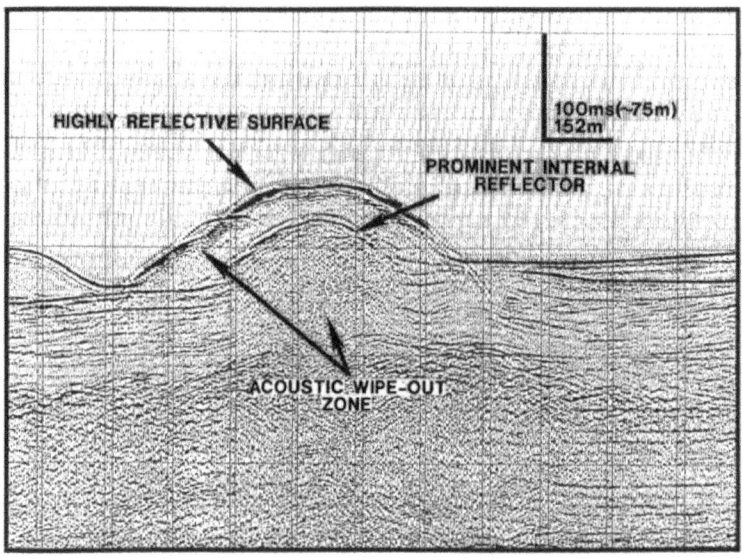

Figure 17. This processed multichannel sparker profile oriented north-south across the GB189 mound clearly illustrates the high amplitude internal reflection event as well as the very reflective upper mound surface. This profile also shows that bedded units terminate against the acoustically opaque center of the larger feature.

Submarine observations indicate that the flanks of the mound are covered with rather featureless hemipelagic sediments while sediments of the top are coarser and have a substantial content of broken shell debris. A rim of scattered, low relief buildups of primarily coralline alga is present (Figure 18). These buildups are scattered over the top of the mound and on the upper flanks of the mound and produce the hard targets on side-scan as well as create a very reflective surface on seismic profiles.

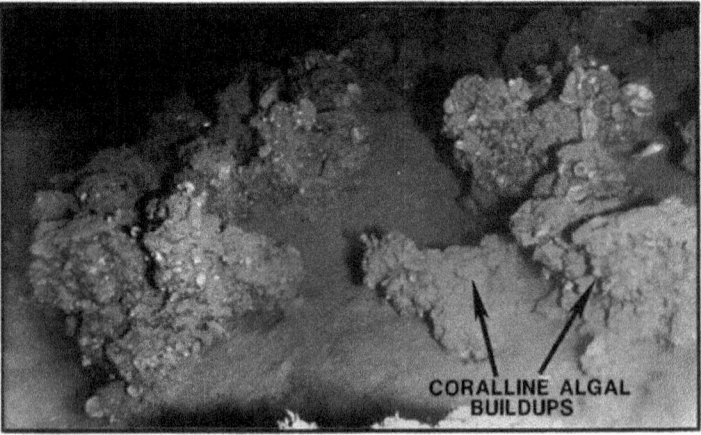

Figure 18. A bottom photograph from JSL-1, Dive 3306, which shows the small coralline algal buildups that occur on the upper mound. These buildups form a rim that is clearly visible in the water gun profile.

30

5.   Feature Synopsis and Interpretation

Initital interpretations of this feature suggested that it originated as a "gas heave structure" that mounded the sea floor (J. Hooper, Fugro-McClelland Marine Geosciences, Inc., personal communication). However, new data sets and further investigations indicate that it currently is not gas-charged and that its present upper surface is mantled with small coralline algal buildups and coarse bioclastic sediments. The biogenic carbonates that occur on the mound top are probably the result of colonization of this positive relief feature during the sea level lowstand following the latest Pleistocene glacial maximum. On seismic records, this surface is an efficient reflector of acoustic energy leading to a high amplitude sea floor reflection event. Surface amplitude maps generated from 3D-seismic data over GC189 indicate an amplitude associated with the mound that is similar to but slightly higher than the response of the surrounding sea floor (Figure 19). Both 3D-sesimic profiles and digital high resolution seismic data acquired as part of this project demonstrate a mound-top phase consistent with that of the surrounding sea floor. The fact that no phase reversal is associated with the surface return from the mound indicates that the mound surface is relatively hard and that surficial sediments are not gas-charged.

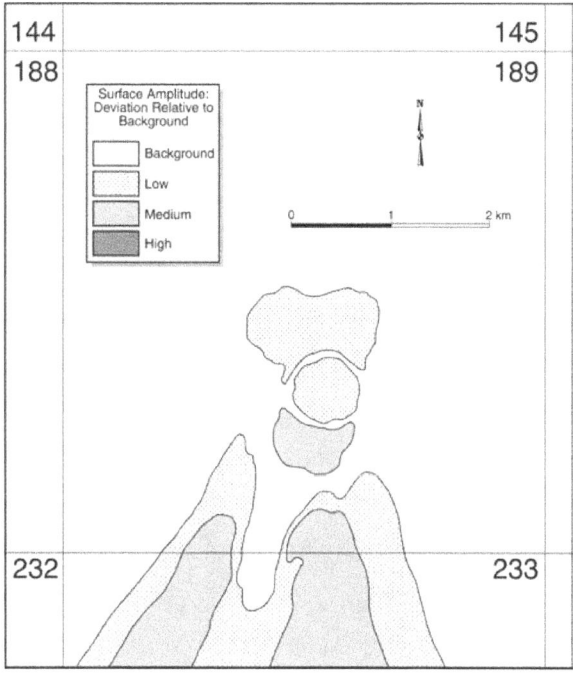

Figure 19. This 3D-seismic amplitude map indicates that this feature has an acoustic impedance similar to the surrounding sea floor with no evidence of a phase inversion over the feature which is generally associated with gas-charged sediments.

Independent of the ultimate origin of this feature, it can now be stated that it has stabilized and at least since the last glacial maximum, approximately 20 kyr BP, this feature has been dormant and has not been a source of gas, fluid, or sediment expulsion. Surficial carbonates are biogenic and do not have light carbon isotope values (unpublished data, H.

Roberts). Shale clasts in cores from the dome flanks (unpublished Fugro-McClelland report) suggest possible expulsion of fluid mud before the final phase of biogenic carbonate mantling of the feature. Recent appraisal of 3D-seismic data suggest the feature may be salt-cored and that the distinct internal reflector represents an acoustic impedance boundary between overlying sediment and underlying salt. The lack of ^{13}C-depleted authigenic carbonates and remains of chemosynthetic organisms, plus the absence of surrounding stratigraphy generally related to mud-extrusion during the mound-building process supports a diapiric salt origin for this feature. The acoustic characteristics of this feature as revealed in geophysical records are tabulated in Tables 6 to 8.

Table 6. Side-scan sonar image characteristics for GB189 case study.

Acoustic Backscatter	Feature	Feature Field	Flanking Areas
Strong	X		
Moderate			X
Weak			
Mixed	X		
Target Shapes			
Bumps	X		
Cones			
Mounds			
Pinnacles			
Depressions			
Irregular	X		
Target Surface			
Smooth			X
Irregular	X		
Variable			
Feature Occurrence			
Isolated	X		
Asymmetric Groups			
Linear			
Circular	X		
Elliptical			
Polygonal			

Table 7. Seismic facies for GB189 case study.

Seismic Facies	Feature	Feature Field	Flanking Units
Gently Divergent-Parallel			
Strongly Divergent			X
Onlapping			
Downlapping			
Drape			
a. Layered			
b. Acoustically Turbid	X		
Sigmoid Progradational			
Oblique Progradational			X
Chaotic			
Contorted-Discordant			
Acoustically Turbid			
a. Complete			
b. Stacked Zones			
c. Chaotic Discontinuous Reflectors	X		
(1) Parallel			
(2) Parabolic	X		
(3) Mixed			

Table 8. Surface reflection characteristics for GB189 case study. F = feature; FF = feature field; FA = feature adjacent are

	3.5 kH Pinger			Intermediate Source			3D Seismic		
	F	FF	FA	F	FF	FA	F	FF	FA
Surface Reflection Strength									
Strong	X			X			X		
Moderate						X			X
Weak			X						
Variable									
Width of Surface Reflectors (MS)									
0-2									
2-5	X			X			X		
>5				X			X		X
Variable									
Reflector Characteristics									
Simple Doublet			X			X	X		X
Stratified									
Prolonged	X			X					
Chaotic									
Windowed									
Bright Spots									
Surface Reflection Geometries									
Planar			X			X			X
Wavy									
Mounded	X			X			X		
Scarped									
Isolated Pinnacle/s									
Isolated Depression/s									
Parabolics									
Isolated	X								
Multiple									
Overlapping									
Phase Inversion									

C. Case Study: Expulsion Centers, Garden Banks Blocks 338 and 382

1.   Introduction

Upslope of the prominent diapiric mound in GB427 are two areas in GB338 and GB382 (Figure 20) from which downslope transport of large volumes of sediment has occurred (Figure 21).

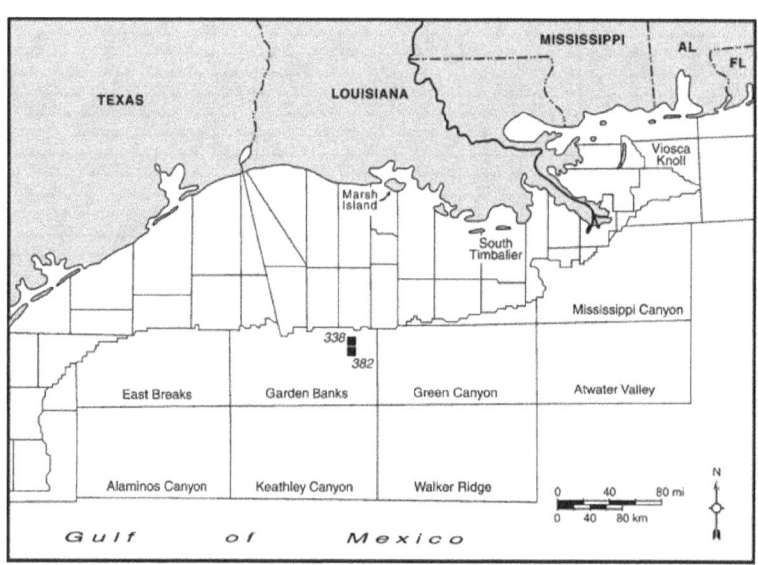

Figure 20. Location map for Garden Banks Blocks 338 and 382 (GB338 and GB382).

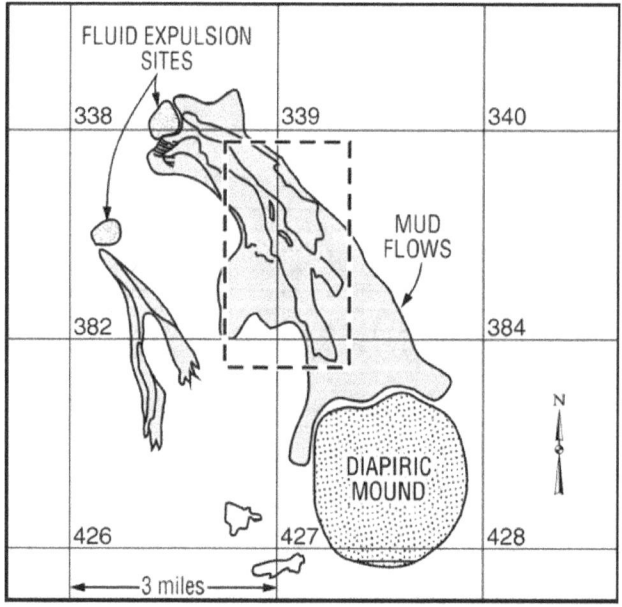

Figure 21. A bottom features map of the GB338-427 area illustrating the expulsion centers in GB338 and GB382, gravity-driven deposits that have been transported downslope, and the large diapiric mound in GB427.

These features were selected for investigation because of the obvious slope failures, fluidized sediment flows, and current near-dormant state of the expulsion centers. It is clear that in the recent past that both expulsion centers were actively extruding large volumes of fluidized sediment onto the sea floor where this extruded sediment traveled toward the a large mound in GB427. Some flows traveled a distance of over 15 km downslope.

The expulsion centers in GB338 (27° 37.80'N; 92° 28.12'W) and GB382 (27° 36.49'N; 92° 29.05'W) clearly are visible on regional bathymetry as mound-like, rounded areas on top of a regional and elongated bathymetric high oriented in a NE-SW direction (Figure 21). Both expulsion centers are in water depths of approximately 500 m. These areas are on the fringes of an excellent deep-tow high resolution geohazards survey conducted in support of Shell's Auger Prospect development. The mudflow deposits originating on the ridge upslope of the proposed drilling site generate concern because flow patterns on the sea floor appear relatively fresh on side-scan sonar data. It is apparent from analysis of the subsurface that large blocks of sediment, obviously derived from slope failures, have been transported into GB426 and GB427 not far from the proposed platform site. Analysis of all data sets from the site survey show that the time frame for the slope failures and expulsion events provide an adequate margin of safety for the project and that additional flows are not to be expected over the production life of the Auger Field. However, it is clear from the surficial geology that the expulsion centers have been very active in the past and now have essentially shut down. This demonstrated history of change in activity level provides an important opportunity to investigate the remotely sensed character of these sites and the actual sea floor conditions that exist there today.

2.   Geology Setting

The ridge on which the expulsion centers are located (Figure 22) is held up by regionally distributed shallow salt. The average off-ridge slopes in the area surrounding GB427, where the diapiric mound is located, are around 2°.

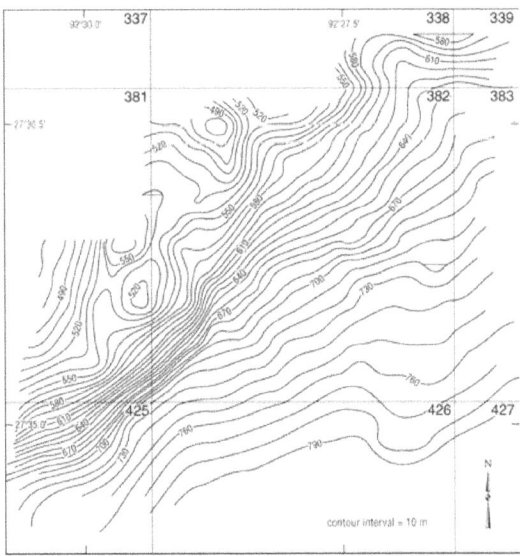

Figure 22. Bathymetric map for the GB338-382 area illustrating the NE-SW ridge-like topography which is a reflection of underlying shallow salt.

However, local slopes associated with the ridge where the expulsion centers are located reach as much as 12°. Berryhill et al. (1987) indicate that the northern part of this salt-cored ridge was completely surrounded by thick late Wisconsinan deltaic depocenters that must have provided abundant sediments to the downslope sedimentary basins both north and south of the ridge. Stratigraphic relationships in high resolution seismic profiles used to construct a synthesis of shelf edge deposition during the late Pleistocene (Berryhill et al., 1987) indicate late falling stage and early rising stage deposition up slope of the GB338 and GB382 areas. Deposition of shelf edge deltas and sediment loading of the slope adjacent to the shelf edge depocenters has been shown to take place in the time frame ~ 23,000 - 16000 yr BP around the latest glacial maximum which occurred 20,000-18,000 yrs BP (Sydow and Roberts, 1994). It is reasonable to assume that his intense sedimentary loading of the basins to the N and S of the salt ridge on which the GB338 and 382 expulsion centers are located triggered salt movement and activated faults that breach the deep subsurface overpressure zone. These events, in turn, would have initiated uplift of parts of the salt ridge, slope failures, expulsion of fluids (including fluidized sediment) and gases at the modern sea floor, and perhaps destabilization of gas hydrates. Sediment samples acquired by manned submersible at the GB382 expulsion center indicate that sediments were brought to the surface from great depth. These sediments were rich in early-middle Miocene microfossils which represent an age of at least 14.6 Ma (Kohl and Roberts, 1994).

The sediment flows that originated from the GB338 and GB382 expulsion centers are spectacularly displayed on the sea floor as viewed on high quality deep-tow side-scan sonar (Figure 23).

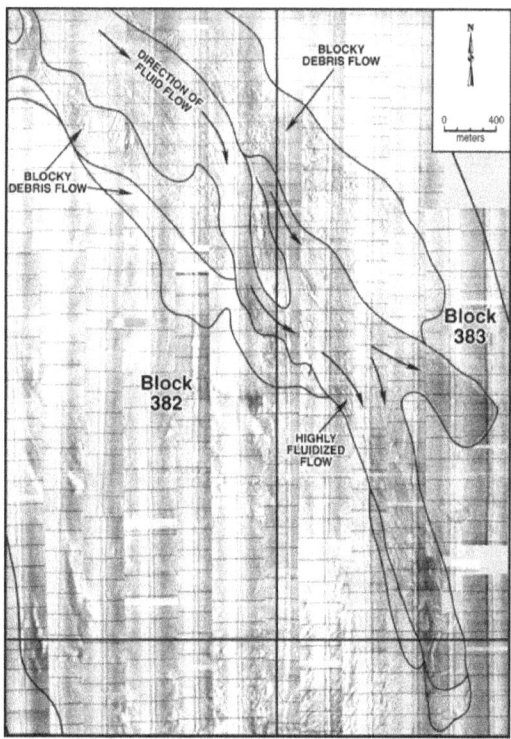

Figure 23. Side-scan sonar mosaic of flows originating from the GB338 expulsion center. Note both the flow as well as irregularities within flows indicating large blocks of sediment associated with debris flows.

36

Flow patterns are easily distinguished from surrounding sediments which suggests a relatively young flow that has not been covered by thick hemipelagic drape deposits typical of some parts of the slope. Most flows do, however, have 1-3 m of hemipelagic drape deposits over them which suggests they were deposited several thousand years ago (hemipelagic depositional rate ~ 1 m/3000 yrs). Close inspection of these flows with both side-scan sonar and subbottom profiles indicates that some are debris flows containing large blocks of sediment while others appear to be highly fluidized. The interpretation of geologic events leading to the creation of these flows and then their abandonment is clearly related to sea level change and upper slope sediment loading by shelf edge deltaic depocenters. As sea level fell prior to the latest Pleistocene glacial maximum, a large shelf edge delta complex developed upslope of the area of interest and loaded the underlying salt causing adjustments. At the same time a decrease in hydrostatic loading forced by falling sea level could have destabilized gas hydrate deposits and perhaps helped initiated slope failures. Sediments continued to be applied till the early stage of sea level rise. At the same time, salt was adjusting to this load by deforming. These events activated existing faults and probably created new ones. Vertical salt movement combined with expulsion of fluids and gases at the sea floor initiated slope failures, fluidized sediment, and downslope transport. Salt adjustment to late Pleistocene sediment loading appears to have waned significantly in the last few thousand years, effectively terminating the mudflow/debris flow episode.

3.   Available Data

Original geohazards data for the Auger Prospect area were acquired by Fugro-McClelland Marine Geosciences, Inc. with a deep-tow high resolution acoustic system for providing details of both the sea floor and shallow subsurface. This system incorporates a 3.5 kHz subbottom profiler with a 100 kHz side-scan sonar. A narrow beam precision depth recorder was used for bathymetry. A high resolution multichannel seismic system was used for moderately deep subsurface penetration. The Tri-Cluster seismic source was used with a ¼ millisecond sampling rate. The data were initially analyzed by Fugro-McClelland personnel and a site evaluation report submitted to Shell Offshore. This report contained side-scan sonar mosaics of the mudflows from expulsion centers in both GB338 and 382 and the diapiric mound in GB427. In addition, the subsurface characteristics of the flows and other important shallow stratigraphic units were summarized. As part of this MMS-CMI project, additional high resolution seismic profiles were acquired over the expulsion centers using both a Seismic Systems S-15 water gun and a 50 in³ air gun (GI gun). Both of these sources were supported by a 50 cfm Hamworthy seismic air compressor. Data were acquired in both digital and analog formats using the Delph II seismic data acquisition and processing software. Digital data were archived on Exobyte tape and analog records were printed on an EPC 9800 graphic recorder. Ground truth observations were made and bottom samples taken using the Johnson Sea-Link manned submersible. Two dives have been made on the mound in GB382 (JSL-1, Dive 3307; JSL-2, Dive 2898) while five dives have been made on the mound in GB338 (JSL-1, Dives 3308, 3565, 3566; JSL-2, Dives 2897 and 2905). The dive made by the author or September 7, 1992 was the dive that discovered the first large and natural barite deposits observed on the northern Gulf of Mexico continental slope. These deposits constitute an interesting part of the expulsion history of this site.

4.   Feature Characteristics

As shown in the bottom features map of Figure 21 and the side-scan sonar mosaic of Figure 23 the two expulsion centers in GB338 and 382 have played an important role in modifying sea floor geology at these sites and downslope where debris flows and more fluidized sediment flows impact the character of the bottom. High resolution seismic profiles (3.5 kHz) acquired across these expulsion features, Figures 24 and 25, indicate that they are acoustically opaque features with a thin layer of rather acoustically transparent material (hemipelagic drape sediments) at the surface.

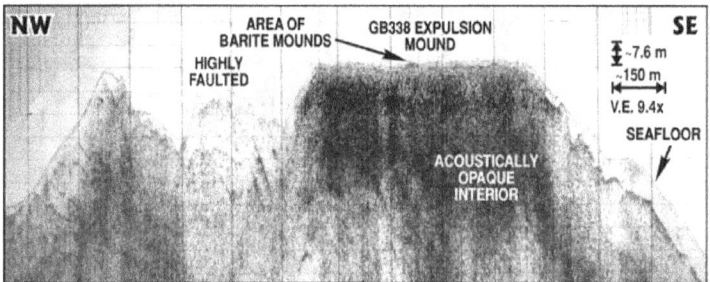

Figure 24. A 3.5 kHz profile across the expulsion center (mound) in GB338.

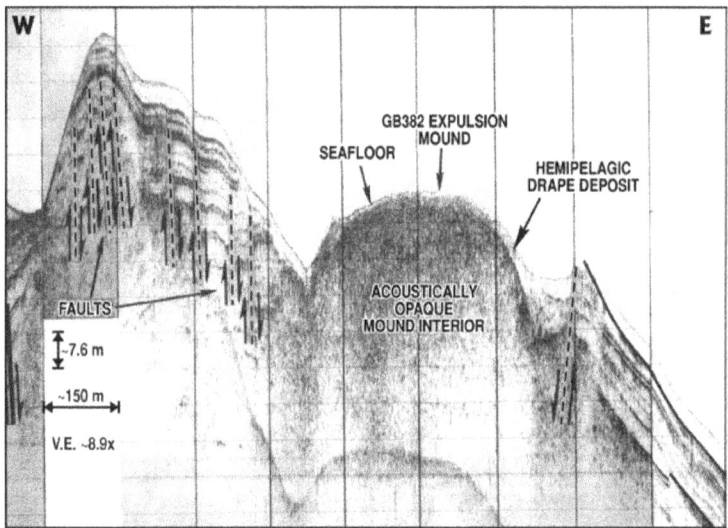

Figure 25. A 3.5 kHz profile across the expulsion center (mound) in GB382.

This surficial sedimentary unit is much more apparent over the GB382 expulsion center as compared to its counterpart in GB338. As is clear from the 3.5 kHz profiles, the GB382 feature is a symmetrical mound whereas the feature in GB338 is relatively flat with evidence of small-scale (<2 m) bottom roughness across the relatively flat area of the mound. Where bedding on the flanks of these two features can be imaged, the sedimentary section is highly faulted. In the case of the GB382 mound (Figure 26), flanking stratigraphy is represented by cyclic units that are probably composed of extruded sediments that were deposited during the active expulsion phase of this feature. They thicken away from the mound and merge with debris flow and fluidized mudflow deposits downslope. A water gun profile across the GB338 feature suggests that bedded sediments on the mound flank appear to be upturned and truncated (Figure 26). The surface of this mound is highly reflective and its interior is an acoustic wipe-out zone even when imaged with more penetration provided by the more powerful water gun.

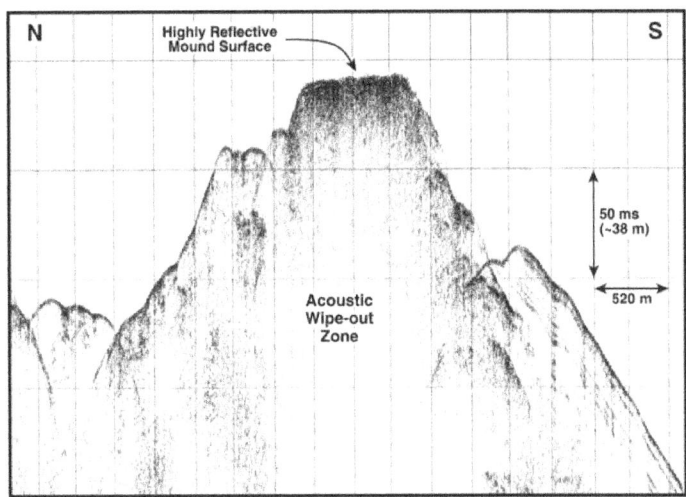

Figure 26. A 15 in³ water gun profile across the expulsion center in GB338.

Side-scan sonar data from the two mounds appears quite different. The smaller of the two expulsion centers (GB382) displays a rather smooth, nonreflective surface with only small relief features (Figure 27). These side-scan sonar targets do not appear as features with highly reflective surfaces at the 200 m swath scale. Instead, they appear as rather soft targets, mounds of various sizes, that are possibly draped with hemipelagic sediments.

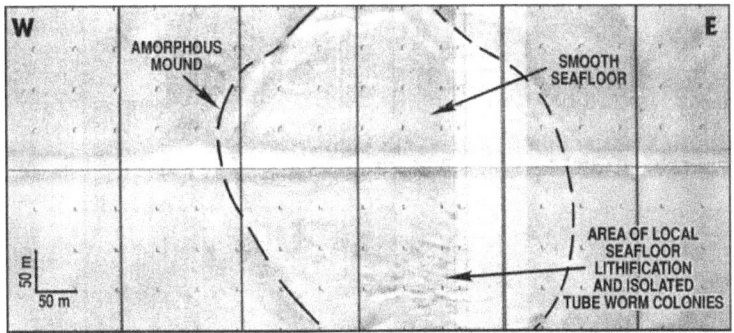

Figure 27. An E-W oriented side-scan sonar swath across the crestal area of the GB382 expulsion center mound.

The 3.5 kHz profile of Figure 25 suggests a thin (1-2 thick) and discontinuous hemipelagic drape across the expulsion center mound. The surface of the GB338 mound has quite a different signature on side-scan sonar records. This mound exhibits numerous highly reflective targets, considerable reflective surface texture changes over short distances, and relief features that cast significant shadows across the side-scan records (Figure 28). Many of the targets are lineated or they are organized into linear patterns suggesting fault control. Other side-scan sonar records indicate flow patterns that originate in the acoustically opaque area of the mound crest and are gravitationally oriented downslope where a blocky bottom topography (debris flow surface) is encountered.

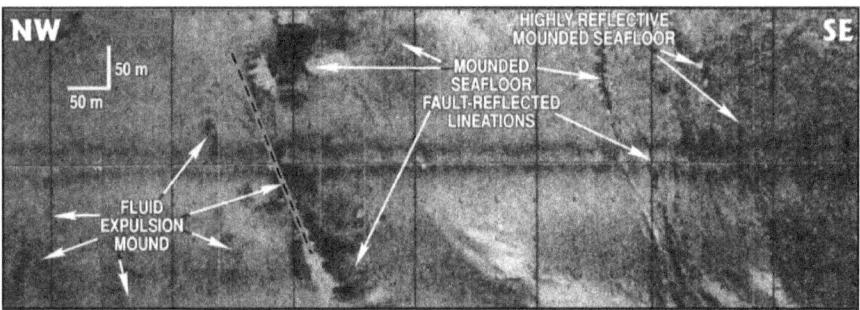

Figure 28. A NW-SE oriented side-scan sonar swath across the crestal area of the GB338 expulsion center mound.

5.   Feature Synopsis and Interpretation

High resolution seismic profiles clearly distinguish the two mound-like features in GB383 and GB382 from surrounding sediments by their reflective surfaces, mounded shapes, and acoustically opaque interiors. Analysis of accompanying side-scan sonar data indicate that each of these mounds has functioned as a focal point for the expulsion of fluidized sediment that has been transported downslope many kilometers from the source. In addition, this expulsion process coupled with possible uplift of the subsurface salt ridge on which the expulsion centers are located plus possible destabilization at gas hydrates caused slope failures leading to fluidized debris flows.

When this general area of the slope is analyzed using 3D-seismic data, a very interesting picture evolves. The expulsion centers as well as the fluidized flow deposits have a much higher amplitude than the surrounding background (Figure 29). The expulsion centers themselves are exceptionally high with the GB338 mound being of a higher amplitude than its smaller GB382 counterpart. An interesting aspect of these amplitudes is that they reflect a hard bottom except for a small central area of the GB382 mound and a slightly larger area central to the GB338 mound. Seismic profiles across these features emphasize strong surface reflectivity suggesting a hard bottom and a central zone characterized by a positive to negative polarity shift suggesting the presence of sedimentary gas (Figure 30).

The two manned submersible dives made on the GB382 mound and five dives made on the large GB338 mound were extremely revealing with regard to real sea floor conditions being reflected in the remotely sensed acoustic data. Dives to the smaller of the two expulsion features (GB382) revealed a highly bioturbated sea floor covered with sediments rich in calcareous microfossil tests (hemipelagic sediments). This character of much of the mound surface correlated well to both the high resolution seismic data (3.5 kHz), both of which show a thin acoustically transparent layer across most of the mound. The general lack of hard reflectors on side-scan sonar data was also consistent with much of the mound surface as viewed directly.

However, not all of the mound surface fits this description. Near the mound's apex bacterial mats became common bottom features and isolated tube worm colonies with associated authigenic carbonate crusts and larger rocks were present. Although gas was never observed to be escaping from the bottom when the bottom was disturbed in the bacterial mat areas, gas bubbles were vented into the water column. These gas-prone sites occurred in the vicinity of the area circled shown on the side-scan sonar record of Figure 27.

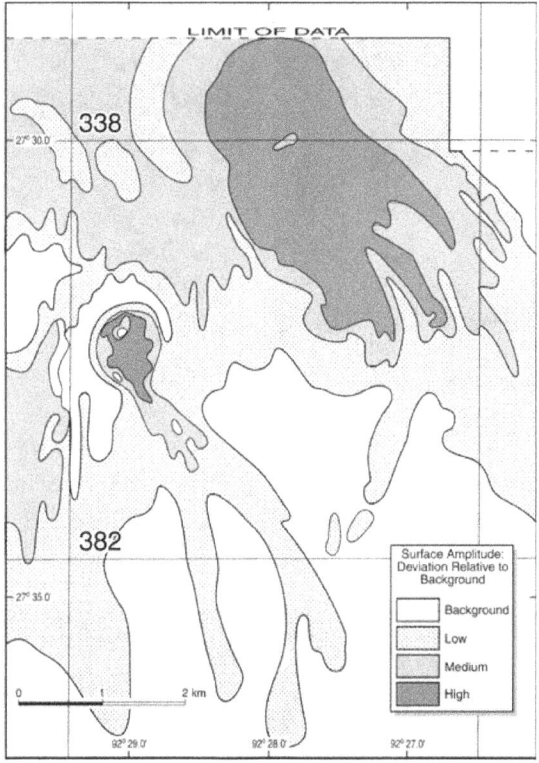

Figure 29. A 3D-seismic surface amplitude map of the GB338 and 382 area illustrating the amplitude deviations from background.

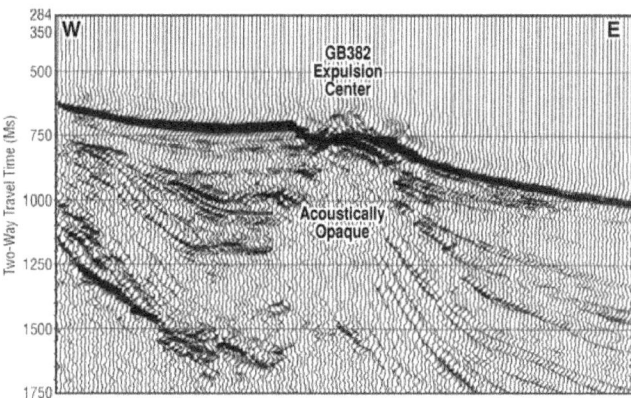

Figure 30. A 3D-seismic profile through the GB382 expulsion center illustrating the acoustically opaque interior of this feature which extends deep within the subsurface, the strong surface reflector defining the mound, and the positive to negative phase reversal over the mound crest.

41

Surface data collection from the GB338 mound provided a much different picture of processes and response features associated with these two expulsion centers. On the first dive to GB338 it became obvious that this mound-like feature was still a marginally active area regarding the flux of fluids and gases to the sea floor. The side-scan sonar data (Figure 28) suggested that there were a number of distinct small-scale buildups, some with relief of up to 3 m. These features turned out to be small mud-rich mounds which had several spectacular volcano-shaped cones near their crests (Figure 31).

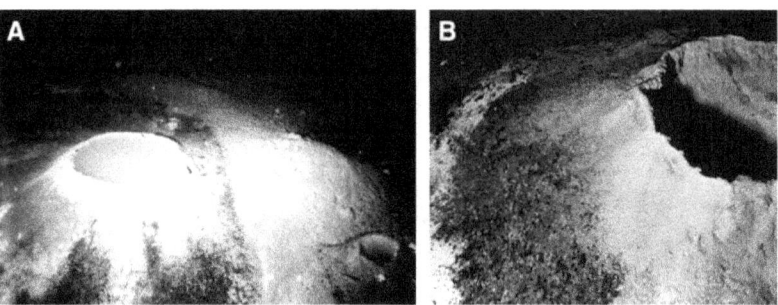

Figure 31. Barite cones found near the apex of the GB338 mound.

Upon laboratory analysis (Roberts and Aharon, 1994) these multicolored and unusual cones were composed of barite. Cones are not the only barite features on the mound top. A large area of the mound surface is occupied by small vents and chimneys resulting from the slow vertical flux of barium-rich fluids (Figure 32).

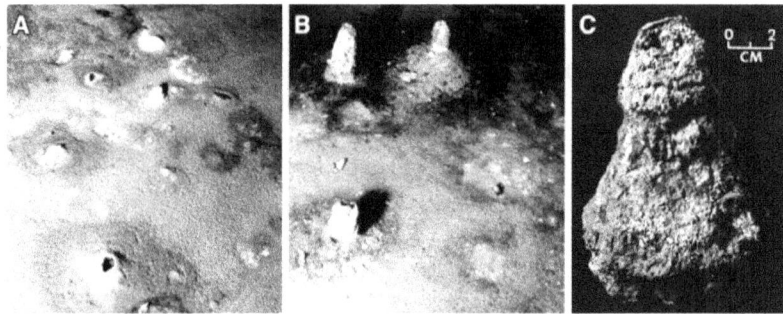

Figure 32. Small barite chimneys common to a large area of the GB338 mound surface.

The largest features of importance are mud volcanoes which are extruding fluidized sediment rich in barium. Barite crusts form on the sides of these features which produces a semi-lithified internal structure. Gas freely escapes from the mud volcanoes and occasionally from the chimneys and cones. Chemosynthetic mussels (*Bathymodiolus sp.*) and bacterial mats are common to some parts of the mound, but tube worms are scarce. As Figure 33 illustrates, benthic communities are cemented with barite as barium-rich fluids seep to the seafloor over a large area of the GB338 mound surface.

Figure 33. Chemosynthetic mussels (*Bathymodiolus sp.*) cemented together with barite.

Analysis of the surface geology of the GB338 and GB382 sites clearly indicates a history of rapid expulsion of fluidized sediment followed by a distinct reduction in the rate of flux to conditions we observe there today. The smaller of the two expulsion centers GB382 has nearly become dormant and a drape of hemipelagic sediments has been deposited over the mound surface and is largely undisturbed except for bioturbation and a crestal site where gas is in the surface sediments. By contrast, the GB338 mound is still actively fluxing gas, fluidized sediment, and barium-rich fluids to the modern seafloor. Analysis of the mud extruded from this area indicates that microfossils as old as Miocene are being extruded onto the modern seafloor (Kohl and Roberts, 1994). The acoustically opaque nature of the mound's interior, its highly reflective surface on both high resolution and exploration-scale seismic, the general hard signature on 3D-surface amplitude data, and the localized polarity shifts over the mound crest are consistent with the characteristics observed on side-scan sonar data and direct observations of the mound surface. The acoustic characteristics of the GB338 feature are tabulated in Tables 9 to 11.

Table 9. Side-scan sonar image characteristics for GB 338, case study.

	Feature	Feature Field	Flanking Areas
Acoustic Backscatter	X		
Strong			
Moderate			X
Weak			
Mixed			
Target Shapes			
Bumps			
Cones			
Mounds	X		
Pinnacles			
Depressions			
Irregular	X		X
Target Surface			
Smooth			
Irregular	X		X
Variable	X		X
Feature Occurrence			
Isolated			
Asymmetric Groups	X		
Linear	X		
Circular	X		
Elliptical			
Polygonal			

Table 10. Seismic facies for GB 338 case study.

Seismic Facies	Feature	Feature Field	Flanking Units
Gently Divergent Parallel			X
Strongly Divergent			
Onlapping			
Downlapping			
Drape	X		X
a. Layered			
b. Acoustically Turbid	X		X
Sigmoid Progradational			
Chaotic			X
Contorted-Discordant			
Acoustically Turbid	X		
a. Complete			
b. Stacked Zones			
c. Chaotic Discontinuous Reflectors	X		
(1) Parallel			
(2) Parabolic			
(3) Mixed			

Table 11. Surface reflection characteristics for GB 338 case study. F = feature; FF = feature field; FA = feature adjacent

	3.5 kH Pinger			Intermediate Source			3D Seismic		
	F	FF	FA	F	FF	FA	F	FF	FA
Surface Reflection Strength									
Strong	X			X			X		X
Moderate			X			X			
Weak				X					
Variable									
Width of Surface Reflectors (MS)									
0-2	X		X						
2-5						X			
>5				X			X		X
Variable	X								
Reflector Characteristics									
Simple Doublet							X		X
Stratified			X			X			
Prolonged	X			X					
Chaotic									
Windowed									
Bright Spots									
Surface Reflection Geometries									
Planar			X				X		X
Wavy	X								
Mounded	X								
Scarped									
Isolated Pinnacle/s									
Isolated Depression/s									
Parabolics			X			X			
Isolated									
Multiple			X			X			
Overlapping									
Phase Inversion				X			X		

44

D. Case Study: Diapiric Mound, Garden Banks Block 427

1.   Introduction

Within the Garden Banks Lease area, block 427 (Figure 34) is dominated by a large mound that occupies most of the southern two-thirds of this block (Figure 35).

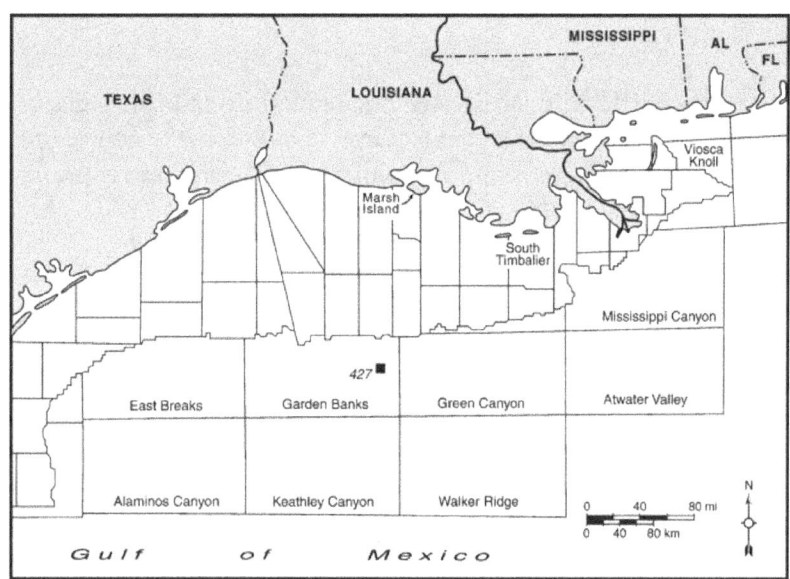

Figure 34. Location map for Garden Banks Block 427 (GB427).

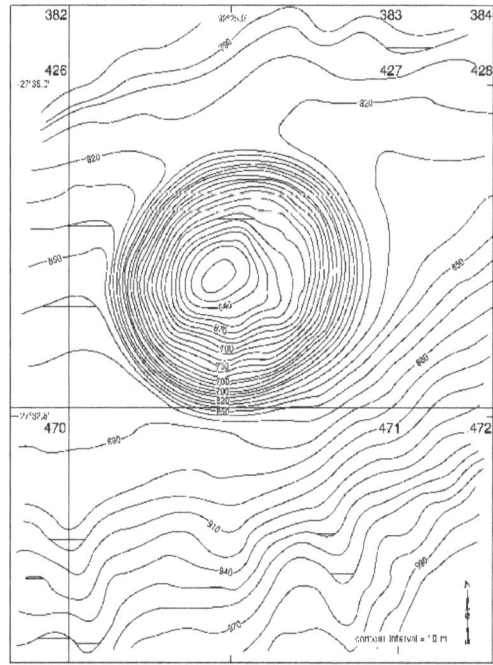

Figure 35. Bathymetric map for GB427 and surrounding areas. Depth contours are in meters.

This impressive feature stands out on regional bathymetric maps, computer-enhanced multibeam images of the upper continental slope, and seafloor renderings of this region of the Garden Banks Lease area (Doyle et al., 1996). The mound (27° 33.59'N; 92°25.53'W) rises over 200 m above surrounding topography and has a base diameter of about 3.8 km. Initial evaluations of this feature for a geohazards assessment of Shell's Auger Prospect area were problematic. Many questions remained, especially concerning details of the sea floor, even after the best high resolution acoustic data and 3D-seismic were acquired over the feature and analyzed to determine its characteristics.

High resolution acoustic data and 3D-seismic renderings indicate areas of extremely high backscatter on the upper flanks and top of the feature. In addition, the cone exhibits linear patterns radiating away from the crest area. A highly reflective surface on the cone flanks highlight the radial patterns that tend to converge at the apex of the mound. These radial patterns were originally interpreted as tensional faults radiating away from a salt-cored and diapiric structure. Attribute mapping using a data base of 3D-seismic, as discussed by Campbell (1997), Hill (1996), Roberts et al. (1996) and Trabant (1996), initially indicated that the mound surface was extremely variable and that making a detailed geologic-sedimentologic interpretation of this variability was difficult without sea floor verification data.

2.   Geologic Setting

The area of interest, GB427, is located on the northwest Gulf of Mexico continental slope approximately 300 km southwest of the modern Balize lobe of the Mississippi River delta (Figure 34). Within this general slope area, the combined effects of massive sediment input (Suter and Berryhill, 1985), primarily at periods of lowered sea level, and the compensating deformation of salt has created a complex slope topography characterized by canyons, troughs, hills, ridges, and intraslope basins. The hills and ridges are, in most cases, a direct reflection of underlying salt. These features have sea floor gradients of 10-12° which are approximately 10X the average gradient of the average continental slope and approximately 30X the gradients of basins (0.2°- 0.4°) that occur as flat areas between the erratic topography created by salt structures. Faults and fluid expulsion features accompany most areas where salt adjustment has created positive sea floor topography.

To the north of GB427 is a topographic ridge oriented roughly NE-SW which is a reflection of underlying and relatively shallow salt masses. Unlike GB427, this area displays the impressive effects of massive fluid expulsions that has been discussed separately in the previous case history. Within this area N-NW of GB427 impressive debris flows and fluidized mudflows have originated from two faulted and acoustically opaque fluid expulsion centers located on a northeast-southwest trending salt ridge upslope of the GB427 diapiric hill.

The diapiric hill in GB427 shares several important characteristics with the fluid expulsion centers to the north. The shallow reflection character over the expulsion area is amorphous on high resolution seismic profiles and there are large areas of patchy high amplitude backscatter on side-scan sonar records. Although the expulsion centers in GB382 and GB338 are also acoustically amorphous and have a few high amplitude backscatter areas on side-scan sonar records, the highly reflective backscatter areas on the top and flanks of the diapiric hill appear darker on side-scan data. These dark areas are much more widespread than in the cases of the upslope expulsion centers. They also function as prevalent reflective surfaces on high resolution seismic profiles. In addition, the diapiric hill exhibits numerous patterns that tend to radiate away from the crest. These features generally have small displacements and therefore do not dramatically offset the seafloor. Vertical displacement is usually 1 m or less.

3.   Available Data

The best possible high resolution acoustic data were acquired for investigation of the Auger Prospect area. Original data were acquired by Fugro-McClelland Marine Geosciences, Inc. using a Tri-Cluster 1/4 millisecond sampled multi-channel digital data for deepest penetration into the subsurface, a deep-tow 3.5 kHz subbottom profiler for configuration of the shallow subsurface, 100 kHz side-scan sonar for seafloor feature detection, and a narrow beam precision depth records for bathymetry. Mosaics of side-scan sonar data and maps of the subsurface were compiled by Fugro-McClelland personnel from geohazards survey data. Ground truth observations and samples were provided by two manned submersible dives on the GB427 diapiric hill using the Johnson Sea-Link research submersible. The first dive (JSL-1, Dive 3305) was made on September 6, 1992 and concentrated primarily on the top of the feature (touchdown at 613 m leave bottom at 608 m). The second dive (JSL-2, Dive 2896) was conducted on August 4, 1997, starting at a depth of 817 m and ended at a depth of 610 m. The objective of this second dive was to traverse the western flank of the hill where high amplitude zones appears on the side-scan sonar data from the base of the hill to its crest. During both dives, video documentation of the seafloor, 35 mm photographs, rock samples, and sediment grab samples were collected. Samples were analyzed for mineralogy using the X-ray diffraction technique (Cook et al., 1995). Stable isotope ratios of carbon ($\delta^{13}C$) and oxygen ($\delta^{18}O$) were provided by a commercial laboratory using PDB as a standard.

4.   Feature Characteristics

The symmetrical shape of the GB427 mound, as reflected on a bathymetric map, is mimicked by a strong internal reflector approximately 50-100 ms beneath the surface of this feature (Figure 36).

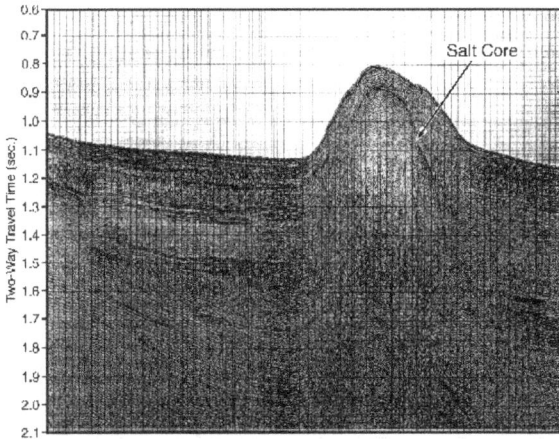

Figure 36. Migrated multichannel seismic profile (TriCluster data) across the GB427 mound illustrating the strong internal reflector which is less than 100 ms from the sea-floor at the mound's apex.

47

Beneath this strong reflector there are no coherent reflection horizons (acoustically opaque) which suggests either a rather homogeneous substance or perhaps the presence of gas. The strong and rather uniform acoustic impedance boundary that defines the mound interior is characteristic of an interface between terrigeous sediments and salt. Original interpretations of this feature suggest that it is salt-cored which certainly is consistent with the geophysical data (personal communication with Fugro-McClelland Marine Geosciences personnel who worked on the Auger Prospect project). Being a salt-cored diapiric structure suggests that existing sediments have been uplifted, faulted, and perhaps forced to fail under the force of gravity creating submarine landslides or slumps. Analysis of the multichannel seismic data indicate that numerous faults with small offsets are present in the sedimentary section above the salt in the crestal part of the mound.

When a somewhat more detailed view of the surface and near-subsurface sediments is analyzed (Figure 37), even the sediments between the salt core and the sea floor have an acoustically opaque nature, especially those sediments directly over the apex of the salt and on the slightly steeper western side of the mound. A side-scan sonar mosaic of the mound emphasized the complexity of the sea floor associated with this feature. During the initial analysis of the deep-tow side-scan and subbottom profile data, the dark reflective areas as well as the radial patterns originating near the mound top were difficult to interpret. Even with 3D-surface amplitude data, analyzed in conjunction with other remotely sensed (acoustic) data sets, a detailed interpretation was not possible till direct sea floor verification data were collected and integrated with other data sets. Additionally, 3D-seismic profiles across the GB427 mound did not indicate a phase inversion over the crest which identifies gas within the near-surface sediments (Figure 38).

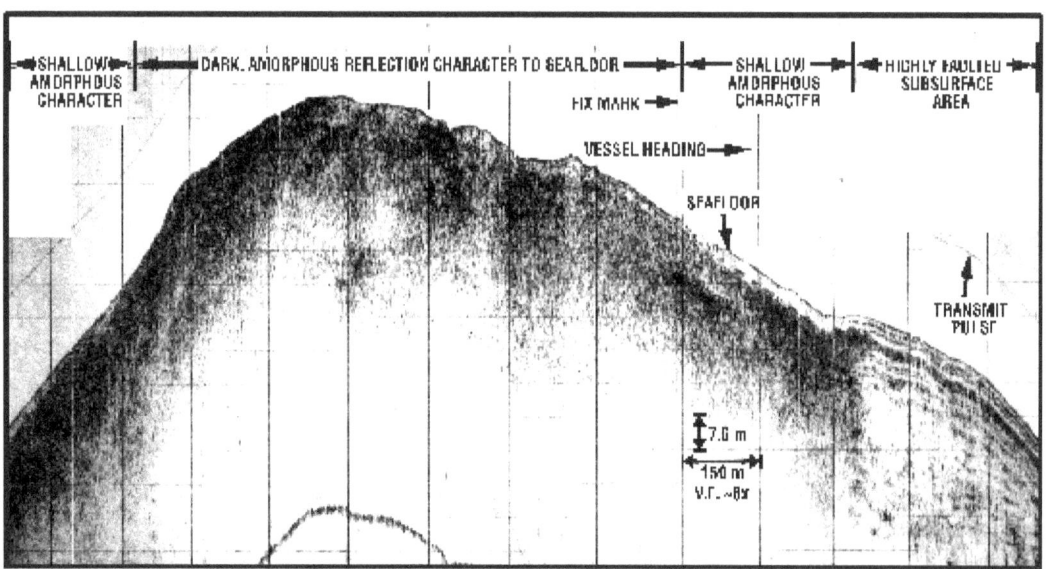

Figure 37. High resolution seismic (3.5 kHz) profile across the GB427 mound illustrating the acoustically opaque mound interior, bedded sediments on the mound flank, remnants of a hemipelagic drape deposit over part of the feature, and its irregular surface of variable reflectivity.

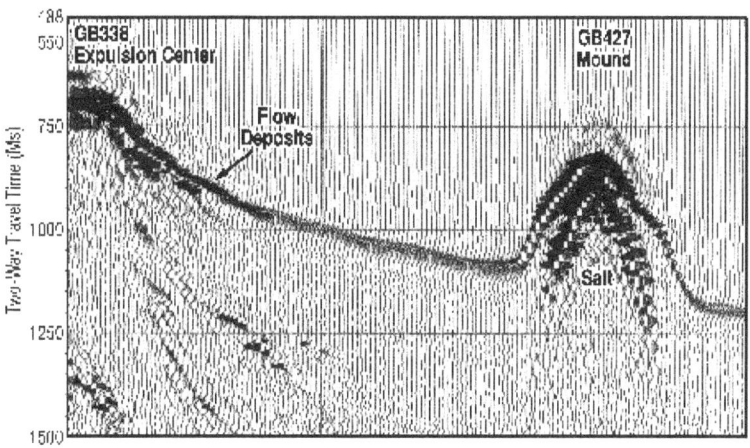

Figure 38. A 3D-seismic profile from the GB338 expulsion center to the GB427 diapiric mound. Note the polarity shift over the expulsion center, but no similar change in phase over the diapiric mound.

5. Feature Synopsis and Interpretation

Analysis of 3D-seismic surface amplitude data in conjunction with the deep-tow side-scan sonar and subbottom data produced a reasonably good correlation between the dark and complex patterns on side-scan data (Figure 39) and patterns of high amplitude on the subbottom profiles and 3D-seismic amplitude map (Figure 40).

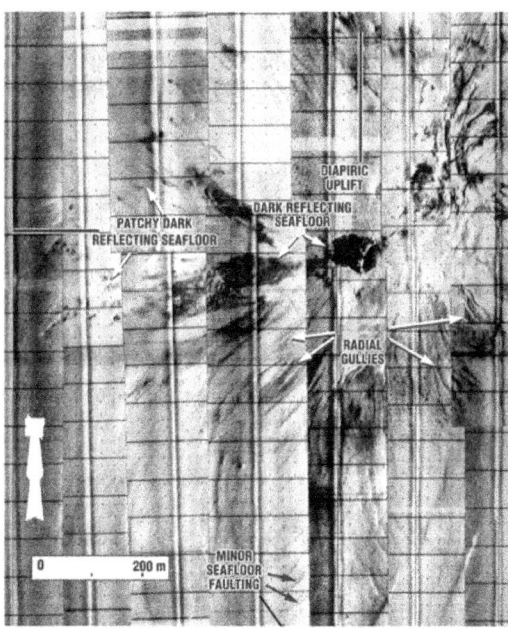

Figure 39. A deep-tow side-scan sonar mosaic of the GB427 mound illustrating important surface characteristics of this feature such as the irregular and highly reflective areas and the linear patterns that are radial to the mound crest area.

Direct observation and sampling of these areas using a manned submersible provided the necessary data to make an improved interpretation of the processes that impacted the mound surface and produced a set of response features identifiable on high resolution acoustic data sets.

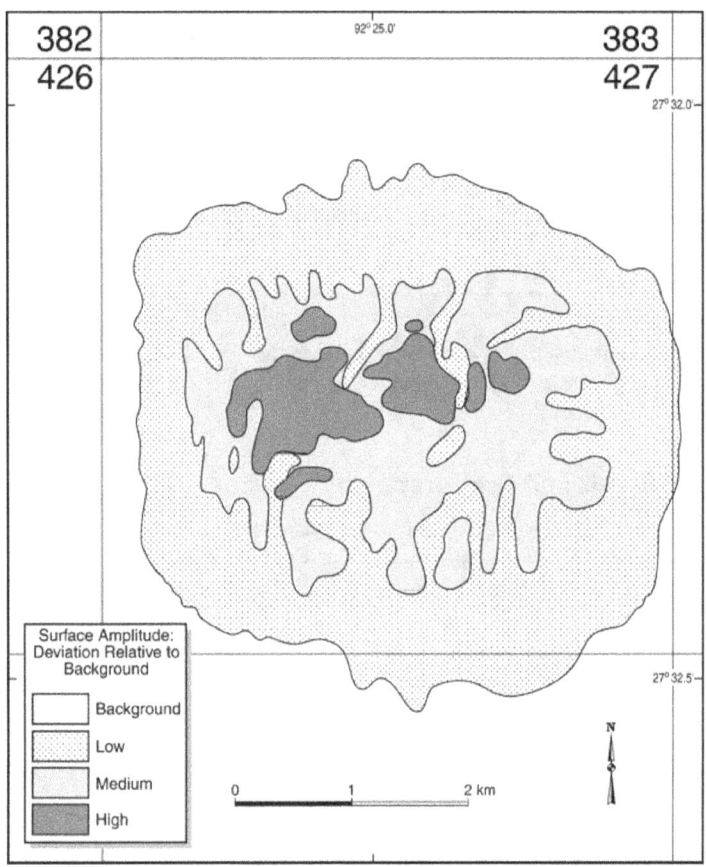

Figure 40. A map of 3D-seismic surface amplitude map of the GB427 mound. The high amplitude zones correlate to areas of lithified seafloor.

Sea floor verification data indicated that high amplitude areas on the 3D-seismic surface amplitude data correlate to regions of the mound top that are hard bottoms. These hard bottom areas resulted from the combined effects of previous fluid-gas expulsion and seafloor lithification. Expulsion centers at the crest of the mound did not appear to be presently active. The two expulsion centers that were directly observed were not degassing or forcing fluids to the surface and appeared to have been dormant for a long time. They were represented as slight depressions with obvious flow pathways oriented away from these depressions and down the mound flanks. The depressions were filled with fine-grained sediment covered with numerous disarticulated lucinid-vesycomyid clams (Figure 41). The fact that no phase reversal was observed on 3D-seismic profiles across the GB427 mound suggests that the vents are currently inactive, the near-surface sediments are not gas-charged. This observation suggests that if gas is still being delivered to the underlying sediments, it is at a slow rate, perhaps enough to cause the near surface sediments to be acoustically opaque on high resolution seismic data.

Figure 41. Disarticulated and scattered lucinid-vesycomyid clams at one of the dormant vent sites near the crest of the GB427 mound.

In close proximity to the dormant expulsion centers, the sea floor is lithified in the form of slabs, boulders, and gravel-sized debris. Samples of the shallow subsurface using short cores indicate that nodular masses of lithified shallow sediment are forming beneath the surface (Figure 42).

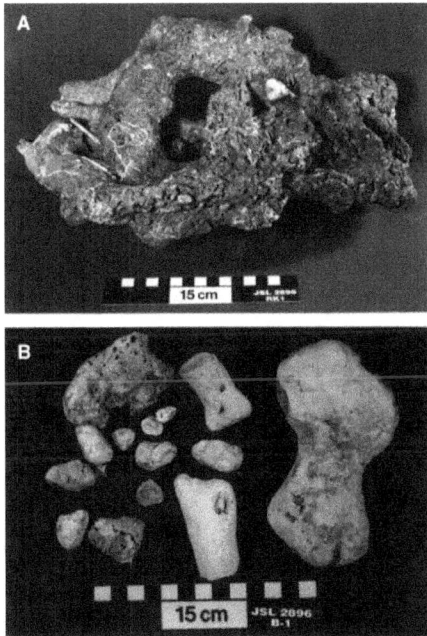

Figure 42. (a) massive rocks of authigenic carbonate are found on the surface and (b) nodular masses of host sediment cemented with ^{13}C-depleted Mg-calcite are found in the subsurface at the mound crest as well as along its flanks, especially near the flow pathways from upslope expulsion centers.

Lithification is not confined to the crestal areas of the mound, but lithified slabs, boulders, and gravel-sized masses are present on the sides of the gullies that radiate down the mound flanks (Figure 43). These radial features were originally interpreted as faults, but with ground truth data, they link directly with fluid expulsion centers at the top of the mound and therefore appear to be erosional in origin and the products of flows originating from the expulsion centers. The lithified surface and shallow subsurface material is composed of fine-grained host sediment (terrigenous clay and quartz silt) cemented with Mg-calcite and dolomite (trace amounts) that are ^{13}C-depleted (δ^{13}C range from -31.2‰ to -45.2‰ in a total of 4 samples tested). Light carbon isotope values indicate a link with hydrocarbons as a carbon source. These results are consistent with similar analyses of other hydrocarbon seep/vent-related carbonates from the northern Gulf of Mexico continental slope.

Figure 43. Lithification on the flank of the GB427 mound.

Finally, rapid expulsion of fluids and sediment, appears to have been a dominant process associated with the GB427 diapiric mound at sometime in the past. However, because the flows are episodic, an environmental setting that provides limited trophic resources to sustain complex and widespread chemosynthetic communities results. In addition, rapid sedimentation during expulsion events is detrimental to fixed bottom dwelling organisms. Only disarticulated lucinid-vesycomyid clam shells scattered on extruded mud surfaces mark the sites of sediments that were once hydrocarbon-charged. The delivery of hydrocarbon-charged fluids and fluidized sediments to the modern seafloor is an episodic process that apparently does not occur often enough to sustain viable and diverse chemosynthetic communities. Migration pathways at the top of the mound are short between the mound surface and underlying salt. Discharge events are apparently not large enough to initiate slope failures. No slumps or larger failure scarps were observed during field verification data collection. Acoustically, the surface of the GB427 mound forms a strong reflector that does not demonstrate a phase inversion that would suggest gas-charged sediments in the shallow subsurface (Figure 44). The acoustic characteristics of the GB427 mound are presented in Tables 12 to 14.

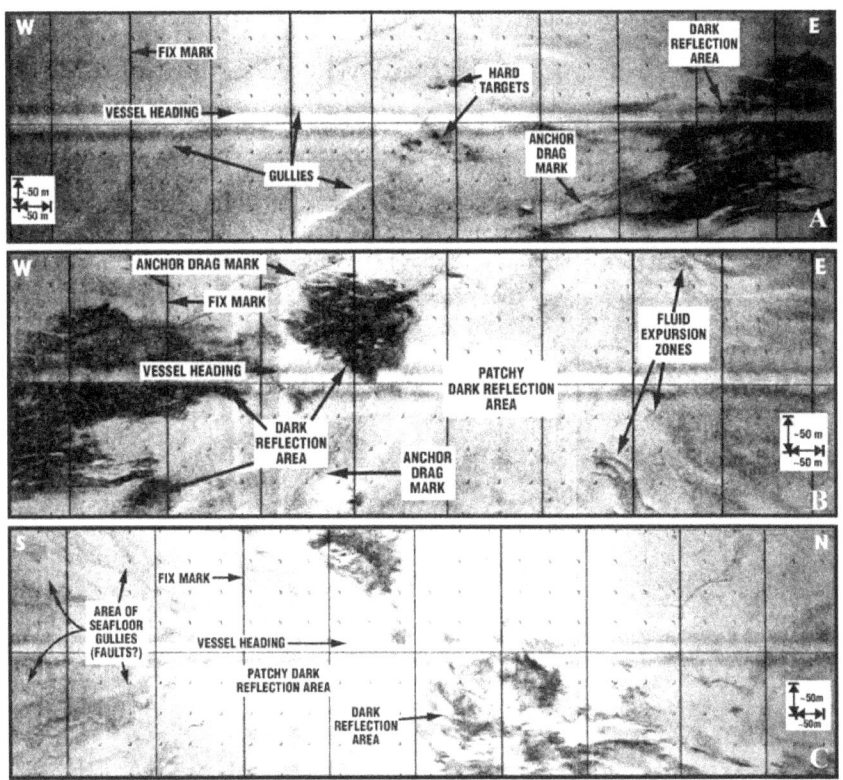

Figure 44. Site-specific areas of side-scan sonar data as extracted from the mosaic of the GB427 mound, illustrated in Figure 38.

Table 12. Side-scan sonar image characteristics for GB 427 case study.

	Feature	Feature Field	Flanking Areas
Acoustic Backscatter			
Strong	X		
Moderate			
Weak			X
Mixed	X		
Target Shapes			
Bumps			
Cones			
Mounds			
Pinnacles			
Depressions			
Irregular	X		
Target Surface			
Smooth			X
Irregular	X		
Variable	X		
Feature Occurrence			
Isolated			
Asymmetric Groups			
Linear	X		
Circular			
Elliptical			
Polygonal	X		

Table 13. Seismic facies for GB 427 case study.

Seismic Facies	Feature	Feature Field	Flanking Units
Gently Divergent-Parallel			
Strongly Divergent			
Onlapping			
Downlapping			X
Drape	X		X
a. Layered			
b. Acoustically Turbid	X		X
Sigmoid Progradational			
Chaotic			
Contorted-Discordant			
Acoustically Turbid	X		
a. Complete			
b. Stacked Zones			
c. Chaotic Discontinuous Reflectors	X		
(1) Parallel	X		
(2) Parabolic			
(3) Mixed			

Table 14. Surface reflection characteristics for GB 427 case study. F = feature; FF = feature field; FA = feature adjacent area.

	3.5 kHz Pinger			Intermediate Source			3D Seismic		
	F	FF	FA	F	FF	FA	F	FF	FA
Surface Reflection Strength									
Strong	X			X			X		
Moderate			X						X
Weak				X		X			
Variable									
Width of Surface Reflectors (MS)									
0-2									
2-5	X			X		X			
>5							X		X
Variable									
Reflector Characteristics									
Simple Doublet									
Stratified	X		X			X			
Prolonged	X			X					
Chaotic									
Windowed	X								
Bright Spots									
Surface Reflection Geometries									
Planar			X			X	X		X
Wavy	X			X					
Mounded									
Scarped	X								
Isolated Pinnacle/s									
Isolated Depression/s									
Parabolics									
Isolated									
Multiple									
Overlapping									
Phase Inversion									

54

E. Case Study: Three Separate Features and Distinct Bottom Types (Mounded Carbonates, Extinct Mud Volcano, and Collapse Depression), Green Canyon Block 53

1. Introduction

The first high resolution geophysical survey of the GC52-53 area was conducted in 1983 by Racal Geophysics, Inc. This initial survey found that much of the sea floor in these blocks was mounded and that the mounds had very little internal acoustic character and highly reflective surfaces. Although there were areas of relatively smooth sea floor outside the mounded zones, some smooth areas had numerous pockmarks. The seafloor geology of GC53 was found to be more complex than that of GC52. In addition to the large areas of hard bottom mounds down the central and western parts of the block, GC53 had a large mound, interpreted as a mud volcano, in the northeast quadrant and a rounded depression in the southwest that showed a signature of gas moving through the water column above it on 3.5 kHz profiles. These three different bottom features of GC53 will be discussed in this case history.

2. Geologic Setting

The lease block GC53 is located at the shelf edge and at the transition between the continental shelf and slope (Figure 45). Water depths in GC53 range from about 100 m in the most northern parts of the block to approximately 220 m in the south (Figure 46).

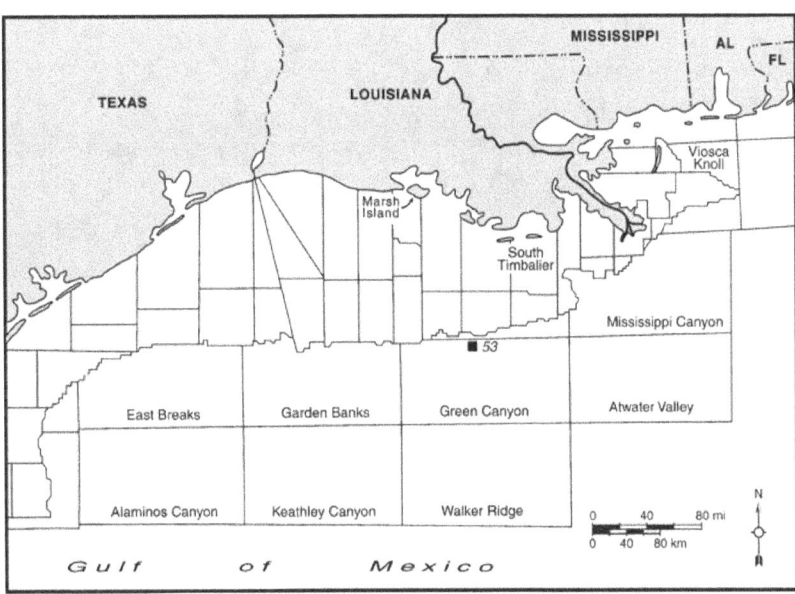

Figure 45. Location map for Green Canyon Block 53 (GC53).

A raised area of sea floor bounded by regional faults trends NW-SE through the northern half of the block. This area and an additional region to the SW are characterized by mounded bottom topography where some individual mounds have over 10 m relief above the surrounding sea floor. Early studies of these shelf edge banks and mounds that characterize much of the shelf-slope transition in the northern Gulf found that some banks (e.g. the Flower Garden Bank of the NW Gulf) supported reef-building communities while most others were veneered with a sponge-coralline algal assmbledge (Bright and Pequegnat, 1974; Rezak and Bright, 1981; Rezak et al., 1985). These reefs, carbonates banks, and mounds seem strangely out of place in a sedimentary province dominated by large volumes of terrigenous clastic sediments transported to the outer shelf and slope during periods of falling to low sea level, especially during the Pleistocene. As Rezak et al. (1985) have pointed out, most of these reefs, banks, and mound complexes are located over shallow allochthonous salt that in recent geologic history has been emplaced near the modern sea floor.

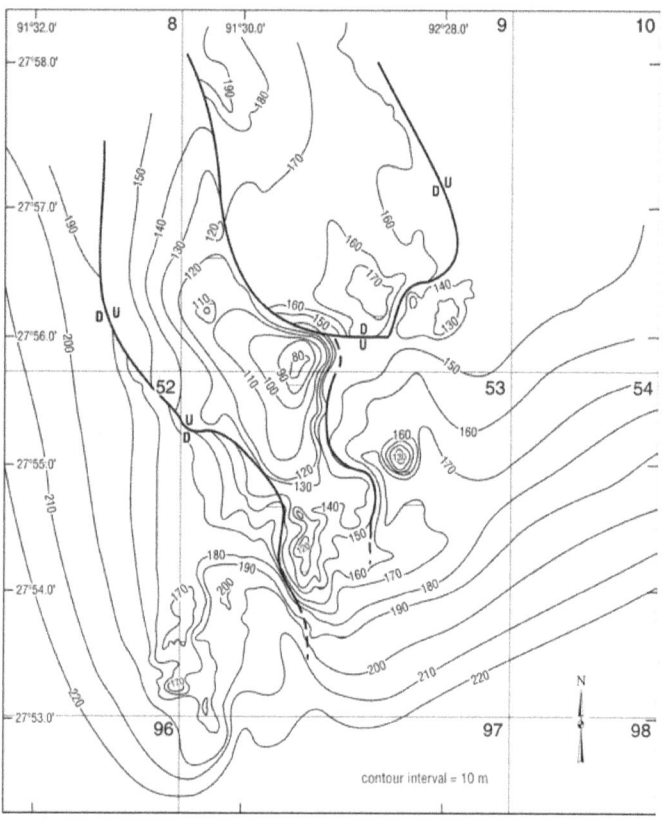

Figure 46. Bathymetric map for GC53 and surrounding areas. The locations of large regional faults have been superimposed on the bathymetry.

Recent studies of structure of the shelf and slope (Diegel et al., 1995; Rowan et al., 1999) emphasize the interplay between application of large volumes of sediment to a system containing thick units of deformable salt. Research by Suter and Berryhill (1985), Roberts and Sydow (1994), and Anderson et al. (1996) clearly demonstrate the relationship between sea level cycles and fluvial-deltaic deposition at the shelf edge and on the adjacent continental slope. During periods of falling-to-lowstands of sealevel the shelf edge becomes a focal point for deposition. Suter and Berryhill (1985) demonstrate that local depocenter development at the shelf edge causes a rapid response in vertical salt migration. These events seem to be responsible for the numerous near-surface salt masses at or near the shelf edge that now support overlying reefs,

56

carbonate banks, and mound complexes. Salt movement also creates faults and reactivates existing faults which can provide a setting for fluid and gas migration to the seafloor.

Roberts (1992) suggested that some of the reefs, banks, and mounds of the shelf edge may be seated on a substrate of authigenic carbonate created as a by-product from the microbial utilization of the hydrocarbons. Even the well-studied Flower Garden Banks may have been initiated on a hard substrate created by this process. Although acknowledged and certainly studied in detail (Bright et al., 1980; Rezak et al., 1985), the hydrocarbon and brine seeps associated with these banks were initially evaluated with ecological impacts to the reef community as a focal point. The significance to reef and bank locations was not realized until studies of seeps from many different settings (Hovland and Judd 1988), and specifically the Gulf of Mexico continental slope (Roberts et al., 1987, 1988), provided a clear association between authigenic carbonates and hydrocarbon seeps. These observations of seeps suggested that the authigenic carbonates provided rather extensive hard substrates on which reef-building biota attached and created buildups in an environmental setting that was otherwise characterized by an abundance of fine-grained siliciclastic sediment, and thus a poor area in which to initiate reef and bioherm growth. Rezak et al. (1985) pointed out that gas plumes have been detected in the water column on many high resolution seismic profiles taken across banks of the northern Gulf.

The GC53 area is at the shelf edge and has a large area of carbonate mounds that are currently veneered with encrusting coralline algae, various types of sponges, and other sessil organisms. Gas has been observed escaping through the mound complex in several locations as well as in off-mound sites. The inactive mud volcano to the east of the mounded seafloor area is evidence of the fact that fluidized sediment and gas are delivered to the sea floor in greater quantities and at higher rates in the recent past than we are able to observe today. Observational data suggest that a collapse depression in the SW portion of the block is still an active gas venting site.

3. Available Data

The original high resolution geophysical survey by Racal Geophysics, Inc. of Houston, Texas was conducted for the GC52-53 area in the summer of 1983. Data were generated from four different surface-tow acoustic sources: a 3.5 kHz subbottom profiler, an 8.4 kilojoule sparker system, a side-scan sonar system, and a precision echosounder (for baythymetry). Survey data were located using the Lorac AA net noting the setback distances of sources and receivers from the Lorac antenna atop the survey vessel's mast. Data from this initial survey confirmed the mounded, bank-like character of GC53 and the presence of gas in the water column at several sites. Later, McClelland Engineers, Inc. conducted an engineering geology and geotechnical assessment of the GC 52-53 area which included the acquisition of high resolution geophysical data as well as piston cores for laboratory testing. Interpretations of sea floor geology for these blocks were based primarily on data from a precision echosounder (Edo Western Model 4077) for bathymetry, surface-tow side-scan sonar (EG&G SMS 960) for geomorphology of the bottom, and an ORE 3.5 kHz subbottom profile plus mini-sleeve exploder for subsurface evaluations. Later, deep-tow side-scan sonar data and 3.5 kHz profiles were collected as part of a pipeline survey between the Jolliet Platform site in GC184 to the Marquette Field in the GC 52-53 area. Finally, both digital high resolution seismic and side-scan sonar data were collected from GC53 as part of this MMS-CMI study. Three high resolution seismic sources were used to image selected targets, and EG&G Uniboom profiler, a Seismic Systems Model S-15 water gun (15 in³), and a Seismic Systems GI air-gun (50 in³). Surface-tow side-scan sonar data were provided by and EG&G Model 260 digital imaging system. These geophysical data were acquired in both analog and digital formats. DELPH 2 acquisition and processing software was used for acquiring the seismic data. Survey planning was accomplished through the hydrographic software program HYPACK. Location data were supplied through HYPACK using differential GPS (Magnavox M4 200d). Seafloor verification data from GC53 on the mud volcano was provided by JSL-1, dive 2582. Mounded carbonates were investigated on JSL-1, Dives 3111, 3112, 3113, 3114. The collape depression was observed and sampled on JSL-1, Dive 2583 and JSL-2, Dive 2894 and 2912.

4. Feature Characteristics

a. Mounded Carbonates Much of the area within GC53 falls within a bottom type category dominated by mounds of various sizes. Topographically, elevated areas in the NW, central, and SW parts of the block are characterized by a sea floor composed of hard, carbonate mounds, some of which have over 10 m relief (Figure 47).

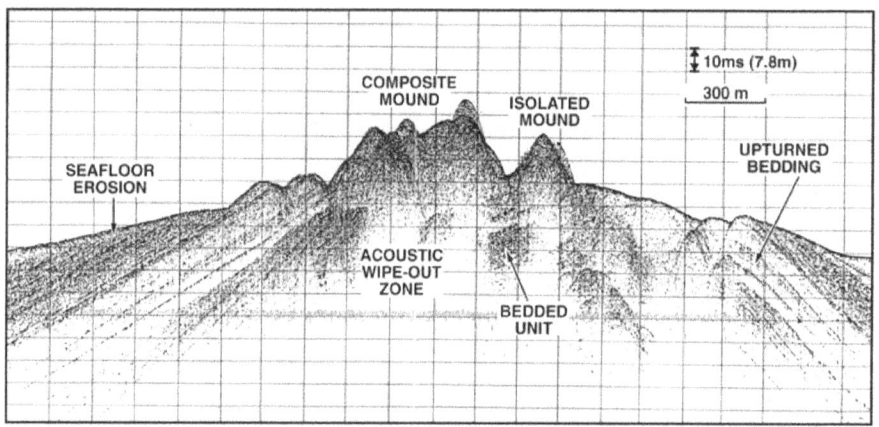

Figure 47. High resolution seismic profile (3.5 kHz) across the mounded area in the SW sector of GC53 (see Figure 45). This profile illustrates the individual and fused mounds of this area.

In the northern Gulf of Mexico both reefs and bioherms have been identified as contributors to the province of mounds and banks along the shelf-slope transition zone (Rezak and Bright, 1981; Rezak et al., 1985). The term reef refers to linear or mound-like buildups that have been constructed by frame-building organisms (e.g. corals) that are both organically and inorganically cemented into a structure that is resistant to significant erosion by physical processes (waves and currents). These types of carbonate buildups are generally associated with the photic zone of warm, tropical oceanic settings. However, special oceanographic conditions in the northwestern Gulf of Mexico allow true coral reefs of the Flower Garden Banks to survive in a subtropical latitudinal setting (Gittings et al., 1992; Lugo-Fernandez, 1998). Bioherms, in contrast, are mound-like buildups that contain the remains of a limited variety of calcareous organisms that are not frame-builders, (Cunnings and Shrock, 1928). Bioherms have no latitudinal restrictions like reefs. Lithoherms are deepwater (below the photic zone) mounded structures formed by submarine lithification of sediment that may contain some skeletal debris (Neumann et al., 1977). A subset of the general class of lithoherms are those mounded carbonates that develop as by-products from the microbial utilization of hydrocarbons. Aharon et al. (1993) and Roberts and Aharon (1994) have informally introduce the term chemoherm to distinguish these special mounded carbonates that are the by-products of chemosynthesis.

The shelf edge mounds and banks of the northern Gulf, of which the GC53 mounds are a part, display rough topography superimposed over shallow salt. Numerous faults accompanied by sea floor scarps are common to this setting. Hydrocarbon and brine vents are commonly associate with these features (Rezak et al., 1985; Roberts et al.,1989). Figure 48 illustrates the shallow salt, numerous faults that intersect the modern sea floor, and the variety of sea floor features that are associated with these faults.

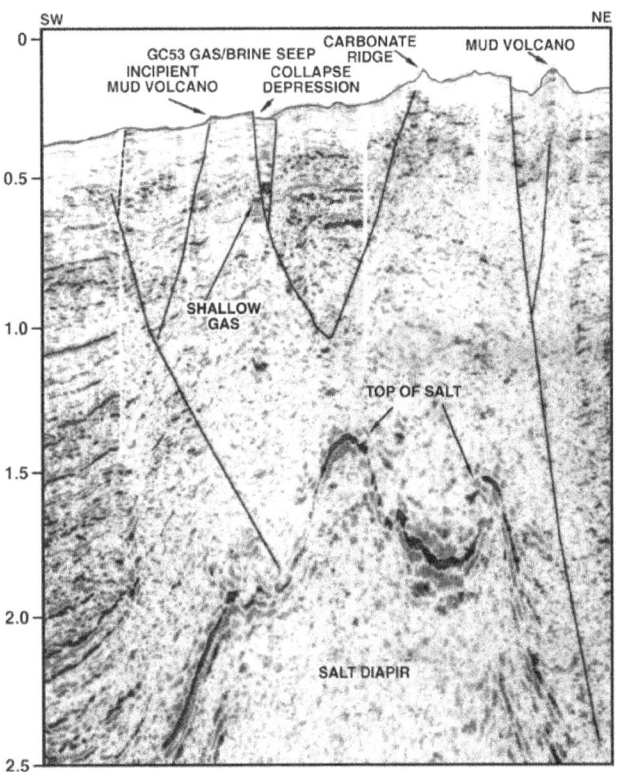

Figure 48. A 3D-seismic profile oriented NE-SW across GC53 showing the relationships between salt, faults, and important surface features.

Direct inspection of the GC53 carbonate mounds indicates that all of the mounds, ranging in depth from approximately 80-200 m, are veneered by actively growing communities of sponges, coralline algal encrustations, leafy algae, antipatharians, crinoids, and hydroids. Figure 49 illustrates typical views of biogenic veneers of the GC53 mounds. Although ^{13}C-depleted

59

authigenic carbon ates were found in local sites with the zones of mounded sea floor, the living biogenic veneer obscures the character of the mound interiors. Therefore, the contention that biogenic growth could have originated on a hard substrate provided by hydrocarbon seep-derived carbonates (Roberts, 1992) cannot be easily tested. Mounds occur as individual features as well as fused groups, as is illustrated on the high resolution seismic line of Figure 47. In many places, sediments immediately surrounding the mounds are coarse and consist of both shell debris and rhodoliths (Figure 49). These coarse sediments, especially associated with the shallowest mounds of the central GC53 area, appear to be the products of physical winnowing of fine-grained components leaving a coarse shell lag. Loop Current intrusions and tropical storm waves are the two most probable physical process agents.

Figure 49. Photographs of the GC53 mounded area in the middle of the block illustrating: (a) a large mound surface encrusted with crinoids sponges, hydroids, and antipatharians on a hard substrate of encrusting coralline alga, (b) a small mound-like buildup of coralline alga with attached sessile organisms, and (c) the edge of a mound with a field of rhodoliths at its base. Water depths range from 105-120 m for these pictures.

Although high resolution seismic profiles of the mounded areas generally indicate that the mounds display hard, reflective surfaces and acoustically opaque interiors, bedding can sometimes be seen in the mound interiors, suggesting possible seep-related lithification of faulted blocks of sea floor as the starting point for biogenic accretions (Figure 47). On side-scan sonar images (Figure 50), mound surfaces are rough and reflective.

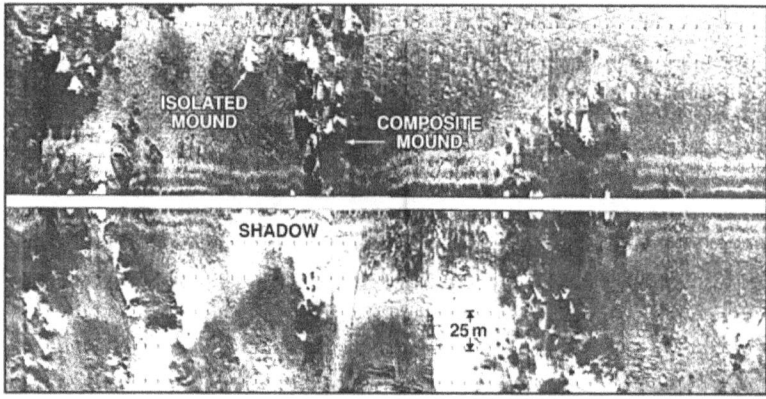

Figure 50. Side-scan sonar image of the central mounded area in GC53. Note the complex nature of the seafloor in this area and the various sizes and shapes of individual mounds. This line is coincident with the 35 kHz profile of Figure 47.

Many mounds merge to make composite features formed from the process of growth and fusion of several smaller mounds to make larger ones. Mound sides appear to be steep on side-scan data, even though the surface-tow high resolution seismic data suggest less steep sides because of parabolic reflector shapes. The steep sides of many mounds have been confirmed by direct observation. Gas has been found escaping through some of the mounds, especially in the SW sector of the block. Analysis of gas samples from the mounded area of GC53 indicates that the gas was methane of biogenic origin (personal communication, Mark Beunas, Chevron).

      b. <u>Extinct Mud Volcano</u> In the NE sector of GC53 the bathymetric contours of Figure 45 clearly define a cone-shaped feature with a base diameter of approximately 600 m and with over 30 m relief above the surrounding sea floor. The base of the feature occurs at a depth of approximately 160 m while the crest is slightly less than 130 m. The 3D-seismic profile that cuts through this feature (Figure 48) suggest that it is directly the product of expulsion of fluidized sediment by way of a deep cutting fault that extends down the flank of a shallow salt mass under the GC53 area. A high resolution seismic profile (3.5 kHz) across this feature illustrates an acoustically opaque interior, but with a distinctive unit having little internal acoustic character (approximately 5 m thick) draping across the entire feature (Figure 51).

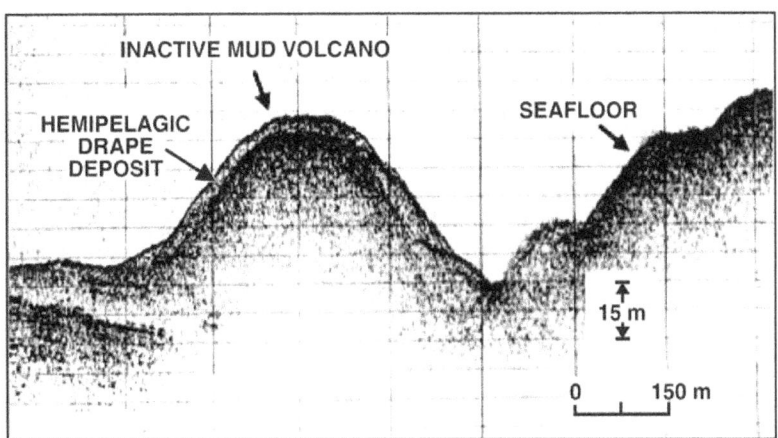

Figure 51. A 3.5 kHz profile across the inactive mud volcano in the NE section of GC53. Note the hemipelagic drape deposit across this feature.

Seismic profiles indicate wedge-shaped sedimentary units flanking the cone-shaped feature suggesting vertical accretion from a sediment source originating from the feature itself. Upon direct visual inspection using a manned submersible, the flanks of the cone are well-burrowed with distinct fluting on the SW side. These few grooves originated near the apex of the structure and extended downslope to the feature base. Ridges between furrows are partially lithified with plate-like slabs of carbonate-rich cemented sediment (Figure 52). These furrows suggest the downslope movement of fluids or fluidized sediment which eroded pathways through the hemipelagic sediments that drape the core flanks. Furrow walls expose thin lithified and thicker unlithified units suggesting alternating periods of sedimentation and exposure resulting the lithification. Cements in these crusts were mostly Mg-calcite that are extremely ^{13}C-depleted, indicating a link to microbial degradation of hydrocarbons (Neurauter and Roberts, 1994). These hydrocarbons were probably incorporated in the muds and deposited with them during the mound-building process.

Figure 52. Bottom photograph of a gully on the flank of the GC53 inactive mud volcano along its SW side. This gully is flanked by slabs of lithified sediments while the gully floor is relatively free of this lithification.

Observation of the mound crest revealed a flattened sea floor with no indication of fluid or gas expulsion and no chemosynthetic organisms except one small area which supported a patch of white *Beggiatoa* sp. (approximately 1 m in diameter). Feature-top sediments were highly burrowed with a few localized areas of hard substrate that supported anemones and a few sea fans (gorgonians). Because of its cone shape, hint of sediment accretion structure on the cone flanks, coincidence with a deep-cutting fault, and acoustically opaque subsurface character far below the modern seafloor, this feature is interpreted as an inactive mud volcano. The furrowed side is interpreted to be a response to the waning phase of activity when only sediment-free fluids welled up from the central vent of the feature and ran down the south side eroding sediment in the process. The lack of a central depression relates to the apparent long period since this feature has been active. The hemipelagic drape over the entire cone suggests it has been inactive for several thousand years since these deposits accumulate at a rate of about 30 cm/1000 years (unpublished data).

c. Collapse Depression On the 3D-seismic profile shown in Figure 48, this unusual feature appears as a graben. The sea floor associated with it is visibly lower than surrounding areas. An early high resolution seismic profile (3.5 kHz) taken by Racal Geophysical in 1983 in the GC53 area crossed this feature and found the small and highly reflective area of depressed sea floor venting gas into the overlying water column (Figure 53). Side-scan sonar data collected as a part of this project indicate that the floor of the collapse depression is very smooth except for a central area characterized by two distinct vents, extruded mud sheets, and semi-concentric low-relief scarps related to local sea floor subsidence (Figure 54).

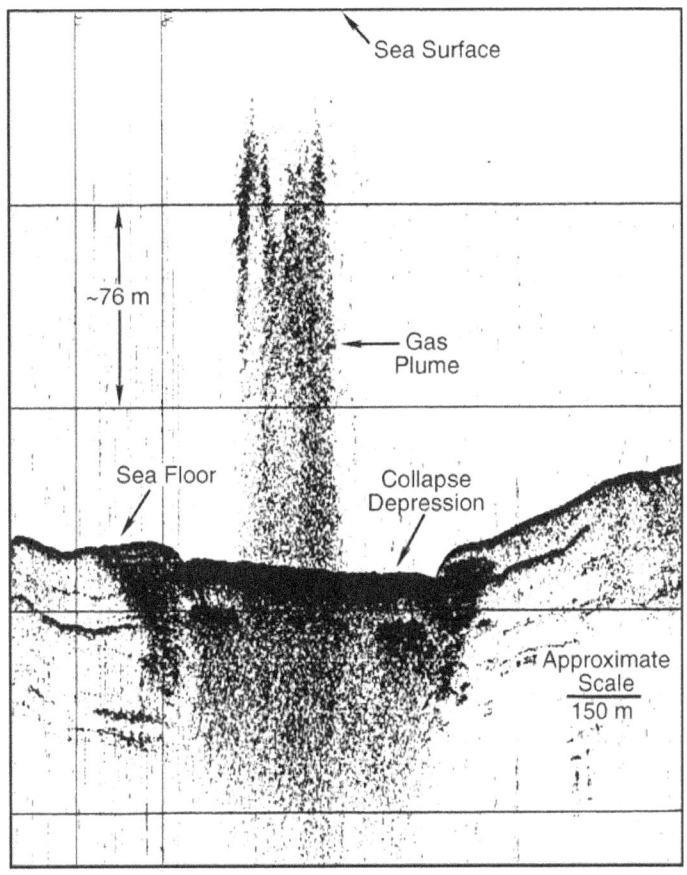

Figure 53. A 3.5 kHz profile across the collapse depression in the SW quadrant of GC53. Note the highly reflective seafloor within the depression and the distinct gas plume in the overlying water column.

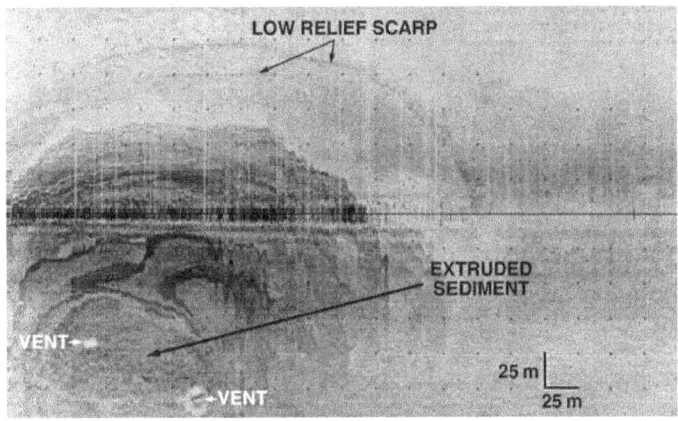

Figure 54. This side-scan sonar record, acquired as part of this project, illustrates the venting area within the collapse depression, newly deposited mud flows, and a set of roughly circular low-relief scarps indicating local subsidence.

Direct observation and sampling of this feature on three occasions confirmed the smooth extruded mud floor of the depression, fresh unoxidized light gray mud sheets originating from the vents illustrated in the side-scan sonar image (Figure 54), and the venting of gas into the water column. On all three visits to this site, *Beggiatoa* mats were observed on the older mud surface of the collapse depression. These sediments were dark and reducing beneath the thin oxidized surficial layer. No other chemosynthetic organisms were observed at this site. Escaping gas was also found at the central venting site on all three dives on this feature. However, the dive in 1997 (JSL-2, Dive 2894) encountered a dynamic event characterized by violent outgassing (Figure 55). This event resulted in gas bubbles traveling from the sea floor to the sea surface and large pieces of mud (up to ~ 15 cm diameter) being propelled into the water column along with an abundance of fine-grained suspended sediment. This event emphasized the episodic and potentially dynamic nature of sea floor outgassing that has never been directly measured, but may have important practical consequences to man's activities in deep water. A follow-up dive at this site five days after the active venting event indicated that the vents were still active but at a much decrease level of intensity.

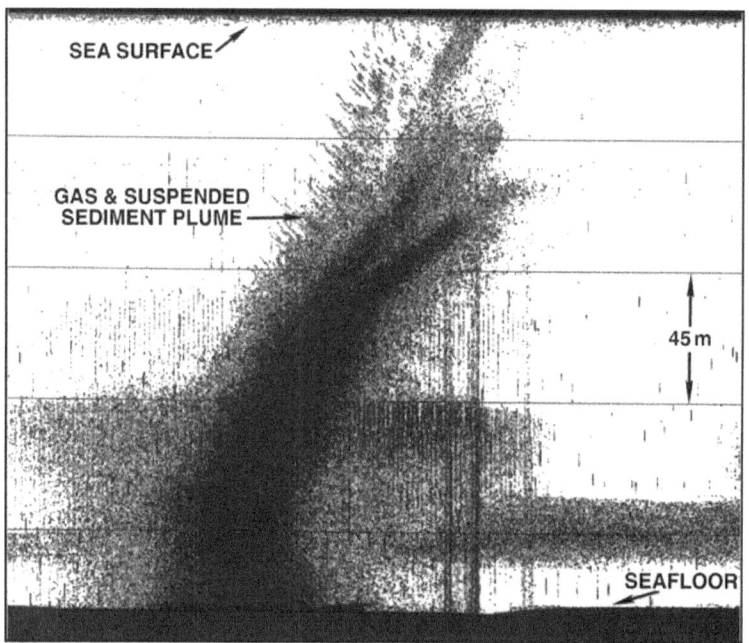

Figure 55. This figure represents the cross section of a combined gas and suspended sediment plume acquired by a precision depth recorder prior to a manned submersible dive on this feature in the summer of 1997. This exceedingly energetic episode of venting resulted in bubble-phase gas reaching the sea surface.

5. Feature Synopsis and Interpretation

High resolution geophysical data clearly distinguish the mounded sea floor, the inactive mud volcano, and the collapse depression as fundamentally different bottom types and features. On the 3D-seismic surface amplitude map of GC53 (Figure 56) sea floor areas representing these three features all display surface amplitudes that significantly deviate from background.

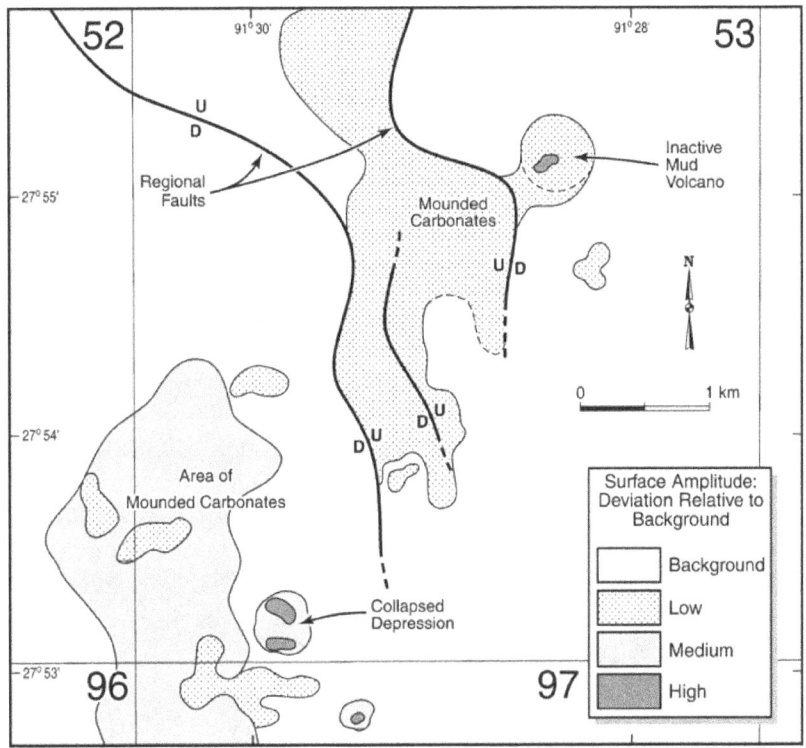

Figure 56. This 3D-seismic surface amplitude map of GC53 clearly identifies that three bottom types and features discussed in this report: (a) mounded carbonates, (b) inactive mud volcano, and (c) gas-emitting collapse depression.

The areas of mounded sea floor are presently covered by a living veneer of organisms, some of which help accrete these features with biogenically precipitated Ca-Mg carbonate (primarily coralline alga). The mounds are hard carbonate structures with a complex surface comprised of small-scale surface roughness elements (local buildups) of 1-2 m and topographic lows containing pockets of sediment. The large complex mounds tend to have relatively steep sides that commonly interface with a shell-rich sediment around the mound base and in pockets across the mound surface. Side-scan sonar images of these mounds corroborate their complex surface structure, steep sides, and the variability of their relief (Figure 52). High resolution seismic profiles across the mounded areas of GC53 confirm the acoustically opaque interiors of these features, the sometimes clear relationship with bedded sediments as a substrate, and the lack of "pull-down" or "pull-up" of reflectors (bedded units) interfacing with the acoustically opaque mound interior. Surface amplitude data derived from 3D-seismic over the GC53 area clearly distinguish the mounded areas as having a moderate amplitude deviation above background. Even though a few small gas seeps were observed by manned research submersible within the areas of mounded seafloor, no phase inversions were noted in the 3D-seismic data. That is, the mounds produced a response in phase with the surrounding sea floor. This result coupled with the evaluated amplitude response suggests a hard bottom that is not associated with sediments or carbonates that are gas-charged. Individual acoustic characteristics of this bottom type as determined on high resolution seismic and side-scan sonar records are summarized in Tables15 to 17.

The isolated and bathymetrically distinct mound in the NE quadrant of GC53 was interpreted as an inactive mud volcano based on its seismic character, geomorphology, and associated surface feature. Although seismic profiles from several acoustic sources indicate an acoustically opaque interior for this feature, a hemipelagic drape appears to have been deposited over this cone-shaped mound. High resolution seismic data also define flanking wedge-like accretion units that suggest vertical growth even through interior stratigraphy of the feature cannot be readily identified. The surface of this cone is relatively smooth, as determined on side-scan sonar records as well as with direct observation (manned submersible), except for limited gully-like fluting of the surface on the cones south side. This fluting is interpreted as a product of sediment-free fluid expulsion during the final stages of mud volcano activity. No "pull-up" or "pull-down" of reflectors interfacing with this feature was observed. The 3D-seismic surface amplitude data indicate that the overall mud volcano deviates slightly above background, but a small area near the apex of the feature displays a high deviation from background (Figure 56). A questionable phase reversal is observable in both the digital high resolution data acquired for this project and on 3D-seismic profiles that cut the apex of the cone. Although there was very little surface expression of a gas seep (one small area of bacterial mat development), perhaps gas-charged sediments still exist in the subsurface feeder system of the cone interior. Individual acoustic characteristics of this feature as determined from high resolution seismic and side-scan sonar data are summarized in Tables 18 to 20.

The collapse depression in the SW quadrant of GC53 is not defined in the regional bathymetry (Figure 46), but is clearly visible in the 3D-seismic surface amplitude data (Figure 56). This feature is depressed 3-4 m below surrounding topography, is roughly circular, and is filled with dark reducing mud covered with bacterial mats (*Beggiatoa* sp.). No other chemosynthetic organisms were observed within the confines of this feature. Although the surface of this sediment is smooth, side-scan sonar data confirm an expulsion area in the north-central area of the depression which shows sheets of recently extruded fluidized mud and concentric scarps caused by local collapse. The surface amplitude data outline the circular nature of this feature and indicate a clear moderate-to-strong deviation from background (Figure 56). Two strong anomalies are present within the circular confines of the feature. The northernmost amplitude anomaly corresponds to the vent areas shown on side-scan sonar (Figure 54). A second vent was not identified on high resolution geophysical data or by direct inspection of the feature using a manned submersible. Perhaps this anomaly is responding to a shallow subsurface gas accumulation which has little or no surface expression. A notable characteristic of the overall feature is that on high resolution seismic flanking reflectors interfacing with the acoustically opaque center of this feature tend to exhibit slight pull-down which is consistent with the presence of gas in the sediments. Individual acoustic characteristics of this feature from high resolution seismic and side-scan sonar data are summarized in Tables 21 to 23.

Table 15. Side-scan sonar image characteristics for GC 53, mounded carbonates, case study.

	Feature	Feature Field	Flanking Areas
Acoustic Backscatter			
Strong	X	X	
Moderate			X
Weak			
Mixed		X	
Target Shapes			
Bumps			
Cones			
Mounds	X	X	
Pinnacles	X	X	
Depressions			
Irregular			
Target Surface			
Smooth			X
Irregular	X	X	
Variable	X	X	X
Feature Occurrence			
Isolated	X		
Asymmetric Groups	X	X	
Linear			
Circular		X	
Elliptical			
Polygonal	X	X	

Table 16. Seismic facies for GC 53, mounded carbonates, case study.

Seismic Facies	Feature	Feature Field	Flanking Units
Gently Divergent-Parallel			
Strongly Divergent			X
Onlapping			
Downlapping			
Drape			
a. Layered			
b. Acoustically Turbid	X	X	
Sigmoid Progradational			
Chaotic			
Contorted-Discordant			
Acoustically Turbid			
a. Complete			
b. Stacked Zones			
c. Chaotic Discontinuous Reflectors		X	
(1) Parallel			
(2) Parabolic		X	
(3) Mixed			

Table 17. Surface reflection characteristics for GC 53, mounded carbonates, case study. F = feature; FF = feature field; FA = feature adjacent area.

	3.5 kHz Pinger			Intermediate Source			3D Seismic		
	F	FF	FA	F	FF	FA	F	FF	FA
Surface Reflection Strength									
Strong	X	X		X	X		X	X	
Moderate			X			X			X
Weak									
Variable									
Width of Surface Reflectors (MS)									
0-2			X						
2-5	X	X		X	X	X			
>5							X	X	X
Variable									
Reflector Characteristics									
Simple Doublet							X	X	X
Stratified			X			X			
Prolonged	X	X		X	X				
Chaotic									
Windowed	X	X		X	X				
Bright Spots									
Surface Reflection Geometries									
Planar			X			X			X
Wavy									
Mounded	X	X		X	X		X	X	
Scarped									
Isolated Pinnacle/s		X							
Isolated Depression/s									
Parabolics									
Isolated									
Multiple									
Overlapping									
Phase Inversion									

Table 18. Side-scan sonar image characteristics for GC 53, extinct mud volcano, case study.

	Feature	Feature Field	Flanking Areas
Acoustic Backscatter			
Strong			
Moderate	X		
Weak			X
Mixed			
Target Shapes			
Bumps			
Cones			
Mounds			
Pinnacles			
Depressions			
Irregular			
Target Surface			
Smooth	X		X
Irregular			
Variable	X		
Feature Occurrence			
Isolated	X		
Asymmetric Groups			
Linear			
Circular			
Elliptical			
Polygonal			

Table 19. Seismic facies for GC 53, extinct mud volcano, case study.

Seismic Facies	Feature	Feature Field	Flanking Units
Gently Divergent-Parallel			X
Strongly Divergent			
Onlapping			
Downlapping			
Drape	X		
a. Layered			
b. Acoustically Turbid	X		
Sigmoid Progradational			X
Chaotic			
Contorted-Discordant			
Acoustically Turbid	X		
a. Complete			
b. Stacked Zones			
c. Chaotic Discontinuous Reflectors			
(1) Parallel			
(2) Parabolic			
(3) Mixed			

Table 20. Surface reflection characteristics for GC 53, extinct mud volcano, case study. F = feature; FF = feature field; FA = feature adjacent area. F = feature; FF = feature field; FA = feature adjacent area.

	3.5 kH Pinger			Intermediate Source			3D Seismic		
	F	FF	FA	F	FF	FA	F	FF	FA
Surface Reflection Strength									
Strong									
Moderate	X		X	X		X	X		X
Weak									
Variable			X			X			X
Width of Surface Reflectors (MS)									
0-2									
2-5	X		X	X		X			
>5							X		X
Variable									
Reflector Characteristics									
Simple Doublet							X		X
Stratified	X		X	X		X			
Prolonged									
Chaotic									
Windowed									
Bright Spots									
Surface Reflection Geometries									
Planar	X		X	X		X	X		X
Wavy									
Mounded			X			X			X
Scarped			X			X			X
Isolated Pinnacle/s									
Isolated Depression/s									
Parabolics									
Isolated									
Multiple									
Overlapping									
Phase Inversion				X			X		

Table 21. Side-scan sonar image characteristics for GC53, collapse depression, case study.

	Feature	Feature Field	Flanking Areas
Acoustic Backscatter			
Strong			
Moderate	X		
Weak			X
Mixed			
Target Shapes			
Bumps			
Cones			
Mounds			
Pinnacles			
Depressions			
Irregular			
Target Surface			
Smooth	X		X
Irregular			
Variable	X		
Feature Occurrence			
Isolated	X		
Asymmetric Groups			
Linear			
Circular			
Elliptical			
Polygonal			

Table 22. Seismic facies for GC53, collapse depression, case study.

Seismic Facies	Feature	Feature Field	Flanking Units
Gently Divergent-Parallel			X
Strongly Divergent			
Onlapping			
Downlapping			
Drape	X		
a. Layered			
b. Acoustically Turbid	X		
Sigmoid Progradational			X
Chaotic			
Contorted-Discordant			
Acoustically Turbid	X		
a. Complete			
b. Stacked Zones			
c. Chaotic Discontinuous Reflectors			
(1) Parallel			
(2) Parabolic			
(3) Mixed			

Table 23. Surface reflection characteristics for GC53, collaspe depression, case study. F= feature; FF = feature field; FA = feature adjacent area

	3.5 kH Pinger			Intermediate Source			3D Seismic		
	F	FF	FA	F	FF	FA	F	FF	FA
Surface Reflection Strength									
Strong									
Moderate	X		X	X		X	X		X
Weak									
Variable			X			X			X
Width of Surface Reflectors (MS)									
0-2									
2-5	X		X	X		X			
>5							X		X
Variable									
Reflector Characteristics									
Simple Doublet							X		X
Stratified	X		X	X		X			
Prolonged									
Chaotic									
Windowed									
Bright Spots									
Surface Reflection Geometries									
Planar	X		X	X		X	X		X
Wavy									
Mounded		X			X				X
Scarped		X			X				X
Isolated Pinnacle/s									
Isolated Depression/s									
Parabolics									
Isolated									
Multiple									
Overlapping									
Phase Inversion				X			X		

F. Case Study: Mounded Carbonates, Green Canyon Block 140

1.   Introduction

In preparation for establishing a pipeline from Jolliet Field in Green Canyon Block 184 (GC184), the upslope and adjacent block (GC140) became an obstacle between the Jolliet Field and a central processing platform in GC52, the Marquette Field. The Jolliet platform, in a water depth of 536 m, was the world's first tension leg well platform. It was placed to the south of higher sea floor terrain in GC140 (Figure 57).

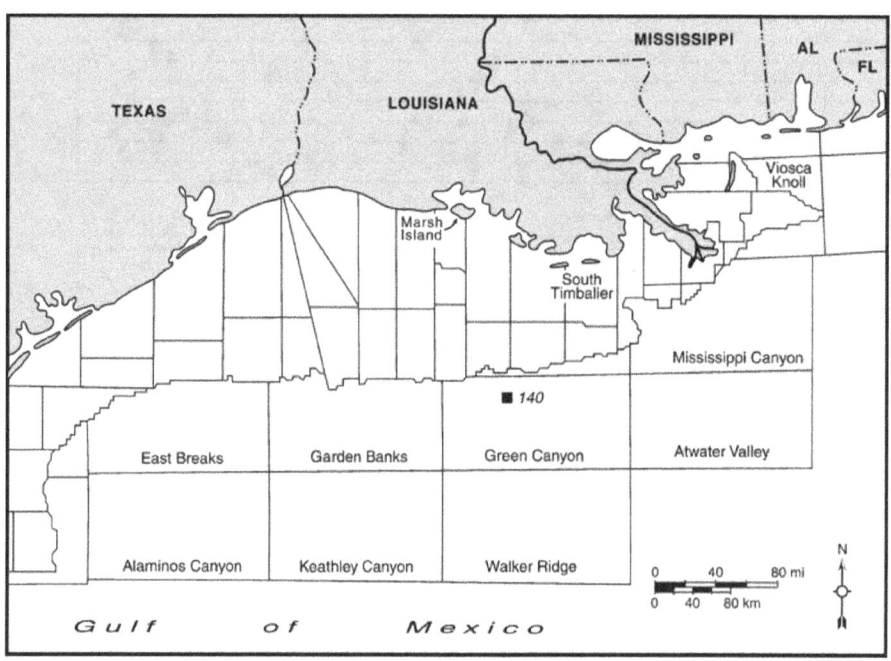

Figure 57. Location map (lease block areas) showing the position of Block 140 in the Green Canyon leasing area.

While acquiring high resolution acoustic data in 1985 for planning a pipeline route, it became clear that GC140 contained sea floor topography that could make pipeline routing difficult. Figure 58 illustrates the regional pattern of relief related to a shallow salt intrusion beneath GC140 creating a broad structural high upwarped by salt movement. The area of mounded sea floor occurs in the southwest part of GC140 (27° 48.17'N; 91° 33.24'W) where the dome-shaped regional feature is shallowest. These mounds were observed on an earlier 1980 high resolution geophysical survey of GC184 and the southern part of GC140 by Racal-Decca Survey, Inc. Water depths at the crest shallow to slightly less than 240 m. Superimposed on regional bathymetric high are numerous mound-shaped buildups that cannot be discriminated at the mapping resolution of Figure 57. This area is located about 16 km from the shelf edge and approximately 240 km southwest of the active Balize lobe of the Mississippi River delta (Figure 57).

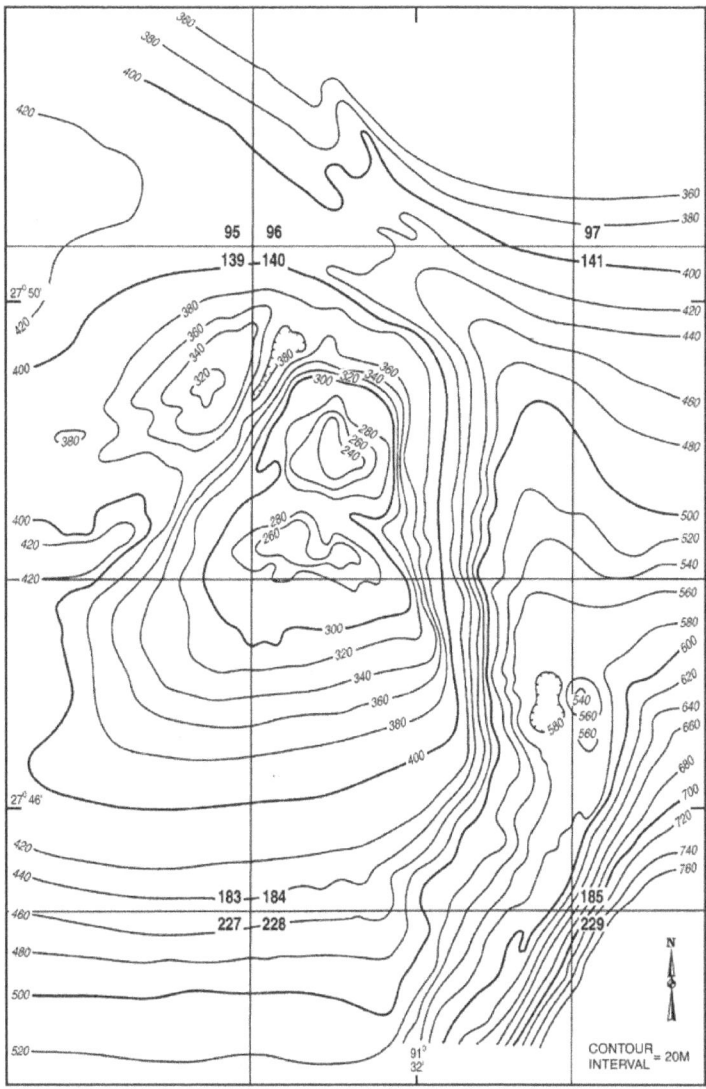

Figure 58. Bathymetric map of the GC140 dome and adjacent areas.

2. Geologic Setting

The dome and basin topography of the Gulf of Mexico's northern continental slope is the result of sediment loading and salt tectonics, processes that created a variety of salt geometries (Jackson and Talbot 1989). The GC140-184 area is underlain by a saddle-shaped salt mass that penetrates to within about 400 m of the sea floor under GC140, but another mass beneath the Jolliet Field in GC184 is much more deeply buried (Cook and D'Onfro 1991). It is now widely accepted that throughout Pleistocene times ancestral Mississippi and other northern Gulf Coast rivers delivered sediments to the outer shelf and slope by propagating across the shelf during periods when the Gulf fell to levels somewhat lower than today. Canyons and feeder channels fed sediment from the shelf edge to downslope depositional sites in intraslope basins as well as onto the Gulf basin floor (Pulham 1993; Winker 1993). Intraslope basins are filled with cyclic

71

deposits that are the products of rapid input of sediments during lowstands and slow deposition of hemipelagic deposits as fluvial sediment sources retreat from the shelf edge as sea level rises. Cook and D'Onfro (1992) indicate that the Jolliet Field occurs in such a basin filled with sand-rich stacked submarine fans deposited as a product of sediment input during sea level lowstands. Twenty-three such coalescing fans were intitially targeted for production in the Jolliet Field (Cook and D'Onfro 1991). As the sedimentary basin between GC140 and GC184 subsided and filled, the salt beneath GC140 remained very close to the sea floor while the salt beneath the Jolliet Field was buried progressively deeper with time during the Pleistocene. Fault pathways over the Jolliet Field developed into deep-cutting networks that tapped hydrocarbon-rich subsurface horizons. The large mound with known gas-hydrates and abundant chemosynthetic communities ("Bush Hill", GC185) is fed by this fault system. By contrast, the thin sedimentary column above the salt mass in GC140 was broken by numerous faults with limited access to overpressured zones of the deep subsurface and a source of hydrocarbons.

3. Available Data Sets

The early (1980) Racal-Decca Survey was conducted with a 7 kHz subbottom profiler, a 8.4 kilojoule sparker, and a magnetometer using Lorac A navigation. Later, geohazards data sets were acquired by John Chance and Associates, Inc. of Lafayette, Louisiana. A precision echo sounder (EDO Western Model 4077) was used to generate a high quality bathymetric map of the GC140-184 area. This system employed a narrow beam (5-10° beam width) output, which helps minimize the problem of side echoes that give false impressions of seafloor features. Shallow subbottom data were obtained with an ORE 3.5 kHz pinger profiler. This system is employed because of the low vertical exaggeration, good resolution of surface cutting faults, and identification of hemipelagic drape deposits deposited over topographic irregularities and fault scarps. Penetration of 50-60 m for this acoustic source is common in slope sediments. Medium-range subsurface penetration (to ~300 m) was provided by a mini-sleeve exploder system. This acoustic source helped define fault planes, bedded as opposed to nonbedded and gas-prone sediments, and buried deposits from mass movement processes. A sparker was used both for collection of single channel and multi-channel data. The frequency range of this acoustic source was 25-2000 Hz with an adjustable energy range from 100-24,000 joules. An SMS 960 EG&G side-scan sonar system, which compensates for slant-range and boat speed distortions, was used to make seafloor mosaics in order to map features that create difficulty in pipeline routing. All geophysical data were spatially controlled with STARFIX navigation which was a high-accuracy (<5 m) satellite positioning and message transmission system provided by John Chance and Associates, Inc. Later, deep tow side-scan sonar and 3.5 kHz data were collected between the Jolliet Platform site in GC184 to the Marquette Field in GC52 in support of pipeline routing.

As part of this research project, high resolution seismic profiles were acquired across the GC140 mound using three sources, and EG&G Uniboom profiler, a Seismic System Model S-15 water gun (15 in^3), and a Seismic systems GI air-gun (50 in^3). These data were acquired in both analog format on EPC Model 9800 seismic recorder and in digital format through the DELPH 2 data acquisition and processing software. Survey planning was accomplished through the hydrographic software program HYPACK and DELPH 2 software programs through a Magnavox M4200d differential GPS system. Using differential GPS navigation data points were

72

located with an accuracy of 3-5 m. Sea floor verification data were provided by JSL-1, Dives 2950, 2592 and 3118.

4.   Feature Characteristics

Bathymetric and high resolution seismic profiles, as well as swaths of side-scan sonar data, clearly indicate that the crestal areas of the GC140 dome are characterized by numerous mound-like buildups that vary in relief from a few meters to over 20 m (Figures 59 and 60).

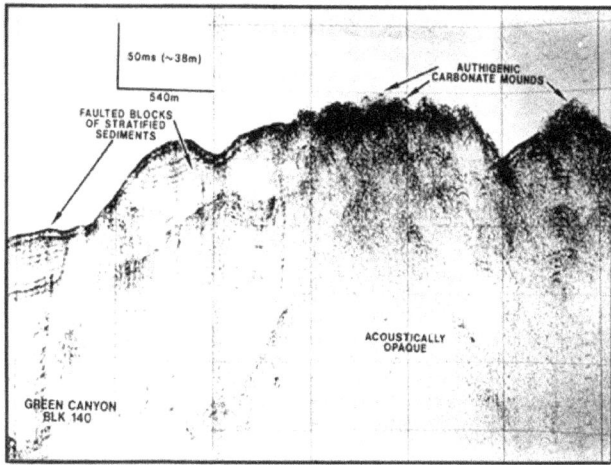

Figure 59. A 50 in³ air gun profile run N-S across the GC140 dome. This profile illustrates the high amplitude surface return from the mounded carbonates on the dome top as well as the bedded sediments on the dome flank. Areas beneath the mounded surface appear as acoustic wipe-out zones.

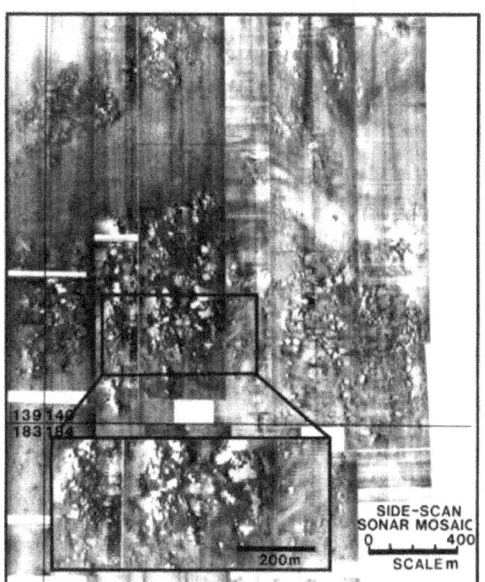

Figure 60. This figure represents a side-scan sonar mosaic of the GC140 dome top area. Note the complex array of hard targets that possess sizable acoustic shadows indicating significant relief above the surrounding seafloor. It is also interesting to note that many of these mounds appear to be aligned, possibly indicating fault control.

To the south of the crestal areas, the regional slope gradient is less than 5%, but in the southern part of GC184 the gradient increases to between 5-10% in a southeasterly direction. However, the fault-controlled slopes to the east and southeast of the dome crest have gradients that vary from 10-25%, with local slope gradients across fault scarps reaching as high as 50%. The flanks of the GC140 dome are draped with fine-grained hemipelagic sediment varying in thickness from approximately 2 m to over 6 m. On the top of the dome, however, the hemipelagic drape is missing, and the sea floor is characterized by complexes of mounds that are clearly visible on high resolution acoustic data sets.

Surface-tow high resolution seismic profiles cannot resolve individual mounds when mounds are closely spaced It is clear that there are many mounds on the crest of the GC140 dome. Some occur in high density clusters when mound distribution is viewed in plan-view on side-scan data (Figure 60). The end result on seismic profiles is a series of overlapping parabolic reflectors (Figure 59). However, the cumulative effect of this reflection response is a high amplitude or strong and irregular surface reflector. On exploration-scale 3D-seismic, the surface mounds are below the resolution of this low-frequency source and are therefore not clearly resolved (Figure 61). Although it is sometimes difficult from seismic and bathymetric profiles to determine if the dome-top mounded surface is composed of a series of lithified buildups or multiple mud volcanoes, the complex structure of individual buildups as viewed on side-scan sonar data suggests that they are not smooth-sided mud extrusion features.

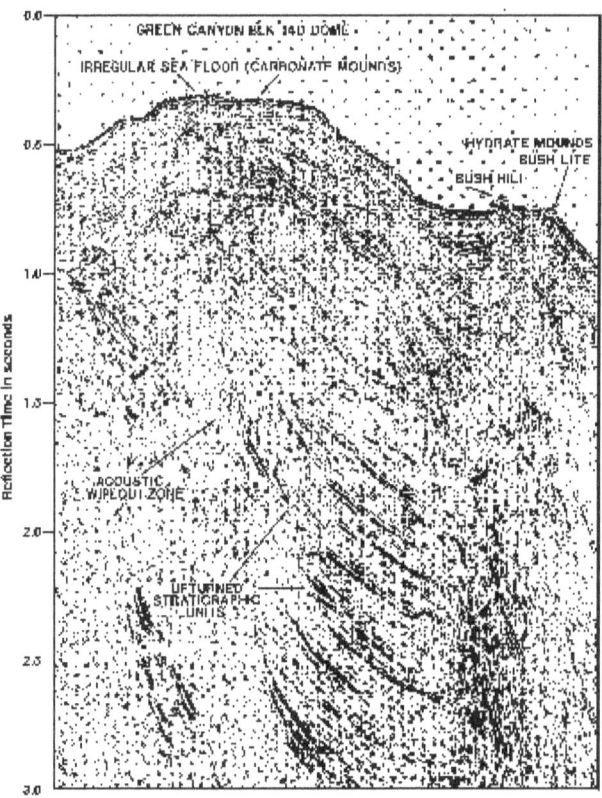

Figure 61. A 3D-seismic profile oriented in a northwest-southeast direction across the GC140 dome to the mounds that are known to contain gas hydrates in GC185. Note that the mounds on the crest of the GC140 dome are not clearly resolved.

74

Submersible observations from the crestal area of the GC140 dome (JSL-1, Dives 2590, 2592, and 3118) clearly indicate that the mounds occupying this area are composed of authigenic carbonates (Figure 62).

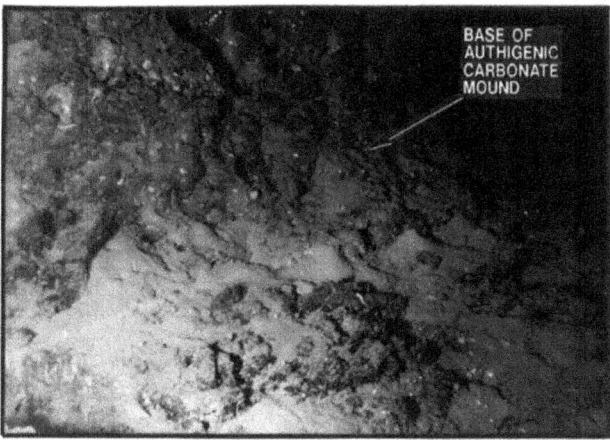

Figure 62. A photograph of the base of an authigenic carbonate mound in GC140 showing large blocks of well-lithified Ca-Mg carbonate forming this feature.

Laboratory work on these carbonates shows that they are extremely ^{13}C-depleted, identifying an origin linked to the microbial utilization of hydrocarbons (Roberts et al. 1992a, b). The mineralogy of the carbonates in GC140 is primarily Mg-calcite with some dolomite. Close inspection of the carbonates reveals the presence of extremely biodegraded crude oil in isolated pores. However, carbon isotope values from carbonate cements suggest that methane was the main contribution of isotopically light carbon (^{12}C) to the carbonates rather than biodegradation of crude oil (Roberts and Aharon 1994). The buildups are composed of chaotically oriented blocks and clasts that are 20-100 m in diameter, up to 20 m high, and most have relief in the 10-15 m range. Surrounding sediments can be quite coarse, containing a high proportion of diagenetic clasts and shell debris. The mounds are cut by fractures and crevices probably related to post-mound movement of underlying salt. Only a single rudimentary community of chemosynthetic organisms was found at this site (Figure 63), living on products expelled through a deep crevice.

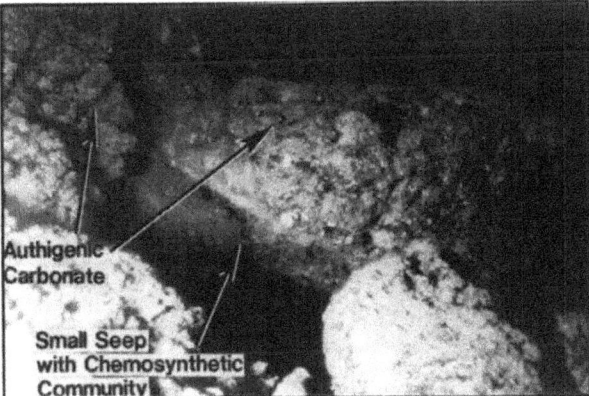

Figure 63. A crevasse in a GC140 authigenic carbonate mound. Note the rudiments of a small chemosynthetic community living in a fracture through the mound.

Evidence of gas or crude oil leaking into the water column was not present in the GC140 area, although the presence of both is indicated by the authigenic carbonates. This area appears to have been one of very slow seepage over a long period of time. Radiometric dates of the buildups (Roberts and Aharon 1994) indicate some mounds date at nearly 200 kyr BP.

5.   Feature Synopsis and Interpretation

The mounded character of the GC140 dome top is clearly displayed on side-scan sonar data. The array of numerous hard targets with highly reflective and irregular surfaces distinguishes these mounds from a field of fluid mud expulsion features. In addition, the highly reflective seafloor, as viewed on high resolution seismic records, tends to support an interpretation of a hard bottom, possibly lithified. This response is in contrast to that of a gas-prone mud-rich sea floor, that would likely exist at the site of an active field of mud volcanoes or other types of fluid and gas explusion features. A key source of supporting data in this regard is 3D-seismic surface amplitude data. Figure 64, a map of 3D-seismic surface amplitude data from the GC140 dome, shows a close relationship between the greatest deviation of amplitudes from background and the distribution of carbonate mounds on the dome top (Figure 60).

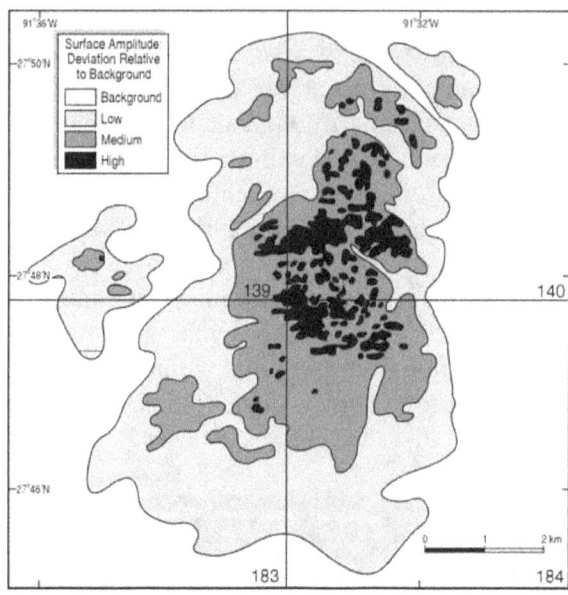

Figure 64. A 3D-seismic surface amplitude map of the GC140 area.

Profiles of 3D-seismic data across this area, such as the one in Figure 61, do not show a phase reversal across the mound crest as in areas of gas-charged sediments in adjacent areas of GC185. The (a) significant surface amplitude shift away from the character of the surrounding sea floor, no phase reversal across the dome crest on the 3D-seismic profiles, (b) a highly reflective and mounded surface on high resolution seismic, and (c) discrimination of complex mounds with irregular surfaces and well-defined and steep sides on side-scan sonar data identifies these features as lithified buildups as opposed to mud mounds or other sediment-derived topographic features. Submersible groundtruth and subsequent laboratory work on mound samples confirms that these features are by-products of microbial degradation of hydrocarbons delivered to the surficial sediments slowly in small amounts. As a general statement, these features in GC140 are not associated with chemosynthetic communities other than small bacterial mats (*Beggiatoa sp.*). Acoustic characteristics, seismic and side-scan sonar, of the GC140 mounds are tabulated in Tables 24 to 26.

Table 24. Side-scan sonar image characteristics for GC 140 case study.

	Feature	Feature Field	Flanking Areas
Acoustic Backscatter			
Strong		X	
Moderate			
Weak			X
Mixed			
Target Shapes			
Bumps			
Cones			
Mounds		X	
Pinnacles			
Depressions			
Irregular			
Target Surface			
Smooth			X
Irregular		X	
Variable		X	
Feature Occurrence			
Isolated		X	
Asymmetric Groups		X	
Linear			
Circular			
Elliptical			
Polygonal		X	

Table 25. Seismic facies for GC 140 case study.

Seismic Facies	Feature	Feature Field	Flanking Units
Gently Divergent-Parallel			X
Strongly Divergent			X
Onlapping			
Drape			
a. Layered			
b. Acoustically Turbid			
Sigmoid Progradational			
Oblique Progradational			
Chaotic		X	
Contorted-Discordant			
Acoustically Turbid		X	
a. Complete			
b. Stacked Zones			
c. Chaotic Discontinuous Reflectors		X	
(1) Parallel			
(2) Parabolic			
(3) Mixed		X	

Table 26. Surface reflection characteristics for GC 140 case study. F = feature; FF = feature field; FA feature adjacent area.

	3.5 kH Pinger			Intermediate Source			3D Seismic		
	F	FF	FA	F	FF	FA	F	FF	FA
Surface Reflection Strength									
Strong		X		X					
Moderate						X		X	X
Weak			X						
Variable									
Width of Surface Reflectors (MS)									
0-2									
2-5		X			X				
>5	X			X			X		X
Variable									
Reflector Characteristics									
Simple Doublet									
Stratified		X			X				X
Prolonged	X								
Chaotic	X			X					
Windowed								X	
Bright Spots									
Surface Reflection Geometries									
Planar		X			X				X
Wavy									
Mounded	X			X			X		
Scarped									
Isolated Pinnacle/s									
Isolated Depression/s									
Parabolics									
Isolated	X								
Multiple	X								
Overlapping	X			X					
Phase Inversion									

☐. ☐ase Study☐☐ound ☐it☐☐as ☐ydrates and ☐☐e☐osynt☐eti☐☐o☐☐unities☐☐reen ☐anyon ☐☐ō☐☐ ☐5

☐   Introdu☐tion

As part of a drilling hazards survey for the GC184 Jolliet field conducted by McClelland Engineers, Inc. in 1985, the mound-like feature on the block border between GC184-185 (27° 46.97'N; 91° 30.47'W) was initially surveyed (Figure 65).

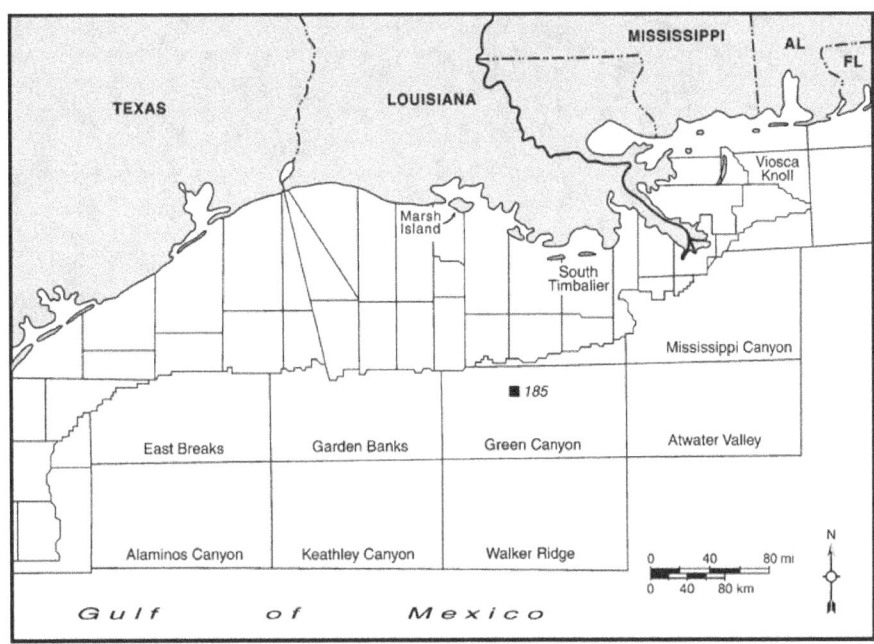

Figure 65. Location map for Green Canyon Block 185 (GC185).

Later in 1985 (November) a high resolution survey, including deep-tow data, was conducted by John Chance and Associates in support of Pipeline survey from GC184 to the Marquette Field (GC52-53). This feature is usually referred to as a single mound, but in fact it consists of two mounds with the northern mound being the larger of the two. The tops of these mounds occur in water depths of about 540 m to 560 m respectively (Figure 66). The larger of the two mounds has a relief above the surrounding seafloor of over 30 m. These mounds occur to the southeast of the large GC140 dome which rises over 300 m above them. The mounds are located in a trough-like regional bathymetric low that is oriented roughly north-south. Roberts et al. (1999) have shown that currents in the vicinity of the GC185 mounds are topographically steered and therefore are biased in north-south directions. The GC185 area is very close to the shelf edge (approximately 20 km) and was a region of rapid deposition from shelf edge sediment sources during the Pleistocene (Cook and D'Onfro, 1991).

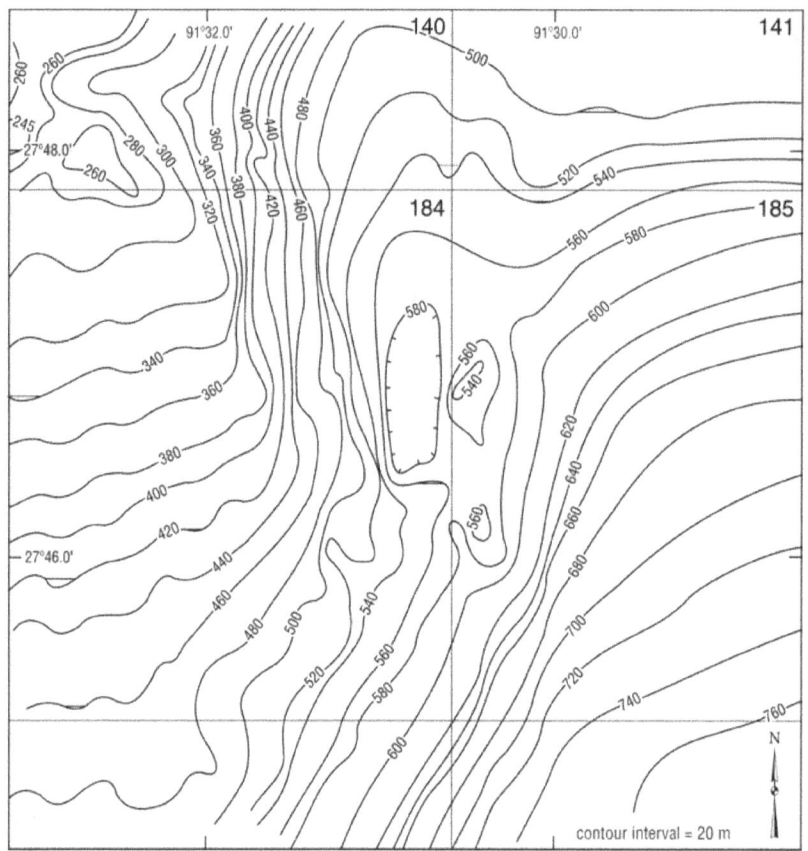

Figure 66. Bathymetric map of the GC185 mound complex indicating that two distinct mound-like features exist along the GC184-185 border.

□   □eo□□i□Settin□

Cook and D'Onfro (1991) clearly illustrate that the GC140 dome is related to the shallow emplacement at allochthonous salt and that faulting associated with basin formation and salt migration accounts for the mounded feature on the GC184-185 boundary which is the subject of this case history.

During the Nebraskan and Kansan stages of the Pleistocene, lowstand deposition of large volumes of sediment in this area triggered underlying salt sheet deformation and movement by differential sediment loading. Salt began to rise in the sedimentary section while salt withdrawal promoted interslope basin formation. (Figure 67). Faults started forming in association with the rising diapirs which probably initiated the flux of fluids and gases to the seafloor. Throughout the Pleistocene, fluctuations of sea level promoted cyclic filling of the rapidly subsiding basins with coarse facies during lowstands and fine-grained and carbonate-rich hemipelagic sediments during highstands. During the final stages of the Pleistocene (Illinoisan) to present the diapir under GC140 continued to rise to a near seafloor position while subsidence continued in the GC185 basin. Faulting occurred in the tensional environment of the rising GC140 dome resulting in an area over the salt characterized by numerous faults of very limited subsurface

80

penetration. The eastern GC185 area, however, was broken into several fault blocks. A prominent reverse fault (Figure 67) created the conduit that fed fluids, sediment, and gas to construct the mound complex that is the subject of this case study.

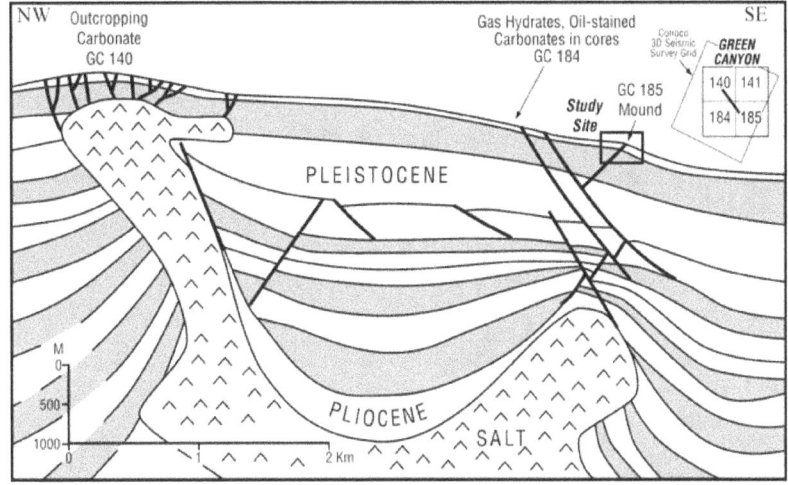

Figure 67. Schematic figure representing the present salt and sediment subsurface configuration of the GC140, 184, and 185 area. Faults and resulting seep-related seafloor geology is shown on this diagram modified from a study by Cook and D'Onfro (1991).

☐   ☐☐ai☐☐é ☐ata

As in the case of the GC140 dome, the original high resolution geohazards data sets were acquired by John Chance and Associates, Inc. using a precision echo sounder (EDO Western Model 4077) for bathymetry and a shallow subbottom profiler (ORE 3.5 kHz pinger) for evaluating the near-bottom subsurface. In sediments not charged with gas, penetration of this profiler commonly reached 60 m. Medium-range subsurface data were acquired using a mini-sleeve exploder which had the acoustic energy to penetrate up to 250-300 m. A sparker system was used for deeper penetration and was used for the collection of both single channel and multi-channel data. Side-scan sonar data were initially collected with an SMS 960 EG&G digital side-scan system. All geophysical survey data were spatially controlled with STARFIX navigation provided by John Chance and Associates with a spatial accuracy of < 5 m. A 3D-seismic survey was acquired by CONOCO that covers both the Jolliet (GC184) and Marquette (GC52) areas. This project was given access to parts of this 3D-seismic data set for incorporation in this report.

In association with this project, both 50 in^3 air gun (Seismic System GI gun) and 15 in^3 water gun (Seismic Systems Model S-15) profiles were acquired by the author across the GC 185 mound complex. The data were collected in digital format using the DELPH 2 high resolution seismic data acquisition and processing software system. Analog records were recorded on an EPC Model 9800 seismic recorder while the digital data were written to Exobyte tapes. Hydrographic Surveying software used on this project for survey planning was HYPACK by Coastal Oceanographics, Inc. Navigation data for input to the program were provided from differential GPS, a Magnavox M4200d which has an accuracy of 3-5 m.

81

4.   Feature Characteristics

The mound complex on the border of GC184 and GC185 occurs southeast of the large GC140 dome. The mounds are clearly visible in the regional bathymetry where the larger northern-most mound (commonly referred to as "Bush Hill") rises over 30 m above the surrounding seafloor to a depth of approximately 540 m (Figure 66). This mound is slightly less than 1 km wide at the base and has a roughly conical shape when viewed in cross section, as is illustrated in the 15 in³ water gun profile shown in Figure 68.

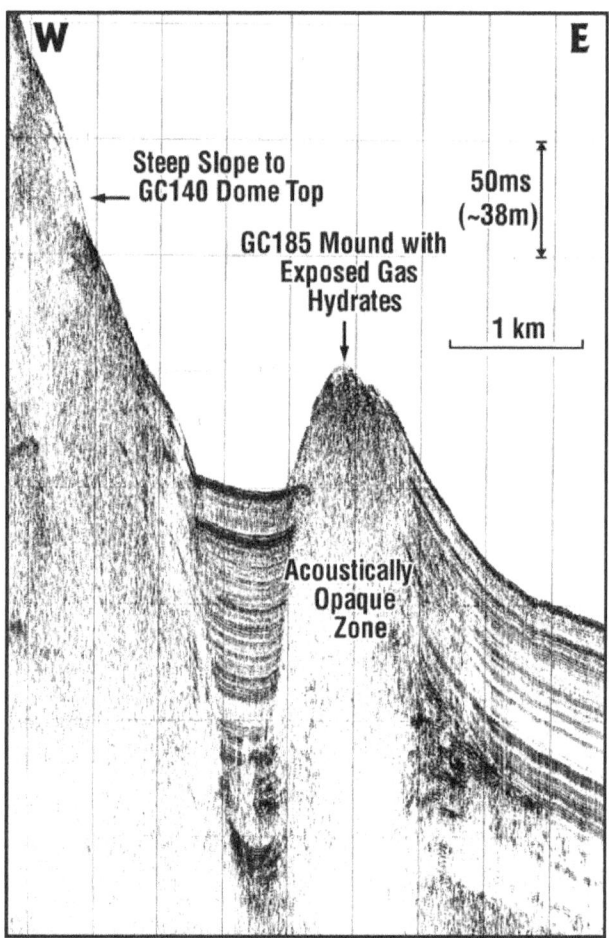

Figure 68. High resolution seismic profile run E-W across the northernmost GC185 mound. Note the mound's acoustically opaque interior, up-turned bedding on its flanks, and highly variable surface return.

Originally, Neurauter and Bryant (1990) attributed the origin of this mound to heave or diapiric processes rather than vertical accretion as in the case of mud volcanoes. This interpretation was based primarily of high resolution seismic data which illustrated an acoustically opaque interior and upturned bedded sediments on the east and southeast side of the feature. Inspection of 3D-seismic profiles through the mound complex suggest a long history of vertical accretion, with the acoustically opaque mound of today being just the latest chapter. However, clear evidence of sediment accretion as a product of mound growth is difficult to identify in high resolution profiles like the one shown in Figure 68. Although deep-tow data were not available for this feature, surface-tow seismic profiles demonstrate three important mound characteristics, (1) the mound has an acoustically opaque interior, (2) surface reflectivity is highly variable, and (3) bedded sediments that truncate against the acoustic wipe-out zone tend to be upturned and thin away from the feature. Side-scan data from the mound surface (MacDonald and Schroeder, 1993; MacDonald et al., 1996) display a high degree of spatial variability in reflectance patterns and reflectance strengths. Hard targets are of a scale that can easily be detected within the typical 100 m swath of a single side-scan channel. Most highly reflective targets have cross-sectional dimensions that fall within the 10-50 m range.

Seafloor verification data of the GC185 mounds were acquired through JSL-1, Dives 3300, 3301, 4063 and JSL-2, Dives 2640 and 2647. The GC185 mud vent site was the subject of data on JSL-2, Dive 2787 and 2899 and JSL-1, Dive 4062.

5. Feature Synopsis and Interpretation

At first inspection of high resolution seismic profiles across the prominent northern GC185 mound, it appears simply as an acoustically opaque feature, the same as many such features observed in geohazard surveys from the northern Gulf's upper slope. However, when viewed in different cross sections and with different acoustic sources it is apparent that this feature exhibits a high degree of surface reflectance variability, even on surface-tow data. Sager et al. (1999) confirm this variability of acoustic response from 25 kHz profiles acquired near the bottom using a submarine (NR-1). Side-scan sonar data (Figure 69) corroborate the variations in surface reflectance observed on profiles generated form various seismic sources. Fields of hard targets cluster around the apex of this feature which occurs at water depths ranging between 550-540 m. These hard targets are scattered throughout the crestal area of the mound which is steeper on its northwestern flank. Therefore, this field of hard targets is biased toward the northwest portion of the overall feature.

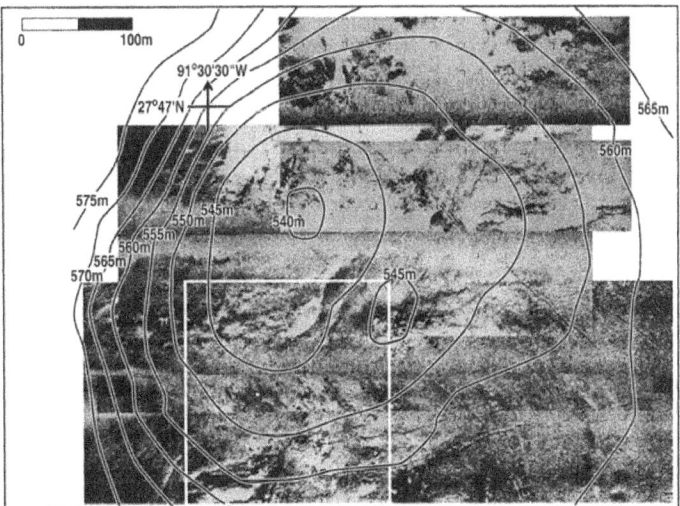

Figure 69. A mosaic of 77 kHz side-scan sonar data collected from the northern GC185 mound (Bush Hill) using the manned submersible NR-1 (MacDonald et al., 1995). Note the complex field of hard targets imaged in this mosaic and the scales of these features.

Extraction of surface amplitude data from a 3D-seismic survey over the area indicates that the main GC185 mound and surrounding region exhibit three areas where amplitude strength is far above the surrounding seafloor (Figure 70).

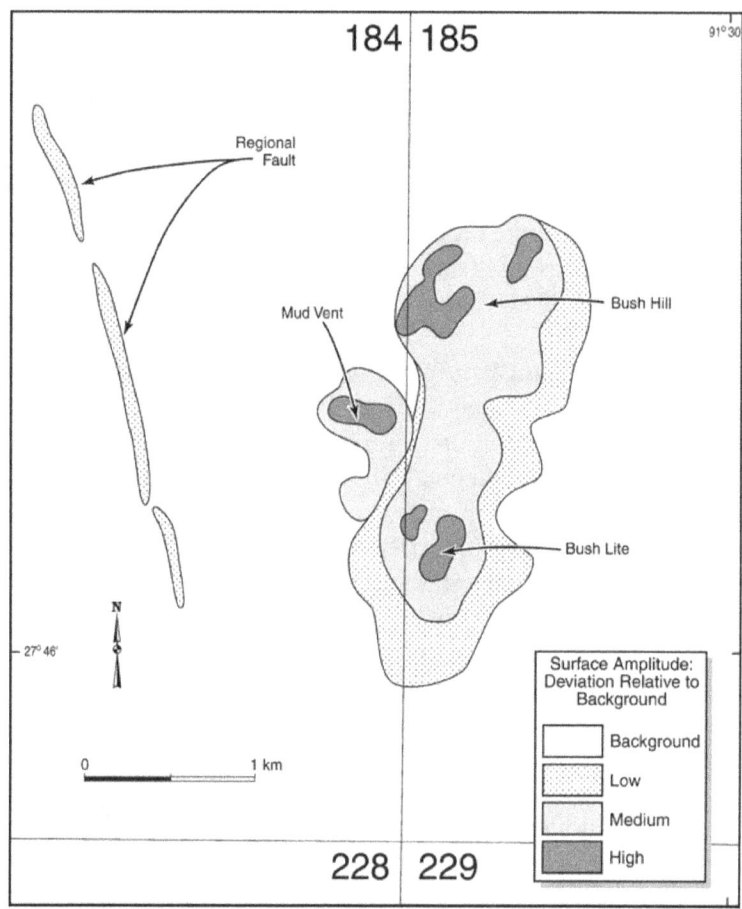

Figure 70. This 3D-seismic surface amplitude map of the GC185 mound complex clearly identifies areas that deviate significantly from the background of seafloor surrounding the mounds. Note that the highest deviations correlate with the highest topography except for the western anomaly which correlates with an active mud vent that constantly leaks gas into the water column.

The northernmost high amplitude zone correlates well with the zone of variable reflectance on high resolution seismic and side-scan sonar records. Analysis of both digital high resolution profiles and 3D-seismic profiles of the main GC185 mound indicates a phase inversion over the highest amplitude zone as compared to the seafloor surrounding the mound (a positive to negative polarity shift), Figure 71. The same phase inversion occurs for the other two high amplitude zones. The one to the south represents the crestal area of a smaller mound (27°46.14'N; 91° 30.32'W) and the western anomaly is an active mud vent (27° 46.17'N; 91° 30.38'W). All of these zones represent areas where gas is trapped in the shallow subsurface and is also being actively vented from the seafloor.

84

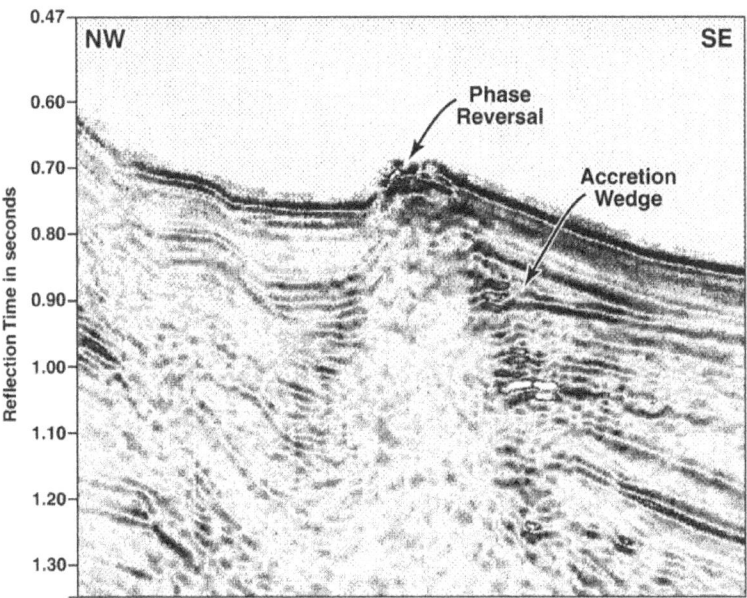

Figure 71. A 3D-seismic profile across the northern GC185 mound (Bush Hill) illustrating (a) the phase reversal of the surface reflector, (b) subsurface accretion wedge on flank of the acoustic wipe-out zone, (c) a prolonged acoustic wipe-out zone, and (d) apparent "pull-up" of north side reflectors entering the acoustic wipe-out zone.

Over a decade of direct observation and sampling of the GC185 mound, using a variety of manned submersibles, has produced a sizeable data based on surface features and conditions (Brooks et al., 1985; Kennicut et al., 1985; Roberts et al., 1992; MacDonald et al., 1996). The GC185 mound has an extremely variable suite of surface features, as the high resolution geophysical data suggest. In the north and northwest sectors where the highest parts of the mound are located, the bottom is characterized by bush-like colonies of tube worms, mussel beds, outcrops of authigenic carbonate from slabs several meters in diameter to small nodular masses in and on the surface of the sediments, and mound-like outcrops of gas hydrates (Figure 72).

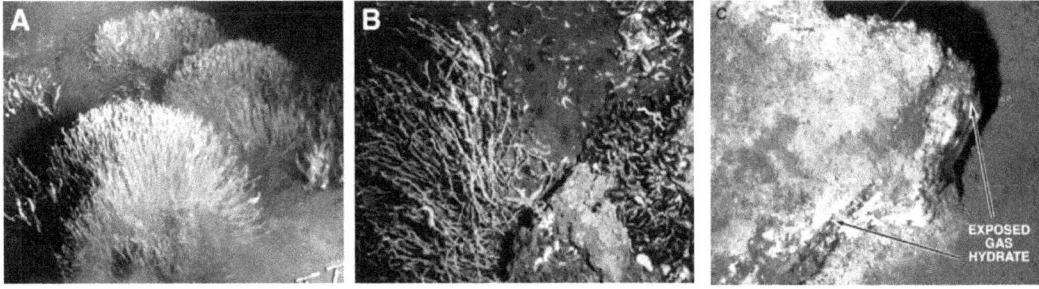

Figure 72. These three photographs are representative of seafloor conditions and communities typical of the high topography of both the northern and southern GC185 mounds: (a) symmetrical colonies of vestimentiferan tube worms (approximately 1.5 m high), (b) bathymodiolid mussels, vestimentiferan tube worms, and slabs of authigenic carbonate are commonly associated at sites of thriving chemosynthetic communities, and (c) an outcrop of gas hydrate.

Areas of the mound which have these characteristics correlate with (a) areas of high reflective and variable scale targets on side-scan sonar records, (b) variable reflectivity of the seafloor on seismic, and (c) a very high amplitude response as well as phase inversion on 3D-seismic surface amplitude maps and seismic profiles suggesting the presence of gas at the seafloor and in the shallow subsurface. Numerous areas have been identified where both gas and crude oil are being vented into the water column. Flanks of the mound and the saddle area between the larger northern mound and its smaller southern counterpart are represented on the 3D-seismic surface amplitude data as slightly deviating from surrounding seafloor amplitudes. However, high amplitude areas associated with the apex of the smaller mound, Figure 70, have similar seafloor characteristics as the larger mound with the exception of gas hydrate outcrops. Figure 72 illustrates typical seafloor scenes in the gas-prone high amplitude areas of the mound.

The strong amplitude anomaly to the west of the mound complex is different (Figure 70). This area consists of an active gas and fluidized mud venting site. Since its discovery in 1992 based on 3D-seismic surface amplitude data, the site has been visited several times. Each dive on this site (mostly with the Johnson Sea-Link) has confirmed both active gas venting and expulsion of very light-gray fluid mud (Figure 73). No diverse chemosynthetic communities are associated with this site. Although, a few disarticulated lucinid-vesycomyid clam shells can be found on old flows with oxidized brown surfaces. On a high resolution seismic profile acquired through this feature, it appears as a graben-like depression.

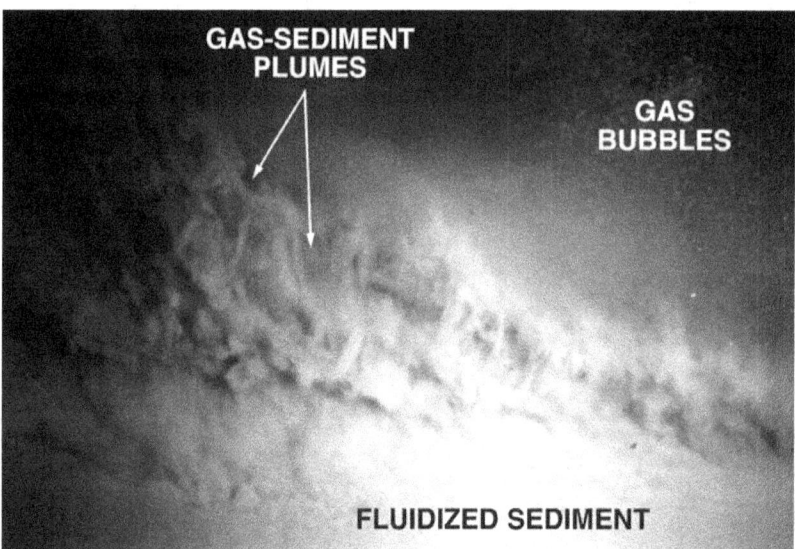

Figure 73. This bottom photograph of the mud vent at the base of the GC185 mound illustrates the active escaping gas and mud extrusion taking place at the site. The field of view is about 3 m wide.

In summary, the mound has been confirmed as a site of scattered, but abundant chemosynthetic communities that become more closely spaced toward the apex areas of both the large and small mounds. Within these areas expulsion of gas as well as crude oil into the water column can be observed. High resolution acoustic data reflect the scattered seafloor features (chemosynthetic communities, outcrops of authigenic carbonates, partially lithified bottom sediments, and gas hydrates). The 3D-seismic surface amplitude data match these areas beautifully, but appear to be responding to surface and near-surface gas since a phase inversion on 3D-seismic profiles is coincident with these zones. The mud vent area on the west side of the mound complex produces the same amplitude and phase response. The phase inversion over these areas is also clearly visible in the digital high resolution seismic profiles taken as a part of this study when analyzed in "wiggle trace" format. Since this feature has an acoustically opaque interior, the interface of bedded sediments with the mound may hold information about the interior character of this feature. Gas-charged sediments may cause local "pull down" because acoustic energy travel slightly slower through this less dense medium. A mound interior characterized by gas hydrate and/or lithified sediments may cause "pull-up" in the interface zone because of slightly faster travel times through this denser medium. A slight pull-up is suggested on the profiles illustrated in Figures 68 and 71. Acoustic characterisitc of the GC185 mound area summarized in Tables 27 to 29.

Table 27. Side-scan sonar image characteristics for GC185 case study.

	Feature	Feature Field	Flanking Areas
Acoustic Backscatter			
Strong	X		
Moderate			X
Weak			
Mixed	X		
Target Shapes			
Bumps	X		
Cones			
Mounds	X		
Pinnacles			
Depressions	X		X
Irregular	X		
Target Surface			
Smooth			
Irregular	X		
Variable	X		
Feature Occurrence			
Isolated	X		
Asymmetric Groups			
Linear			
Circular			
Elliptical			
Polygonal			

Table 28. Seismic facies for GC185 case study.

Seismic Facies	Feature	Feature Field	Flanking Units
Gently Divergent-Parallel			X
Strongly Divergent			
Onlapping			
Downlapping			
Drape			
a. Layered			
b. Acoustically Turbid			
Sigmoid Progradational			
Oblique Progradational			X
Chaotic			X
Contorted-Discordant			
Acoustically Turbid	X		
a. Complete	X		
b. Stacked Zones			
c. Chaotic Discontinuous Reflectors			
(1) Parallel			
(2) Parabolic			
(3) Mixed			

Table 29. Surface reflection characteristics for GC185 case study. F= feature; FF - feature field; FA = feature adjacent area.

	3.5 kH Pinger			Intermediate Source			3D Seismic		
	F	FF	FA	F	FF	FA	F	FF	FA
Surface Reflection Strength									
Strong	X								
Moderate									
Weak			X						
Variable									
Width of Surface Reflectors (MS)									
0-2									
2-5			X			X			
>5	X			X			X		X
Variable	X			X					
Reflector Characteristics									
Simple Doublet							X		X
Stratified			X			X			
Prolonged	X			X					
Chaotic									
Windowed									
Bright Spots	X								
Surface Reflection Geometries									
Planar			X			X			X
Wavy									
Mounded	X			X			X		
Scarped									
Isolated Pinnacle/s									
Isolated Depression/s									
Parabolics									
Isolated									
Multiple									
Overlapping									
Phase Inversion				X			X		

III. Summary of Project Results

Through the analysis of numerous data sets taken for geohazards surveys or engineering projects, review of 3D-seismic data, and seafloor verification from research submersible observations it has become clear that the rate of supply of fluids (including fine-grained sediment) and gases to the seafloor largely controls geologic and biologic responses. In this section of the report, a summary of project results will be presented. This section of the report will first will summarize the general observations concerning geologic and biologic responses to various hydrocarbon venting and seepage settings. This interpretive section is designed to provide a simple framework for understanding the geologic and to a lesser extent the biologic variability of hydrocarbon seepage and venting sites. Along with this summary characteristic of each major part of the feature spectrum will be presented for interpreting this variability from high resolution acoustic data (seismic and side-scan sonar) and 3D-seismic surface attribute data.

A. Geologic and Biologic Responses to Venting and Seepage

As previously discussed in the introductory parts of this report, the geology of the northern-northwestern Gulf's continental slope is complex and sometimes bewildering when viewed in a high resolution perspective. Although domes, ridges, and basins dominate regional slope topography, at a smaller scale slope failures, mounds, depressions, and scarps become apparent. When a focus is placed on those seafloor features judged to be products of fluid and gas expulsion they always appear to be situated over or near well-defined faults and accompanying subsurface acoustic wipe-out zones (Behrens, 1988; Roberts et al., 1990). On high resolution seismic and side-scan sonar records it is common to observe alignments of pock marks, mud volcanoes, small mud flows, and a variety of mounded features. This linearity in the spatial distribution of these features caused by fluid and gas expulsion can usually be directly correlated to a fault that intersects the modern seafloor (Roberts, 1995). Figure 74 illustrates the alignment of authigenic carbonate mounds along a fault crossing Garden Banks Block 304.

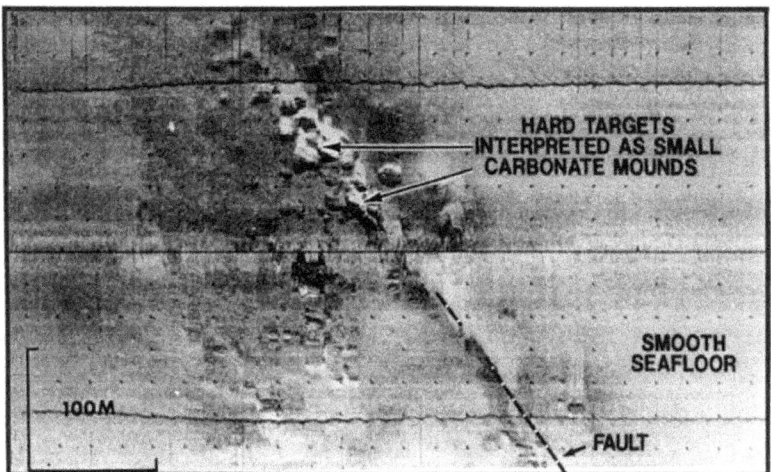

Figure 74. Authigenic carbonate mounds are aligned along a fault that is clearly visible in high resolution seismic data. This relationship confirms the importance of faults as conduits for the transport of fluids and gases to the modern seafloor.

This close relationship between faults and venting/seepage-related features emphasizes the importance of faults as conduits for fluids and gases moving upward through the sedimentary column to the seafloor. The actual mechanics of this process are poorly understood and this subject is currently under investigation (e.g. Roberts and Nunn 1995; Roberts et al. 1996). Studies of reservoir recharge by hydrocarbons migrating vertically along faults have demonstrated that fluid and gas movement up faults can involve an extremely complex set of geologic conditions including pressure release from overpressured zones at depth (Anderson et al. 1991; Anderson 1993). Considering our present state of understanding concerning fluid and gas transport along faults, there is little argument that faults function as conduits. It is also clear that formation waters, hydrocarbons, fine-grained sediments, and gases are transported from depth at various rates to the modern seafloor. Kohl and Roberts (1994, 1995) have convincingly demonstrated that relic microfossil assemblages are being actively spread over the continental slope in some areas through the extrusion of fluid muds that originated at considerable depths beneath the present ocean bottom. Even though these vent-seep features are commonly and clearly associated with faults, the controls on frequency of fault movements and flux rates are not known. The consistent presence of oil slicks over the continental slope, as viewed from satellite imagery (MacDonald et al., 1993, 1994) suggests that the expulsion of crude oil and gas is an on-going process that may be episodic on the short term, but is consistently impacting the geology and biology of the Gulf's continental slope.

. Feature Spe ̄tru ̄

From approximately a decade of direct observations of the hydrocarbon-impacted seafloor using research submersibles (e.g. Brooks et al., 1985; Roberts et al., 1988; MacDonald et al. 1995) coupled with the systematic analysis of remotely sensed data of the slope surface and shallow subsurface associated with this study, it is clear that geologic and biologic responses are highly variable. Compilation, review, and interpretation of data assembled in support of this MMS-CMI study have shown that there is a relationship between the qualitative rate at which venting-seepage products are delivered to the seafloor and both geologic and biologic responses. Although rates of delivery of these products have never been satisfactorily quantified, episodic releases of fluids and gases from deep overpressured subsurface environments have been recorded in Gulf Coast Basin mineral deposits (Cathles and Smith 1983; Cathles 1990) and have been predicted from numerical modeling (Roberts et al. 1996). Perhaps the best example that relates to a discussion of Louisiana's continental slope comes from the occurrence of thin sulfide layers in the anhydrite caprock of Winnfield salt dome (Ulrich et al. 1984). These sulfides are interpreted as products of the episodic release of reducing waters from geopressured zones deep in the stratigraphic section. Sulfides are precipitated at the salt-anhydrite interface when reducing fluids are released from the subsurface by way of faults along the flanks of the dome (Hallager et al. 1990). Paleomagnetic dating of these sulfides suggests that expulsion events may have occurred at a frequency of around 300 years (Kyle et al. 1987). These results are compatible with recent numerical modeling solutions that suggest that fluid expulsion from geopressured sediments of the northern Gulf of Mexico occurs in short-lived events (Roberts and Nunn 1995). This and other studies (Ranganathan and Hanor, 1989; Roberts and Nunn 1995) suggest that expulsion events create local, transient anomalies in overlying sediments in short periods of time, perhaps less than 100 years. A recent two-dimensional finite element model of a South Eugene Island Block 330 area sedimentary basin (Roberts et al. 1996) suggests that excess fluid pressure in abnormally pressured sediments would drop to approximately half its original value after about 10,000 years of expulsion. They also estimate by variable fault permeability simulations, where compaction of fault zone sediments closes the fracture network, that fault permeability decreases by 1-2 orders of magnitude within 200 years after fluid expulsion begins. In order to produce the thermal and baric anomalies observed in the subsurface overlying the South Eugene Island area geopressured zone Roberts et al. (1996) suggest that faults must remain open for 20-30 years. These model results support episodic expulsion of fluids and gases from geopressured zones and for the first time provide insight into timing for these events from numerical modeling.

Even though only qualitative data concerning flux rates and durations of delivery events exists for the Gulf's hydrocarbon seeps and vents, it is clear some areas are dominated by rapid venting of hydrocarbons and associated fluid plus sediment while other areas are affected only by very slow seepage. The terms venting and seepage are used in this report as qualitative expressions of comparative rates at which hydrocarbons, fluidized sediment, and other carrier fluids are delivered to the modern slope surface. Venting implies rapid delivery while seepage suggests slow flux rates. Figure 75 summarizes, in a schematic way, the geologic responses to the flux rate spectrum. On one end of the spectrum are those features that result from the rapid expulsion of large volumes of fluid mud frequently containing crude oil and hydrocarbon gases. On the other end of the spectrum are features related to the very slow seepage of hydrocarbon gas or hydrocarbon-charged (gas and/or crude oil) waters. In this setting, precipitation of calcium and magnesium carbonates, as well as exotic minerals like barite takes place (Roberts and Aharon 1994). While some features clearly have been produced in a single flux rate environment (rapid flux, slow flux, or somewhere between the two extremes), it is also clear that some areas of seafloor have evolved from one extreme to the other because of a change in the rate of the fundamental forcing process, vertical flux of fluids and gases. Enough comparative work has now been completed, as a part of this investigation between acoustic response on high resolution seismic profiles and direct observations of the seafloor, to know that most areas of hydrocarbon venting-seepage are represented as zones of acoustic wipe-out or acoustic turbidity (Roberts 1995, 1996). A goal of this MMS-CMI research is to build a better understanding of the geologic and biologic variability that these zones represent and develop criteria for interpretations using a high resolution acoustic and 3D-seismic data base.

Figure 75. A schematic illustration of the relationship between rate of delivery of fluids and gases to the seafloor and geologic/biologic response.

Table 30 summarizes the general relationships between vent-seep features and chemosynthetic communities with delivery rate of hydrocarbons plus carrier fluids (including

91

fine-grained sediment). End member and transition cases are discussed below starting with the rapid delivery, mud-prone case.

Table 30. General relationships between delivery rate of fluids and gases to the seafloor and response in seafloor geology, biology, and hydrocarbon degradation.

Flux Rate	Rapid (Venting)	Transitional	Slow (Seepage
Feature Spectrum	Mud Prone	———————	Mineral Prone
Dominant Feature Types	Mud Volcanoes Mud Flows Gas Expulsion Features	Gas Hydrate Mounds (Isolated Authigenic Carbonates) Small-scale Gas/Fluid Expulsion Features	Authigenic Carbonate •Mounds/Hardgrounds •Crusts/Nodules Mineralized Cones/Chimneys
Chemosynthetic Communities	Localized •Bacterial Mats •Lucinid Vesycomyd Clams •Pogonophoran Tube Works	Dense, Diverse, Widespread •Bacterial Mats •Lucinid/Vesycomyid Clams •Pogonophoran Tube Worms •Bathymodiolid Mussels	Very Localized •Bacterial Mats •Lucinid/Vesycomyid Clams •Vestimentiferan Tube Worms Bathymodiolid Mussels
Hydrocarbons and By-product*	Non-biodegraded •Cruide Oil •Thermogenic Gases •Biogenic Methane	Moderately Biodegraded •Crude Oil •Thermogenic Gases •Biogenic Methane HS and H_2S	Highly Biodegraded •Crude Oil •Thermogenic Gases •Biogenic Methane HS and H_2S (limited)

* The types of hydrocarbons found at any given site depend on the numbers and types of sources being tapped by the delivery system(s).

a. Mud-Prone Cases Hedberg (1974) recognized that the vertical migration of gas and fluids through unconsolidated-to-semiconsolidated sediments may create a slurry-like mixture of sediment, gas, and water that can produce mud volcanoes and other fluid expulsion features at the seafloor. Mud volcanoes and extruded mud sheets have been observed from many different geological settings (Hovland and Judd, 1988) ranging from areas where accretionary prisms are being degassed and dewatered by the process of subduction (e.g. Barber et al. 1986; Breen et al. 1986; Brown 1990; Henry et al. 1990; Orange and Breen 1992; Zhao et al. 1986) to areas of active salt deformation like the Gulf of Mexico (Neurauter and Bryant 1990; Neurauter and Roberts 1992, 1994). They have also been reported from Trinidad (Arnold and Macready 1956) the Caspian Sea (Hedberg 1974), the Black Sea (Ivanov et al. 1989) Beaufort Sea (Pelletier 1980), offshore Panama (Reed et al. 1990), the Arabian Sea (Hovland and Judd 1988), the Northeast shelf of New Zealand (Nelson and Healy 1984), as well as many other places.

An example of a mud-prone feature from the northern Gulf of Mexico slope that has formed in a rapid flux regime is the active mud volcano in the north central part of Green Canyon, Block 143 (Neurauter and Roberts,1994). This feature (Figure 76) has formed in a water depth of ~ 335 m, is cone-shaped, has built to a height of 35 m above the surrounding seafloor, and has a base of about 450-500 m diameter. Short cores into the sides of this feature indicate that it is composed of fine-grained sediment (clay to fine silt sized mud) with no indication of post depositional cementation at the surface. However, a similar but dormant mud volcano in GC53 (Neurauter and Roberts 1994), discussed as a case study in this report, displays lithification, as exposed in an eroded gullies on the cone flank. This lithification occurs in multiple layers as if the deposition of cone-building mud was episodically turned-on and turned-off allowing time for surficial lithification, at least in localized areas. Both cases, GC53 and GC143 clearly indicate demonstrate that these features are acoustically opaque on high quality geohazards-scale seismic profiles.

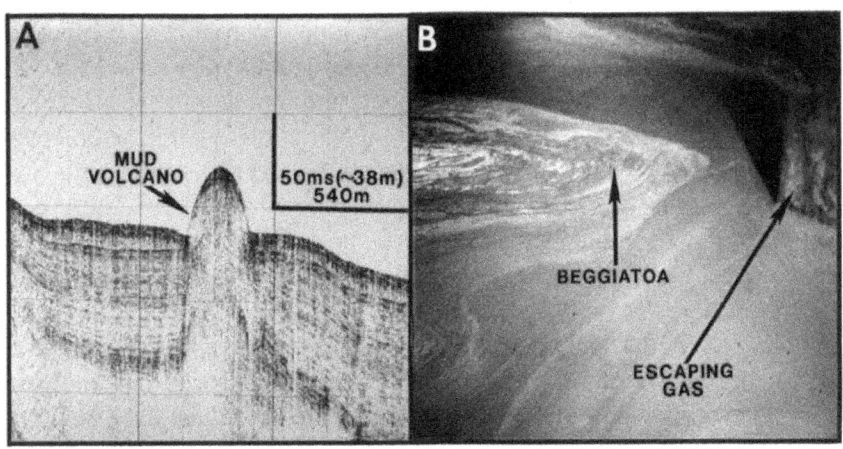

Figure 76. (a) A high resolution seismic profile (15 in^3 water gun) across a mud volcano in Green Canyon Block 143. (b) This submersible-acquired picture shows gas escaping from the central crater of the GC143 mud volcano. The white streaks on the fluid mud surface are Beggiatoa bacteria.

The GC143 mud volcano has been observed and sampled on four occasions (JSL-1, Dives 2587, 2588, 3115, and 3298). On a 1992 dive (JSL-2, Dive 3298), fluid mud saturated with crude oil and gas was actually spilling from the central caldera-like crater (approximately 50 m diameter) onto the flanks of the core. During other observation periods, gas was escaping from the central crater. The fluid mud in the crater was being convectively mixed as interpreted from the swirl-like patterns of thin orange and white bacterial mats (*Beggiatoa* sp.) on the mud surface. Escaping gas probably forced the convective mixing and caused fine-grained sediment, gas, and droplets of crude oil to be entrained in the overlying water column. Terrace-like features around the mud-filled central depression indicate the dynamic nature of the fluid mud level. No macroscale chemosynthetic organisms were observed in the central crater or on the cone flanks. Kohl and Roberts (1994, 1995) have demonstrated that this process causes fossil foraminifera to be spread over considerable areas on the modern slope. In the GC 143 mud volcano case, late Pleistocene foraminifera are being deposited. At other sites, for example the mud expulsion area in GB 338, discussed as a case study in this report, microfossils as old as early-to-middle Miocene are being deposited at the surface (Kohl and Roberts, 1994). At this site large quantities of extruded mud and associated slope failures have transported sediment nearly 10 km downslope (Figure 21). The case studies of the GC53 and GC185 mud vents are similar in that gas and fluidized sediment are being forced to the modern seafloor where the sediment spreads into well-defined sheets.

93

In areas where the seafloor is impacted by a rapid flux of fluidized sediment, complex chemosynthetic communities have problems becoming established because of unstable substrates and high sedimentation rates, even though the necessary trophic resources may be available. In fact, sediments from rapid flux sites commonly contain hydrocarbons that have experienced minimal biodegradation. The soft sediments of venting and seep environments may be inhabited by chemosynthetic lucinid-vesycomyid clams and occasional tubeworms. Both employ bacterial symbionts to derive food from the oxidation of hydrogen sulfide, and both require relatively firm sediments in order to maintain a stable life position. It is easy to appreciate that life position, literally how an animal is positioned so as to survive in an environment, is especially important for species exploiting the gradients of two toxins, oxygen and hydrogen sulfide. Lucinids are typically infauna, living within sulfide-rich sediments and maintaining respiratory contact with oxygenated water via a burrow and siphon. The vesycomyid live at the sediment-water interface, extending a foot down into sulfide-rich sediment while a short siphon keeps the body oxygenated. Pogonophorans (tube worms) dwell in a tube which extends into the sulfide rich sediments, leaving the anterior end exposed a few centimeters above the seafloor. In rapid flux, mud-rich environments, lucinids are the most common members of the infauna that exploit rapidly deposited sediments from hydrocarbon vents while *Beggiatoa sp* inhabit the surface. Sheets of crude oil soaked fluid mud extruded from mud volcanoes and other types of expulsion sites commonly display scattered lucinid shells on the surface. Cores through fluid mud deposits reveal concentrated layers of lucinid-vesycomyid clam shells separated by mud containing few infauna constituents. These observations suggest episodic influx of fluid muds burying the lucinid shells that probably represent the remains of a community that had depleted its trophic resource, hydrogen sulfide.

Sites of rapid venting with fine-grained sediment deposition both from suspension and as fluid mud are extremely hostile environments for all fauna. Suspended sediment deposition can restrict respiratory organs and blanket bacterial mats. Fluid muds make life positioning impossible except for bacteria which might float at the interface. These rapid flows may come from reservoirs with little sulfide and flow rates preclude sulfide-producing anaerobic oxidation of hydrocarbons. These conditions are consistent with the observations of Sassen et al.(1994) that hydrocarbons in such venting are not highly biodegraded. Infaunal lucinids could not survive in the fluid muds, but might colonize some areas of greater sediment stability on the periphery of the feature so long as a sulfide source is present. Therefore, areas of the continental slope where fluid mud is being rapidly forced to the surface by pressure release in the deep subsurface, buoyant forces created by gas pressure, and other poorly understood mechanisms are regions where chemosynthetic communities are absent or poorly developed.

b. Transitional Cases - Figure 75 schematically identifies this class of feature and the processes that produce them between the rapid venting mud-prone end numbers and mineral-prone features produced by slow seepage on the other end of the feature spectrum. When venting rates decrease from the mud-prone rapid venting case, substrates and trophic resources become available and the seafloor environment becomes favorable to the establishment of complex local chemosynthetic communities. Conversely, when seepage rates increase in mineral-prone settings of slow seepage, trophic resources increase and local conditions become favorable to complex community support. Chemosynthetic species at environmentally suitable Gulf of Mexico vent/seep sites are vestimentiferan tube worms, bathymodiolid mussels, and vesicomyid clams along with lucinid clams and pogonophoran worms (Carney, 1994). These groups of specialized organisms constitute the complex chemosynthetic communities referred to in this report. Along with the occurrence of chemosynthetic communities, there is evidence of seafloor lithification, which takes a variety of forms ranging from nodular masses in sediment to hardgrounds, slabs, and/or mound-like buildups (Roberts et al. 1992a, b).

Vent-seep related features and communities that fall into the transitional category generally occur in water depths below ~ 500 m and are coincident with the occurrence of surface-to-near surface gas hydrate deposits. These unusual deposits are stable-to-metastable at temperatures and pressures associated with water depths below about 400-500 m in the Gulf of Mexico (Brooks et al. 1985). The stability window shifts with temperature, pressure, and types (mixtures) of hydrocarbon gases (Sloan 1990). As observed by Roberts and Carney (1997), viable chemosynthetic communities in the Gulf's upper-to-middle continental slope province seem to be concentrated in the same depth ranges and at known gas hydrate sites. Only infrequent occurrences of chemosynthetic organisms have been reported shallower than the gas hydrate window (Roberts et al. 1990). This association is probably not fortuitous since gas hydrate areas store the trophic resources necessary to sustain long-term and complex chemosynthetic communities. Such communities require sustainable sources of methane and sulfide. As Carney (1994) suggests, "solid-phase gas hydrates of methane and water, which are stable at the pressure and temperature conditions below 400-500 m of water depth in the Gulf of Mexico, may be that unique aspect of deep ocean methane and sulfide chemistry that allows for chemosynthetic community development." Although slow migration of methane through the sediment column will cause gas-hydrates to form at the lower boundary of the pressure/temperature stability zone (Hyndman and Davis 1992), the many faults on the Gulf of Mexico continental slope introduce boundary instabilities causing methane to be transported vertically to the seafloor where gas-hydrate formation takes place near the sediment-water interface. Once at the seafloor, methane comes in contact with sea water sulfate and microbial communities, and sulfide is generated by methane oxidation-sulfate reduction. Sassen et al. (1993) suggest that there is a strong coupling between microbial mats (*Beggiatoa* sp.) common to the seafloor over gas hydrates and hydrocarbon concentrations in the sediment. The mats function as semi-permeable membranes that trap vertically migrating hydrocarbons beneath. Bacterial oxidation of hydrocarbons depletes oxygen which encourages bacterial sulfate reduction to produce hydrogen sulfide needed for *Beggiatoa* growth and mat development. Sassen et al. (1993) also re-emphasize the point made by other researchers that bicarbonate and carbon dioxide from microbial oxidation of hydrocarbons is probably responsible for initiating the precipitation of authigenic carbonates, nodular masses in the sediment as well as slab-like hardgrounds and more massive rocks.

The observations of gas hydrates outcropping on the seafloor (Figure 77), first made by the author in 1991 (GC232) and later observed by other researchers (MacDonald et al., 1994), suggest that they are localized along fault trends such as those crossing GC 232, 233, and 234, as well as mounds like the one in GC 185 (discussed as a case study in this report). Within either of these areas of known gas hydrate exposure, individual outcrops are only a few meters across. This localization of surface gas hydrates reflects the high spatial variability of seafloor types that occurs over gas hydrate areas. Within a few tens of meters one can move from a newly formed area of outcropping gas hydrates covered with bright orange and white bacterial mats (*Beggiatoa sp.*), Figure 78, to complex and densely arranged chemosynthetic communities of mussels and tube worms mixed with outcrops of authigenic carbonate (Figure 78) to small areas of seafloor where fluid muds have been extruded and lucinid clam shells litter the surface (Figure 79). Variability of benthic communities and seafloor geology is characteristic of transitional areas that fall between the rapid venting and slow seepage end members of the seafloor features spectrum. Areas characterized by transition fluid and gas expulsion environments are acoustically opaque with variable surface reflectivity on high resolution seismic profiles, and reflect a variety of hard target spacings and geometries on side-scan sonar.

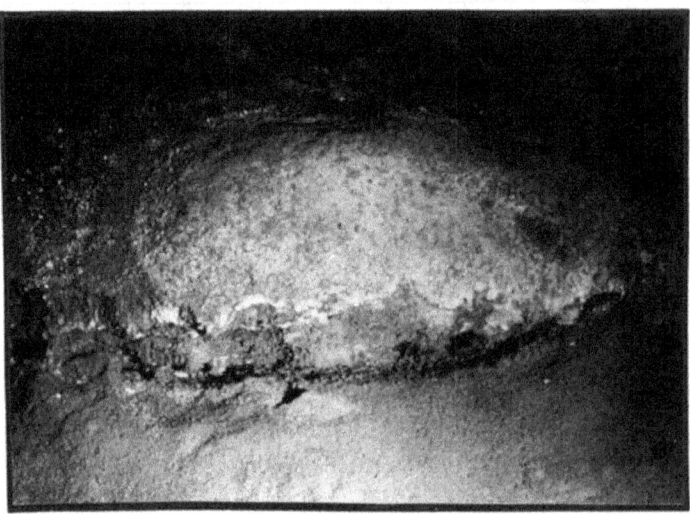

Figure 77. A small gas hydrate mound in Green Canyon Block 232 showing outcropping ledges of gas hydrate at its base and along its flanks and orange bacterial mats on the surface. This mound is about 2.5 m in diameter.

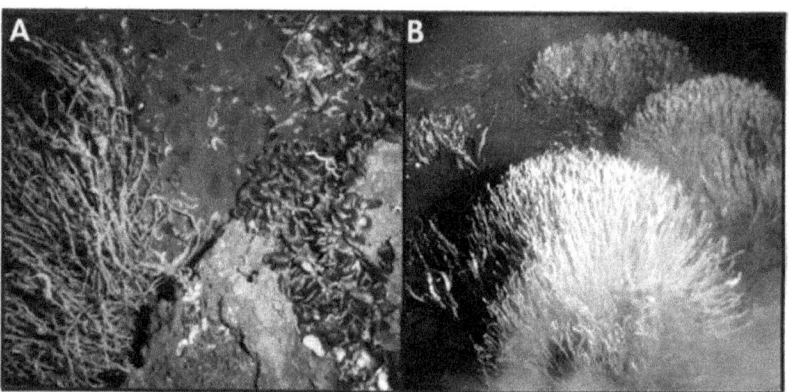

Figure 78. (a) This outcrop of authigenic carbonate with associated tube worms and mussels occurs in Green Canyon Block 232. Gas was observed escaping the mussel bed in this field of view. (b) Tube worm colonies and bacterial mats on a known gas hydrate area in Green Canyon Block 185.

Figure 79. Small fluid mud expulsion areas in Green Canyon Block 232 exhibit sheets of extruded mud on which lucinid clam shells litter the surface.

Known gas hydrate features geomorphically may be associated with mounds, such as "Bush Hill" in GC 185, oblate in plan-view but flat (GC 180-181), or elongate along a fault line (GC 232-234). Direct observations of gas hydrate areas indicate: (a) abundant complex chemosynthetic communities usually associated with hardgrounds and more massive authigenic carbonate rocks; (b) occasional low-relief carbonate mounds (usually <2-3 m relief); (c) abundant bacterial mats (both white and orange); (d) occasional outcrops of gas hydrate breaching the surface (MacDonald et al. 1994); and, (e) small-scale fluid and gas expulsion features. The localized authigenic carbonates (Figure 78) that are present at the best-studied sites of known gas hydrates (GC 185, GC 232, GC 234, GC 272, and MC 709) are composed dominantly of Mg-calcite and aragonite and frequently occur as imbricated slabs suggesting an episodic formational history. High reflectively on both high resolution seismic profiles and side-scan sonar swaths across gas hydrate areas occur in well-defined zones characterized by seafloor lithification and complex chemosynthetic communities.

c. Mineral-Prone Cases When rates of delivery of hydrocarbons and carrier fluids to the ocean floor are very low, either through primary supply or by a systematic decrease from higher rates, mineralization within surface and near-surface sediments is an important geologic process. Positive regional relief features (domes) that occur above shallow salt masses of the upper continental slope are common sites of mineral-prone features that result from a slow seepage environment. Most observations are limited to < 1000 m by the maximum diving depth of commonly used research submersibles. These sites generally exhibit complex fault networks that have limited depth penetration because of shallow salt. Unlike carbonate buildups at the shelf edge that have similar morphologies but are covered with thick biogenic carbonate veneers, seep-derived authigenic carbonate buildups below depths of ~ 200 m display little encrustation by carbonate-secreting organisms. As suggested in an earlier paper (Roberts 1992), the carbonate buildups at the shelf edge may be seated on substrates of seep-related authigenic carbonates. However, during late Pleistocene periods of lower sea level, reef-building organisms colonized these sites because they were more environmentally suitable than under today's conditions, particularly because of more light for photosynthetic zooxanthellae and the absence of a continental shelf where shallow water becomes cold during the winter because of limited heat storage capacity.

As summarized by Roberts and Aharon (1994), most of the mineralization associated with transitional and mineral-prone areas of the Gulf's continental slope is represented by the deposition of Mg-calcite, aragonite, and dolomite. These mineral phases are distinguished as being hydrocarbon-related by their ^{13}C -depleted compositions inherited from microbial oxidation of hydrocarbons (both crude oil and gas) and incorporation of abundant ^{12}C into the various mineral phases. Similar carbonates have been reported from other seep environments like the base of the Florida Escarpment (Neumann et al. 1988; Paull et al. 1992) and the subduction zone off the coasts of Oregon and Washington (Ritger et al. 1987). Although carbonates of mixed mineralogies occur at nearly every site where carbonate cementation occurs, there is usually a clear dominance of one phase over another. The most common carbonate mineralogy found in seep sites of northern Gulf slope is Mg-calcite (Roberts and Aharon 1994). Unlike the mineralogy, stable carbon and oxygen isotope compositions do not occur in well defined patterns. For example, ^{13}C values can range 1 ‰ to values more negative than -55‰. Values for $^{18}0$ also have quite a range (1°/00 to ~ 6 ‰). This range in stable isotope values and carbonate mineralogies presents a complex picture of formational processes.

One area, previously discussed as a case study, that demonstrates both transitional and mineral-prone responses to various venting and seepage rates is the GC 140-185 area. Cook and D'Onfro (1991) indicate that important faulting in this area resulted from salt movement in the lower Pleistocene. At this time a major thrust fault was initiated by salt movement responding to lowstand deposition of sand-rich gravity flows on the continental slope. Over Pleistocene times these types of deposits and intervening condensed sections filled a basin created by salt withdrawal. Figure 67 of the GC140 case study illustrates the present subsurface configuration of salt, sediments, and major fault networks. Seafloor features associated with the two major fault zones shown on this figure are quite different, one over a shallow salt diapir and the other where normal and antithetic faults intersect a deep-cutting thrust fault. Numerous faults cutting the thin sedimentary sequence over the shallow salt mass of GC 140 appear poorly connected to the deep subsurface and therefore have provided a slow seepage environment that has produced a complex field of authigenic carbonate mounds, as discussed above. In contrast, the antithetic fault that has intersected a family of eastward dipping normal faults, which connect with a deep-cutting reverse fault, has produced a complex of mounds containing gas hydrates. They are interpreted as features arising from moderate rates of fluid and gas flux to the seafloor that are intermediate between mud volcanoes and the aforementioned authigenic carbonate mounds.

The top of the regional dome expressed primarily in GC140 has been to a slow seepage environment provided by numerous shallow-cutting faults that are connected to a deep subsurface hydrocarbon source by a complex plumbing system. This seafloor area is characterized by many distinct carbonate mounds ranging in relief of a few meters to over 20 m. These mounds are composed of authigenic carbonates (Mg-calcite and dolomite primarily) that are ^{13}C -depleted (Figure 60) and clearly the by-product of microbial utilization of hydrocarbon gas, primarily methane (Roberts et al. 1992a, b). Although a very localized occurrence of dead tube worms and mussels was reported in a crevice (water depth ~ 290 m) in one of these features (Roberts et al. 1990), the general absence of fossil shell debris and tube worm molds from the mound-building carbonates suggests that seepage has been too slow to sustain a complex chemosynthetic community, but carbonate precipitation was mediated by methanotrophic bacteria.

The mineral-prone features of GC 140 have not only developed in a slow seepage environment but are interpreted to have formed over a relatively long period of time. Radiometric dates from six samples acquired from a carbonate mound in Green Canyon Block 140 range from 194.5 to 13.3 ka (Roberts and Aharon 1994). In contrast, samples from carbonate slabs exposed at the surface of the largest gas hydrate mound (transitional between mud-prone and mineral-prone features) in GC 185 yielded ages ranging from 3.2 to 1.4 ka (Roberts and Aharon 1994). In addition to developing in an environment of slow seepage, dome-top carbonate mounds of the upper slope have also developed under conditions of erosion. Seismic profiles across these areas clearly indicate truncation of stratified units and general sediment stripping from dome crests. Processes of erosion are poorly understood in slope-depth environments, but expanding knowledge of the Gulf's Loop Current indicates that currents capable of transporting sand-sized sediment occur to depths of approximately 600 m (Hamilton 1990). Surface sediments of the GC 140 dome top contain sand and gravel-sized diagenetic clasts and shell debris interpreted as a long-term lag deposit created by the dome-top erosional setting. Seismically, the GC 140 area is an acoustic wipe-out zone that has a strongly reflective and topographically variable surface.

Some areas that now are in slow seepage environments illustrate geologic and sedimentologic characteristics that suggest a progressive evolution from a rapid venting area to a present state of slow seepage. Good examples of areas evolving from one stage to another are found within the previous discussed case studies from GB 338 and 382, which overly a subsurface salt ridge. There are well-defined sites within each lease block area from which vast quantities of mud have been expelled, creating mud flows and fluid debris flows that are clearly recognizable on side-scan sonar data. These flowed sediments originated from two circular expulsion centers and have been deposited over hummocky landslide-debris flow deposits that probably developed as a result of slope instability related to movements of the underlying salt ridge. Although no absolute dating exists for the late stage mud flows, geomorphology of these deposits suggests they are very young. Sediment transport pathways and boundaries of depositional lobes are still clearly visible on side-scan sonar images. In addition, the thicknesses of the mudflow deposits diminish stratigraphically upward, suggesting a slowing of the expulsion process. A thin (< 3 m thick) hemipelagic sediment drape occurs over much of the present seafloor in this area but is thin to indistinguishable on high resolution seismic records over the latest flow channels and deposits, suggesting a very young age. The thickness of hemipelagic drape deposits outside the mudflow deposit areas is comparable to the drape on other parts of the continental slope (Doyle et al. 1992). These highly calcareous hemipelagic drape deposits have developed as the sources of fluvial sediments have retreated landward following the latest Pleistocene glacial maximum, leaving the slope without a direct source of terrigenous sediments. Therefore, the thin drape over the latest mudflows suggests that they were deposited sometime after sea level started to rise from the last glacial maximum.

The fluid mud expulsion centers are mounded areas that appear acoustically amorphous on high resolution seismic profiles, but the one in GB 338, which is slightly larger than its counterpart in GB 382 (~ 825 m vs 700 m diameter), has a flattened top. Direct observation and sampling of these two areas has revealed that the expulsion of large volumes of fluid mud has stopped. A few small mud volcanoes have been observed in GB 338, but they appear to only extrude small volumes of fluid mud. At present, the seafloor of these areas is in the initial stages of mineralization by both Ca-Mg carbonates, but primarily by more exotic mineral species such as barite (Roberts and Aharon 1994; Fu et al. 1994). Figure 32 illustrates barite cones and chimneys that occur on top of the GB 338 mound. Pyrite is also a common constituent in mound-top sediments, as well as a minor component in barite and carbonate deposits (Fu et al. 1994). Equivalent features have not been found on the GB 382 mound, but Ca-Mg carbonate crusts and slabs are abundant. These areas have evolved from producing mud-prone features to producing mineral-prone features as the pressure drive responsible for venting of large volumes of fluid mud has progressively waned in favor slow seepage of mineral-rich fluids. The time frame for this transition has not been quantified. However, it seems reasonable to suggest that the rapid expulsion of mud followed the latest Pleistocene lowstand sediment loading event. The onset of a mineral-rich phase appears to relate to a slowing of salt movement as sediment sources have retreated landward with rising sea level and the lowstand sediment load has largely equilibrated with underlying salt. Seismically, both GB 338 and 382 exhibit an acoustic wipe-out signature on high resolution profiles.

☐. ☐riteria ☐or ☐a☐in☐☐etter Interpretations o☐Seep☐☐ent ☐e☐ated Sea☐oor Features ☐ro☐ ☐☐busti☐☐ata

This summary section of the report is based on the criteria used in each case study to characterize and identify each feature used in this investigation. These criteria include (a) high resolution seismic reflection characteristics, (b) seismic facies of the feature and surrounding units, (c) acoustic backscatter and target shapes from side-scan sonar data, (d) 3D-seismic surface amplitude and phase relationships, and finally (e) ground truth observations provided by submersible work. These data are summarized for each major feature group ranging from rapidly deposited mudflows and mud volcanoes to slowly accreted authigenic carbonate mounds.

a. Mud-Prone Cases Rapid extrusion of sediment as a part of carrier fluid and gas expulsion tends to create a rather smooth seafloor since many small-scale bottom roughness elements are buried by the process. Depending on the local setting, fluidized sediment extrusion can result in sheet-like flows as discussed with regard to GC53 collapse depression, GC185 mud vent, or the GB338, 382 mudflow case studies or in mound or cone shaped mud volcanoes as investigated in GC53 and 143. As a general statement these features have a smooth surface texture on side-scan sonar records with a low level of backscattered energy. Localized mud flows tend to have rather concentric patterns since they generally originate from a central vent or set of vents. Only in cases like the large-scale GB338, 382 flows where slope collapse is also obviously involved would side-scan sonar records contain highly apparent flow patterns and hard targets related to blocks of displaced sediment. Since only a few chemosynthetic communities have been found in association with mud-prone settings, a high degree of small-scale surface roughness and textured changes associated with these communities is not to be expected. This relationship is true of mud volcanoes and both small-scale and larger-scale mud sheets or flow.

Seismically, the thickness of individual mud-prone sheets is generally below the resolution limit of commonly used high resolution seismic sources and they are positioned over a zone that has little or no acoustic character (acoustic wipe-out zone). However, larger scale features like mud volcanoes commonly exhibit clear downlap of mud-prone deposits onto the surrounding slope surface because of vertical accretion from a central venting site. Even though most mud volcanoes have an acoustically turbid character, the flanks of these features frequently exhibit stratigraphy and downlap onto the adjacent slope surface. Reflector strength over mud-prone features is moderate-to-strong with a prolonged character over obvious gas-charged areas. On 3D-seismic surface amplitude data active mud vents and extruded mud sheets strongly deviate from background and display a positive-to-negative polarity shift. In the case of the GB338 and GB382 expulsion centers with associated flows, the extensive barite deposition over the mound crests and incorporated in the fluidized flows makes them appear as hard reflective surfaces on surface amplitude data.

b. Transitional Cases Transitional settings are characteristically variable regarding local seafloor topography, types and numbers of small-scale bottom roughness elements, and presence or absence of gas in surface sediments. This spatial complexity is reflected in side-scan sonar records as groups of scattered hard targets separated by areas of seafloor with varying "texture" or backscatter response. This high degree of backscatter and feature variability can be separated from areas characterized, for example, characterized by multiple small mud mounds in that the side-scan targets associated with transitional areas are generally more reflective. They consist of hard bottoms (authigenic carbonate slabs or nodular masses in the sediments), upturned carbonate slabs or small cemented mound-like features, outcrops of gas hydrate, numerous tube worm colonies, small-to-large fields of mussels, small mud extrusion features with lucinid-vesycomyid clams, and scattered areas of bacterial mats. Grouped in this matrix of diverse bottom features are active gas and crude oil expulsion sites where trains of bubbles and crude oil droplets can be observed in the water column. Roberts et al. (1998) have shown that some of this gas derives from decomposition of surface and near-surface gas hydrates as a product of thermal loading from the water column. In general, transitional areas at or below the gas hydrate stability zone (~ 500 m depth in the Gulf) can be characterized as having a broad spatial array of irregular hard targets that frequently occur in linear patterns, presumably along faults. Acoustic backscatter strength is generally strong and "texture" changes from area-to-area are usually moderate to high with high spatial variability. Feature outlines are irregular and usually of limited relief (usually < 2 m high).

Seismically, the subsurface of transitional areas is basically represented as an acoustic wipe-out zone with occasional chaotic reflection events. However, careful inspection of high resolution seismic profiles across these areas demonstrates extremely variable surface reflection strength, with localized zones being highly reflective. Reflector characteristics vary from prolonged and chaotic to bright spots with windowed reflections in transitions to flanking areas. Reflector geometries are irregular to isolated and multiple small parabolic reflectors. Sediments flanking transitional features are generally well-stratified, commonly demonstrate divergent facies, and exhibit both "pull-up" and "pull-down". Areas where flanking reflectors are upturned may represent areas where gas hydrates (relatively dense medium) may be present while down-turned reflectors may reflect the slower velocities associated with free gas in the sediments. Analysis of 3D-seismic surface amplitude data over these areas indicates the presence of bright spots or high amplitude zones, which suggest gas in near-surface sediments. Profile data support the interpretation of gas-charged sediments by demonstrating a positive-to-negative polarity shift or phase inversion over these areas.

     c. <u>Mineral-Prone Cases</u> The best examples of mineral-prone cases are characterized by areas of seafloor with a high degree of surface roughness. In the most dramatic cases, such as the GC140 case study presented earlier in this report, surface topography is dominated by mounds of various dimensions that are composed of ^{13}C-depleted authigenic carbonates. On side-scan sonar records these mounds present clear targets with sharp edges, irregular surfaces, and variable relief. They cast well defined acoustic shadows which can indicate relief of many meters above the surrounding seafloor. Intermound areas demonstrate a variety of backscatter patterns, but reflectance values are much lower than the mounds themselves. Sediments between the mounds vary from fine-grained hemipelagic muds to coarse lags of shell debris and diagenetic clasts. On high resolution seismic profiles these mounded areas are represented as highly reflective surfaces that are organized into isolated and overlapping parabolic reflectors. The subsurface beneath this highly reflective seafloor is represented dominatly by acoustically turbid or somewhat chaotic signature. Because of the interpreted low quantity of bubble phase gas in the near subsurface of many mineral-prone sites, particularity the mounded sites, acoustic windows occur that reveal subsurface stratigraphy. Frequently, these windows occur at locations where considerable distance occurs between mounds or groups of mounds. Sediments flanking mounded areas are generally upturned, eroded, and highly faulted since most mineral-prone sites are located over shallow salt. On 3D-seismic surface amplitude data mounded mineral-prone seafloor is highly reflective and stands out as compared to surrounding seafloor. However, 3D-seismic and digital high resolution profiles across these areas show no phase reversal and therefore indicate a hard bottom with no substantial amounts of bubble-phase gas in the shallow sediment column.

I□. □ro□e□t □on□□sions

During the course of this project detailed data sets were collected on 29 features of the northern Gulf of Mexico upper continental slope (<1000 m water depth). Each one of these sites was represented by a shallow subsurface acoustic wipe-out zone on high resolution seismic. In addition to high resolution seismic, side-scan sonar, 3D-seismic, and direct seafloor verification data sets were analyzed for each feature and a synthesis of feature characteristics derived. This program has led to an improved understanding of hydrocarbon seep/vent-related phenomena on the Louisiana-Texas continental slope by helping clarify the relationships between rate of delivery of fluids and gases to the seafloor and geologic as well as biologic response. Specific conclusions from this project are as follows:

1. Not all acoustic wipe-out zones are related to hydrocarbon seepage and venting sites. Areas of seafloor that are extremely compacted, coarse grained (gravel lag), mounded, or cemented (diagenetically altered) are highly reflective and scatter acoustic energy resulting in acoustic wipe-outs on high resolution seismic records. In addition, areas where allochthonous salt is near the seafloor with only a thin sediment drape over it can appear as an acoustic wipeout zone, but these areas are not prone to have hydrocarbon seeps/vents and the chemosynthetic communities that are commonly associated with them.

2. Areas of continental slope seafloor impacted by hydrocarbon venting and seepage are nearly always represented on high resolution seismic profiles as acoustic wipe-out zones. These zones correlate with the occurrence of gas in surface and near-surface sediments. Through an appraisal of the variability of seafloor features within these zones, feature types can be conveniently grouped into those that are the result of rapid delivery of fluids and gases at one end of the spectrum to those that are the result of slow seepage on the other. The rapid delivery features are mud-prone while the slow delivery features are mineral-prone.

3. Considering the data reviewed for this project, no areas shallower than a water depth of ~500 m and characterized by acoustic wipe-out zones were accompanied by macro-scale chemosynthetic communities.

4. Through an appraisal of the variability of seafloor features within areas characterized by acoustic wipe-out zones plus fluid and gas expulsion, feature types can be conveniently grouped into those that are the result of rapid delivery of fluids and gases at one end of the spectrum to those that are the result of slow seepage on the other. The rapid delivery features are mud-prone while the slow delivery features are mineral-prone.

5. Mud-prone features such as mud vents, mud flows, and mud volcanoes do not generally support complex chemosynthetic communities, and hydrocarbons reaching the seafloor are only slightly biodegraded. Bacterial mats and lucinid clams are the most common chemotrophic forms. On high resolution seismic records these mud-prone features usually have a vertical acoustic wipe-out zone ("gas chimney") that connects the surface form to the subsurface. Gas in the water column, as interpreted by "plumes" on high resolution seismic records, is common. The flanks of mud volcanoes, as well as stacked mudflows, may have internal stratigraphy detectable on high resolution seismic mounds. These mound-flanking

103

sediments commonly downlap onto adjacent slope sediments. The surfaces of mud volcanoes and mud flows are not highly reflective on side-scan sonar records. Vent areas may be identified on side-scan sonar records by concentric patterns that reflect former fluid levels or localized mud flows. Flow lines are sometimes visible on mud flows. Active mudflows, mud vents, and mud volcanoes will appear "bright" on 3D-seismic surface amplitude maps, and a phase change or positive to negative polarity shift is present when compared to the surrounding seafloor (indicating a slower velocity caused by gas-charged sediment). Ground truth verification of areas where fluidized sediments, fluids, and gases are being rapidly delivered to the seafloor indicates that both regional and small-scale fluid/gas expulsion features are present and that sediments in expulsion areas are highly charged with gas and frequently mixed with crude oil. Evidence of chemosynthetic organisms is limited to scattered bacterial mats and lucinid clams.

6. Mineral-prone features such as mounded carbonates, hardgrounds, or barite-carbonate encrusted areas do not support densely populated and complex chemosynthetic communities. Hydrocarbons that reach the seafloor in these slow seepage areas, especially crude oil and associated products, are badly biodegraded. On high resolution seismic records across these mineral-prone areas are represented as acoustic wipe-out zones with highly reflective surfaces (high amplitude). Commonly, complex interfingering of parabolic reflectors characterizes the seafloor on surface-tow high resolution seismic profiles. On deep-tow records it is clear that these surfaces are mounded. Small "plumes" of gas are occasionally observed on high resolution seismic records in the water column above these areas, but the general case is for no gas to appear on acoustic records. Shallow subsurface seismic returns are variable from total acoustic wipe-out zones to alternating acoustic wipe-out and chaotic zones to windows of stratified sediments that are usually faulted and inclined. Side-scan sonar data indicate discrete mound-like buildups that have complex and reflective surfaces. Data from this project suggest that these buildups vary in relief above the surrounding seafloor from less than 1 m to over 20 m. Outside the mounded seafloor areas variable backscatter intensities on side-scan records suggest variable sediment types. On 3D-seismic surface amplitude data mineral-prone areas are highly reflective and have no phase inversion as compared to surrounding seafloor areas. Research submersible verification of these areas indicates the presence of authigenic carbonate buildups, coarse surface sediment lags of diagenetic clasts, and little evidence of chemosynthetic communities or escaping hydrocarbons. Isolated tube worm, clams, and mussels can be found in these areas, but they are certainly not plentiful and occur in isolated patches. Most mineral-prone areas that have thus far been studied have only marginal chemosynthetic communities. The general case is for no macro-scale chemosynthetic communities to be present.

7. The best examples of areas of seafloor that fall between the two end members of rapid versus slow delivery of fluids (including fluidized sediment) and gases and are in water deeper than ~500 m. These areas are the most diverse with regard to surficial geology and biology. High resolution acoustic data reflect this variability in spatially varying patterns of reflection strength and backscatter. Areas of known gas hydrate occurrence at or near the modern seafloor best fit this intermediate or transitional case. Many areas impacted by the formation of gas-hydrates appear as simple mounds to larger low-relief mounded complexes. Most of these areas are characterized by complete acoustic turbidity in the shallow subsurface. Occasionally, discontinuous and sometimes chaotic high amplitude reflection events can be observed in the shallow subsurface. The strength of surficial returns on high resolution seismic profiles varies

104

over short distances from weak to extremely strong. Surface amplitude maps from 3D-seismic data demonstrate a surface variability characterized by scattered "bright areas" that correlate to phase reversals (positive to negative polarity shift) as compared to background seafloor areas. On side-scan sonar data these areas are characterized by scattered, low-relief hard targets and variable seafloor backscatter outside the hard target areas. Hard targets are usually of low relief (< 2 m), have irregular shapes, and commonly occur in lineated patterns. Research submersible verification of the surface of these intermediate flux cases verifies that the surficial variability in geology and biology reflected in amplitude variations on seismic and numerous hard targets on side-scan records is related to scattered tube worm colonies, mussel beds, low-relief outcrops of authigenic carbonate, and mounded gas-hydrates.

8. The quality of interpretation of seafloor geology using remotely sensed acoustic data is dependent on a wide variety of variables, including frequency and firing rate of the source, towing configuration, filtering, and recording-data storage modes. Results of research associated with this project clearly identify the benefits of digitally acquired high resolution acoustic data as opposed to analog. These benefits primarily fall in the realm of post-data collection processing and play-back. Digital acquisition preserves the frequency content of the data, allows for post-acquisition filtering, deconvolution, stacking, and other manipulations of the data to help understand the time character of the seafloor. Not only does digital data provide the benefits of processing for higher quality images, but polarity changes in the data can be easily recognized when data are displayed in appropriate format.

9. Surface-tow data derived from high resolution acoustic seismic sources are depth-limited. Digital acquisition and processing enhances surface-tow data, and this project produced excellent data to water depths of about 850 m. However, it is the author's opinion that 1000 m is the outside limit for surface-tow data adequate for reliable appraisals of seafloor geology. Below this depth, deep-tow technologies must be employed for reliable high resolution data sets. In extremely complicated topographic and geologic settings the maximum depth for reliable high resolution seismic data is even shallower than 1000 m. This reservation is especially true for side-scan sonar data, which become difficult to acquire because of cable length and fish location problems.

10. Utilization of 3D-seismic surface amplitude and phase data provides a powerful additional element for interpreting seafloor geology and, to some extent, biology when used in conjunction with good quality high resolution seismic and side-scan sonar data. The 3D-seismic amplitude and phase data can help discriminate hard and soft seafloor types, surface and near-surface sediments that are gas-charged and geohazards like subtle faults that may be difficult to image with other acoustic methods.

☐. ☐e☐o☐ ☐endations

As one of the deliverables for the final report, recommendations are to be made to the Minerals Management Service regarding feature detection, upgrades for surface-tow data acquisition, and merits of digitial processing of acoustic data, and the role for 3D-seismic in geohazards evaluations. The accumulation of data for this project has lead to the development of a convenient scheme for describing areas and features that are either impacted by or have developed from the delivery of fluids and gases to the modern seafloor. This spectrum of mud-prone to mineral-prone features helps us understand the variability of seep/vent-related phenomena and it introduces a level of predictability not only for seafloor geology, but also for hydrocarbon vent/seep biology. The characteristics of seafloor areas that have acoustic wipe-out zones and fall into these areas are discussed in the project conclusions.

Regarding surface-tow acquisition of high resolution seismic data, computer programs are now readily available for digital acquisition and processing. Analog data should no longer be acceptable because of the post-processing options available to upgrade record quality. However, surface-tow data have water depth limitations. In the author's opinion, surface-tow data are not reliable proxies for the seafloor below water depths of 1000 m. In extremely complex seafloor settings, this maximum depth can be somewhat shallower. Deep-tow high resolution data represent the seafloor better in continental slope water depths than any other option. This option is best for both side-scan sonar and high resolution seismic.

New options using 3D-seismic data for seafloor evaluations should be used in conjunction with higher resolution data sets. Surface amplitude and phase data are extremely valuable for interpreting areas of hard and soft bottom, as well as gas-prone sediments. However, even the best 3D-seismic has resolution problems when one is interested in small-scale features like mounds, small slumps, gas hydrate outcrops, chemosynthetic communities as well as other features common to the northern Gulf of Mexico continental slope. Therefore, multiple data sets are required for the best interpretations. In the author's opinion 3D-seismic profiles coupled with seafloor renderings incorporating multibeam bathymetry and 3D-seismic amplitude data are sufficient for clearing a block for areas that are probable sites for potential geohazards or protected benthic communities. However, for determining pipeline routing and platform locations more detailed data sets are required.

Finally, the northern Gulf of Mexico continental slope is such a complex and diverse area of ocean bottom that more work must be focused on understanding its geologic-sedimentologic variability and how this variability impacts slope biology. It is the author's opinion that as the oil and gas industry moves deeper, more seafloor verification of acoustic data must be accomplished before geologists,geotechnical engineers, and regulatory personnel can be confident of seafloor interpretations based on remotely sensed acoustic data (both high-resolution data including Seabeam bathymetery and low frequency exploration-scale seismic).

XI. References

Aharon, P., H.P. Schwarcz, H.H. Roberts, and S. Valastro. 1993. A feasibility study of chronology of submarine venting in the northern Gulf of Mexico by radiometric isotope techniques. Geological Society of America Abstracts with Programs 25:A443.

Aharon, P and J Chappell. 1986. Oxygen isotopes, sealevel changes, and temperature history of a coral reef environment in New Guinea over the last 105 years. Paleogeography, Paleoclimatology, and Paleoecology 56:337-379.

Anderson, J.B., K. Abdulah, S. Sarzalego, F. Siringan, and M.A. Thomas. 1996. Late Quaternary sedimentation and high-resolution sequence stratigraphy of the least Texas shelf, pp. 95-124. In DeBatist, M. and P. Jacobs, eds. Geology of Siliciclastic Shelf Seas. Geological Society of American Special Publications, No. 117.

Anderson, R.N. 1993. Recovering dynamic Gulf of Mexico reserves and the U.S. energy future. Oil and Gas Journal 11:85-91.

Anderson, R.N., W. He, M.A. Hobart, C.R. Wilkinson, and H.R. Nelson. 1991. Active fluid flow in the Eugene Island area, offshore Louisiana. Geophysics: The Leading Edge of Exploration, pp. 12-17.

Arnold, R. and G.A. Macready. 1956. Island forming mud volcano in Trinidad, British West Indies. American Association of Petroleum Geologists Bulletin 40:2748-2758.

Barber, A.J., S.R. Tjokrosapoetro, and T.R. Charlton. 1986. Mud volcanoes, shale diapirs, wrench faults, and melanges in accretionary complexes, eastern Indonesia. American Association of Petroleum Geologists Bulletin 70(11):1729-1741.

Behrens, E.W. 1988. Geology of a continental slope oil seep, northern Gulf of Mexico: American Association of Petroleum Geologists Bulletin 72:105-114.

Berryhill, H.L. 1987. Late Quaternary facies and structure, northern Gulf of Mexico. AAPG Studies in Geology 23, 289 pp.

Berryhill, H.L., J. R. Suter and N.S. Hardin. 1986. Late Quaternary facies and structure, northern Gulf of Mexico: American Association of Petroleum Geologists Bulletin 72:105-114.

Breen, N.A., E.A. Silver, and D.M. Hussong. 1986. Structural styles of an accretionary wedge south of the island of Sumba, Indonesia, revealed by Sea MARCII side scan sonar. Geological Society of America Bulletin 97:1250-1261.

Brooks, J.M., M.C. Kennicutt II, R.R. Bidigare, and R.A. Fay. 1985. Hydrates, oil seepage, and chemosynthetic ecosystems on the Gulf of Mexico slope. EOS Transactions American Geophysical Union 66:106.

Brown, K. 1990. The nature and hydrogeologic significance of mud diapirs and diatremes for accretionary systems. Journal of Geophysical Research 95:8969-8982.

Campbell, K.J.. 1997. Fast track development: The evolving role of 3D seismic data in deepwater hazards assessment and site investigation, Proceeding offshore technology Conference, OTC 8306:15 p.

Carney, R.S. 1994. Consideration of the oasis analogy for chemosynthetic communities at Gulf of Mexico hydrocarbon vents. Geo-Marine Letters 14:149-159.

Cathles, L.M. 1990. Scales and effects of fluid flow in the upper crust. Science 248:323-329.

Cathles, L.M and A.T. Smith. 1983. Thermal constraints on the formation of Mississippi Valley-type lead-zinc deposits and their implications for episodic basin dewatering and deposit genesis. Economic Geology 78:983-1002.

109

Coleman, J.M., D.B. Prior, and J. Lindsey. 1983. Deltaic influences on shelf edge instability processes. In D.J. Stanley, and G.T. Moore, eds. The Shelf Break: Critical Interface on Continental Margins. Society of Economic Paleontologists and Mineralogists Special Publication 33, pp. 121-137.

Coleman, J.M., D.B. Prior, and H.H. Roberts. 1986. Geologic development and characteristics of the continental margins, Gulf of Mexico. Gulf Coast Association of Geological Societies Transactions 36: 61-64.

Cook, H.E., Johnson, P.D., Matti, J.C. and Zemmels, I. 1975. Methods of sample preparation and X-ray diffraction analysis data analysis: X-ray Mineralogy Laboratory. Deep Sea Drilling Project, University of California, Riverside, Initial Reports of the Deep Sea Drilling Project, 28. Washington (U.S. Government printing Office). P. 999-1007.

Cook, D. and P. D'Onfro. 1991. Jolliet Field thrust fault structure and stratigraphy, Green Canyon block 184, offshore Louisiana. Transactions Gulf Coast Association of Geological Societies 41:100-121.

Cunnings, E.R. and R.R. Shrock. 1928. Niagaran coral reefs of Indians and adjacent states and their stratigraphic relations. Geologic Society of American Bulletin 39:579-619.

Diegel, F.A. and R.W. Cook. 1990. Palinspastic reconstruction of salt-withdrawal growth-fault systems, northern Gulf of Mexico. Geological Society of America Abstracts with Programs 22:A48.

Diegel, F.A., J.F. Karlo, D.C. Schuster, R.C. Shoup, and P.R. Tauvers. 1995. Cenozoic structural evolution and tectono-stratigraphic framework of the northern Gulf Coast continental margin, pp. 109-151. In M.P.A. Jackson, D.G. Roberts, S. Snelson, eds. Salt Tectonics: A Global Perspective. AAPG Memoir 65:109-151.

Doyle, E.H., M.J. Kaluza, and H.H. Roberts. 1992. Use of manned submersibles to investigate slumps in deep water Gulf of Mexico. Proceedings Civil Engineering in the Oceans V, p. 770-782.

Doyle, E.H., J.S. Smith, P.R. Tauvers, J.R. Booth, M.C. Jacobi, A.C. Nunez, F.A. Diegel, and M.J. Kaluza. 1996. The usefulness of enhanced surface renderings from 3D-seismic data for high resolution geohazard studies. Proceedings Minerals Management Service Gulf of Mexico 16th Information Transfer Meeting, Dec. 11, 1996, New Orleans: 9 p.

Fu, B., P. Aharon, G. R. Byerly and H. H. Roberts. 1994. Barite chimneys on the Gulf of Mexico slope: Initial report of their petrography and geochemistry. Geo-Marine Letters 14:81-87.

Gittings, S., R.G.S. Boland, K.J.P. Deslarzes, C.L. Combs, B.S. Holland, and T.J. Bright. 1992. Mass spawning and reproductive viability of reef corals at East Flower Garden Banks, northwest Gulf of Mexico. Marine Science 51:420-428.

Hallager, W.S., M.R. Ulrich, J.R. Kyle, P.E. Price, and W.A. Gose. 1990. Evidence for episodic basin dewatering in salt-dome caprocks. Geology 18:716-719.

Hamilton, P. 1990. Deep currents of the Gulf of Mexico. Journal of Geophysical Research 20:1087-1104.

Hedberg, H.H. 1974. Relation of methane generation to under compacted shales, shale diapirs, and mud volcanoes. American Association of Petroleum Geologists Bulletin 58:661-673.

Henry, P., X. LePichon, S.Lallemant, J.P. Foucher, G. Westbrook, and M. Hobart. 1990. Mud volcano field seaward of the Barbados accretionary complex: A deep-towed side-scan sonar. Journal of Geophysical Research 95:8917-8929.

Hill, A.W. 1996. The use of exploration 3-D data in geohazard assessment: Where does the future lie? Proceedings Offshore Technology Conference; OTC 7966:113-117.

Hovland, M. and A.G. Judd. 1988. Seabed pockmarks and seepages: Impact on geology, biology and the marine environment. Graham and Trotman. London. 293 pp.

Hovland, M., M. Talbot, H. Quvale, S. Olanssen, and L. Asaberg, 1987, Methane-related carbonate cements in pockmarks of the North Sea. Journal of Sedimentary Petrology, 57:881-892.

Hyndman, R.D. and E.E. Davis. 1992. A mechanism for the formation of methane hydrate and sea floor bottom-simulating reflectors by vertical fluid expulsion. Journal of Geophysical Research 97:7025-7041.

Ivanov, M.K., A.I. Konyukhov, L.M. Kul'nitskii, and A.A. Musatov. 1989. Mud volcanoes in the abyssal area of the Black Sea. Moscow University Geology Bulletin 44(3):43-49.

Jackson, M/P.A. and C. Talbot. 1989. Salt canopies. Tenth Annual Research Conference of the Gulf Coast Section of Society of Economic Paleontologists and Mineralogists Foundation, pp. 72-78.

Jorgensen, N.O. 1992. Methane-derived carbonate cementation of marine sediments from the Kattegat, Denmark, Geochemical and geological evidence. Marine Geology, 103:1-13.

Kennicut, M.C. II, J.M. Brooks, R.R. Bidigare, R.A. Fay, T.L. Wade, and T.J. McDonald. 1985. Vent-type taxa in a hydrocarbon seep region on the Louisiana slope. Nature 317:352.

King, L.H. and B. MacLean. 1970. Pockmarks on the Scotian Shelf. Geological Society of America Bulletin, 81:3141-3148.

Kohl, B. and H.H. Roberts. 1994. Fossil foraminifera from four active mud volcanoes in the Gulf of Mexico. Geo-Marine Letters 14:126-134.

Kohl, B. and H.H. Roberts. 1995. Mud volcanoes in the Gulf of Mexico: A mechanism for mixing sediments of different ages in slope environments. Gulf Coast Association of Geological Societies Transactions 45:351-359.

Kyle, J.R., M.R. Ulrich, and W.A. Gose. 1987. Textural and paleomagnetic evidence for the mechanism and timing of anhydrite caprock formation, Winnfield salt dome, Louisiana, pp. 497-542. In Lerche, I. And J.O'Brien, eds. Dynamical geology of salt and related structures: Academic Press, Orlando, Florida.

Lugo-Fernandez, A. 1998. Ecological implications of hydrography and circulation to the Flower Garden Banks, northwest Gulf of Mexico. Gulf of Mexico Science 2:144-160.

McBride, B.C. 1995. Evaluation of subsalt petroleum potential using structural restorations. AAPG Annual Convention Program 4:62A.

McBride, B.C. 1996. Geometry and evolution of allochthonous salt and its impact on petroleum systems, northern Gulf of Mexico Basin: studies in three- and four-dimensional analysis. Ph.D. Thesis. University of Colorado, Boulder, Colorado.

McDonald, I.R., N.L. Guinasso, Jr., S.G. Ackleson, J.F. Amos, R. Duckworth, R. Sassen, and J.M Brooks. 1993. Natural oil slicks in the Gulf of Mexico visible from space. Journal of Geophysical Research 98:16,351-16,364.

MacDonald, I.R., N.L. Guinasso, Jr., R. Sassen, J.M. Brooks, L.Lee, and K.T. Scott. 1994. Gas hydrates that breach the sea floor on the continental slope of the Gulf of Mexico. Geology 22: 699-702.

MacDonald, I.R. and W.W. Schroeder. 1993. Chemosynthetic ecosystems studies. Interim report: OCS Study MMS 93-0032. 94 pp.

MacDonald, I.R., W.W. Schroeder, and J.M. Brooks. 1995. Chemosynthetic ecosystems studies final report. Prepared by Geochemical and Environmental Research Group: U.S. Department of the Interior, Minerals Management Service, Gulf of Mexico OCS Region, New Orleans, La., OCS Study MMS 95-0023. 338 pp.

MacDonald, I.R., W.W. Schroeder, and J.M. Brooks. 1996. Northern Gulf of Mexico chemosynthetic ecosystems study. Final Report: OCS Study MMS 95-0022, vol. 2 (Technical Report), 317 pp.

Martin, R.G. 1980. Distribution of salt structures in the Gulf of Mexico; map and descriptive text. U.S. Geological Survey Map MF-1213, 2 sheets.

Nelson, C.S. and T.R. Healy. 1984. Pockmark-like structures on the Poverty Bay sea bed - possible evidence of submarine mud volcanism. New Zealand Journal of Geology and Geophysics 27:225-230.

Neumann, A.C., J.W. Kofoed, and G.H. Keller, 1977, Lithoherms in the straits of Florida. Geology 5:4-11.

Neumann, A.C., C.K. Paull, R. Commeau, J. Commeau, J. Chanton, C. Martens, M. Gardemal, W. Trumbull, and W. Showers. 1988. Abyssal seep site cementation: West Florida Escarpment. American Association of Petroleum Geologists Bulletin 72:228.

Neurauter, T.W. and W.R. Bryant. 1990. Seismic expression of sedimentary volcanism on the continental slope, northern Gulf of Mexico. Geo-marine Letters 10:225-231.

Neurauter, T. and H.H. Roberts. 1994. Three generations of mud volcanoes on the Louisiana continental slope. Geo-marine Letters 14:120-125.

Neurauter, T.W. and H.H. Roberts. 1992. Seismic and visual observation of seepage-related structures on the continental slope, northern Gulf of Mexico. Proceedings 24th Offshore Technology Conference, Houston, Texas, OTC 6850, pp. 355-362.

Neurauter, T.W. and H.H. Roberts. 1994. Three generations of mud volcanoes on the Louisiana continental slope. Geo-Marine Letters 14:120-125.

Norrany, I. 1984. Phase relations in marine soils. ASCE Journal of Geotechnical Engineering; Paper 18706:4.

Orange, D.L. and N.A. Breen. 1992. The effects of fluid escape on accretionary wedges, II: Seepage force, slope failure, headless submarine canyons, and vents. Journal of Geophysical Research 97:9277-9295.

Paull, C.K., J.P. Chanton, A.C. Neumann, J.A. Coston, C.S. Martens, and W. Showers. 1992. Indicators of methane-derived carbonates and chemosynthetic organic carbon deposits: Examples from the Florida Escarpment. Palaios 7:361-375.

Peel, F.J., C.J. Travis, and J.R. Hossack. 1995. Genetic structural provinces and salt tectonics of the Cenozoic offshore US Gulf of Mexico: a preliminary analysis. In: M.P.A. Jackson, D.G. Roberts, S. Snelson, eds., Salt Tectonics: A Global Perspective: AAPG Memoir 65, pp. 153-175.

Pelletier, B.R. 1980. Review of surficial geology and engineering hazards in the Canadian Offshore. Marine Sediments 15:55-91.

Poag, C.W. 1973. Late Quaternary sea levels in the Gulf of Mexico. Transactions Gulf Coast Association of Geological Societies 43:394-400.

Pulham, A.J. 1993. Variations in slope deposition, Plio-Pleistocene, offshore Louisiana, northeast Gulf of Mexico, pp. 199-234. In Weimer, P. and H.W. Posamentier, eds. Siliciclastic sequences stratigraphy: recent developments and applications. American Association of Petroleum Geologists Memoir 58.

Ranganathan, V. and J.S. Hanor. 1989. Perched brine plumes above salt domes and dewatering of geopressured sediments. Journal of Hydrology 110:63-86.

Ratcliff, D.W. 1993. New technologies improve seismic images of salt bodies. Oil and Gas Journal 91:41-49.

Reed, D.L., E.A. Silver, and J.E. Tagudin. 1990. Relations between mud volcanoes, thrust deformation, slope sedimentation, and gas hydrate, offshore north Panama. Marine and Petrol. Geol. 7:44-54.

Rezak, R. and T.J. Bright, 1981, Northern Gulf of Mexico topographic features study. Final Report to USDI-BLM, Contract No. AA551-CT8-35, Technical Report 81-2-T, Texas, A&M, Department of Oceanography, 1-5.

Rezak, R., T.J. Bright, and D.W. McGrail, 1985, Reefs and banks of the northwestern Gulf of Mexico, Theis geological, biological, and physical dynamics. John Wiley and Sons, New York, 1-259.

Ritger, S., B. Carson, and E. Suess. 1987. Methane-derived authigenic carbonates formed by subduction-induced pore-water expulsion along the Oregon/Washington margin. Geological Society of America Bulletin 98:147-156.

Roberts, H.H., R. Sassen, and P. Aharon. 1988. Petroleum-derived authigenic carbonates of the Louisiana continental slope. Proceedings of the Ocean '88, Baltimore, Md., pp. 101-105.

Roberts, H.H., R, Sassen, R. Carney, and P. Aharon. 1989. Carbonate buildups on the continental slope off central Louisiana. Proceedings 21st Annual Offshore Technology Conference, OTC 5953, pp. 655-662.

Roberts, H.H., P. Aharon, R. Carney, J. Larkin, and R. Sassen. 1990. Responses to hydrocarbon seeps, Louisiana continental slope. Geo-Marine Letters 10: 232-243.

Roberts, H.H., D.J. Cook, and M.K. Sheedlo. 1992a. Hydrocarbon seeps of the Louisiana continental slope: Seismic amplitude signature and sea floor response. Gulf Coast Association of Geological Societies Transactions 42:349-362.

Roberts, H.H., R.H. Fillon, B. Kohl, AlH. Bouma, and J. Sydow. 1991. Lithostratigraphy, biostratigraphy and isotopic inestigation of a boring in Main Pass Area, block 303: a calibration of high resolution seismic stratigraphy. Proceedings of Twelfth Annual GCS-SEPM Research Conference, Houston, Tex., Dec. 8-11, pp. 271-277.

Roberts, H.H., P. Aharon, and M.M. Walsh. 1992b. Cold-seep carbonates of the Louisiana continental slope-to basin floor, pp. 95-104. In Rezak, R. And D. Lavoie, eds. Carbonate Microfabrics. Springer-Verlag, Berlin.

Roberts, H.H. 1992. Reefs, bioherms, and lithoherms of the northern Gulf of Mexico: The importnat role of hydrocarbon seeps. Proceedings of 7th International Coral Reef Symposium, Guam, June 22-26.

Roberts, H.H. and P. Aharon. 1994. Hydrocarbon-derived carbonate buildups of the northern Gulf of Mexico continental slope: A review of submersible investigations. Geo-marine Letters, 14:135-148.

Roberts, S.J. and J.A. Nunn. 1995. Episodic fluid expulsion from geopressured sediments. Marine and Petroleum Geology 12:195-204.

Roberts, H.H. 1995. High resolution surficial geology of the Louisiana middle-to-upper continental slope. Gulf Coast Association of Geological Societies Transactions 45:501-508.

Roberts, S.J., J.A. Nunn, L. Cathles, and F.D. Cipriani. 1996. Expulsion of abnormally pressured fluids along faults. Journal of Geophysical Research 101:28,231-28,252.

Roberts, H.H., E.H. Doyle, J.R. Booth, B.J. Clark, M.J. Kaluza and A. Hartsook. 1996. 3D-seismic amplitude analysis of the seafloor: An important interpretive method for improved geohazards evaluations. Proceedings Offshore Technology Conference; OTC 7988:283-292.

Roberts, H.H. and R. Carney. 1997. Evidence of episodic fluid, gas and sediment venting on the northern Gulf of Mexico continental slope. Economic Geology, 92:863-879.

Roberts, H.H., and E.H. Doyle. 1998. Seafloor calibration of high resolution acoustic data and amplitude rendering of the "diapiric hill", Garden Banks 427. Proceedings Offshore Technology Conference; OTC Paper' 8592:19-30.

Roberts, H.H., B. Kohl, D. Menzies, and G.D. Humphrey, 1999, Acoustic wipe-out zones - A paradox for interpreting seafloor geologic/geotechnical characteristics (An example from Garden Banks 161). Proceedings 31st Annual Offshore Technology Conference, OTC 10921:1-6.

Rowan, M.G. 1995. Structural styles and evolution of allochthonous salt, central Louisiana outer shelf and upper slope, pp. 199-228. In M.P.A. Jackson, D.G. Roberts, and S. Snelson, eds. Salt Tectonics: A Global Perspective: AAPG Memoir 65.

Sager, W.W., C.S. Lee, I.R. MacDonald, and W.W. Schroeder, 1999, High-frequency near-bottom acoustic reflection signatures of hydrocarbon seeps on the northern Gulf of Mexico continental slope. Geo-Marine Letters, 18:267-276.

Sassen, R., I.R. MacDonald, A.C. Reguejo, N.L. Guinasso, Jr., M.C. Kennicutt II, S.T. Sweet, and J.M. Brooks, J.M. 1994. Organic geochemistry of sediments from chemosynthetic communities, Gulf of Mexico slope. Geo-Marine Letters 14:110-119.

Sassen, R., H.H. Roberts, P. Aharon, J. Larkin, E.W. Chinn, and R. Carney. 1993. Chemosynthetic bacterial mats at cold hydrocarbon seeps, Gulf of Mexico continental slope. Organic Geochemistry 20:77-89.

Sloan, E.D. 1990. Clathrate hydrates of natural gases. Marcel Drekker. New York. 641 pp.

Suter, J.R. and H.L. Berryhill. 1985. Late Quaternary shelf margin deltas, northeast Gulf of Mexico. American Association of Petroleum Geologists Bulletin 69: 77-91.

Sydow, J. and H.H. Roberts. 1994. Stratigraphic framework of a Late Pleistocene shelf edge delta, northeast Gulf of Mexico. American Association of Petroleum Geologists Bulletin 78:1276-1312.

Trabant, P.K. 1996. Use of 3-D exploration seismic data for geohazards analysis. Proceedings Offshore Technology Conference; OTC 7991:319-326.

Ulrich, M.R., J. R. Kyle, and P.E. Price. 1984. Metalic sulfide deposits in the Winnfield salt dome, Louise; evidence for episodic introduction of metalliferous brines during caprock formation. Gulf Coast Association of Geological Societies Transactions 34:435-442.

Vendeville, B.C. and M.P.A. Jackson. 1992. The rise of diapirs during thin-skinned extension Marine and Petroleum Geology 9:331-352.

Volkes, H.E. 1963. Studies on tertiary and recent grant *linidae*:. Tulane Studies in Geology 1:75-92.

Whelan, T., III, J.M. Coleman, J.N. Suhayda, and H.H. Roberts. 1977. Acoustical penetration and shear strength in gas-charged sediment. Marine Geotechnology, 2:9-44.

Winker, C.D. 1996. High-resolution seismic stritigraphy of a late Pleistocene submarine fan ponded by salt-withdrawal mini-basins on the Gulf of Mexico continental slope. Transactions Offshore Technology Conference, OTC 8024 1:619-628.

Winker, C.D. 1993. Pleistocene "lowstand" deposits of the Mississippi, Mobile, and Trinity Rivers: Models for turbidite sedimentation in the Gulf of Mexico (abs.): American Association of Petroleum Geologists Convention Program. 202 pp.

Winker, C.D. and M.B. Edwards. 1983. Unstable progradational elastic margins,p. 139-158. In Stanley, D.J. and G.T.Moore, eds. The shelfbreak: Critical interface on continental margins. Society of Economic Paleontologists and Mineralalogists Special Publication 33.

Worrall, D.M. and S. Snelson. 1989. Evolution of the northern Gulf of Mexico, with emphasis on Cenozoic growth faulting and the role of salt, p. 97-138. In A.W. Bally and A.R. Palmer, eds. The geology of North America; an overview. Geological Society of America Decade of North American Geology A.

Zhao, W.L., D.M. Davis, F.A. Dahlen, and J. Suppe. 1986. Origin of convex accretionary wedges: Evidence for Barbados. Journal of Geophysical Research 91:10.246-10.258.

Appendix A

Industry Data Sets Reviewed for MMS-CMI Project

Data sets acquired by individual companies in the petroleum industry formed the data base from which this MMS-CMI funded project evolved. Some data sets were given to Coastal Studies Institute for research purposes and others were either loaned or the PI was provided access. After an initial review of the data, a determination was made by the PI as to data quality and interest level in the area regarding project goals and objectives. Within any given area that fit the project guidelines, features of interest were selected , and the site was put on a high priority list. All data sets were eventually evaluated, and a high priority list was compiled. In order to make this list, acoustic wipe-out zones had to be present in the data set and data had to be of high quality. The next level of selection was based on the willingness of the participant company to share the data for publication and the availability of complimentary data sets, such as 3D-seismic and ground truth observations. When selected early enough, ground truth was planned for the following year's submersible program.

AREA	GREEN CANYON											
BLOCK	6	9	10	11	17	18	19	25	26	34	35	40
CONTRACTOR	MTS	RGI	RGI	JCA	RM		ME	MTS	JCA	GSI	GSI	JCA
COMPANY	Texaco	Conoco	Conoco	Chevron	Shell		Shell	Conoco	Texaco	Amoco	Amoco	Texaco
HAZARD REPORT				X		X			X	X	X	X
ENGINEERING REPORT	X	X	X	X	X		X	X	X	X	X	X
BATHYMETRIC MAP	X	X	X	X	X	X	X	X	X	X	X	X
DEEP TOW												
SURFACE TOW					X							
3.5 kHz	X	X	X	X	X	X	X	X	X	X	X	X
Boomer												
Sparker		X	X	X	X	X		X	X	X	X	X
Minisleeve							X					
Air-Gun												
Water-Gun						X						
Side-Scan	X	X	X	X	X	X	X	X				
3D-SEISMIC SURFACE AMPLITUDES												
WATER DEPTH (m)	85-271	79-274	79-274	160-245	329-805	215		262-501	253-457	553-663	538-601	564-488
CORES						X						
SUBMERSIBLE OBSERVATIONS						X						
FM=Fugro-McClelland												
ME=McClelland Engineers, Inc.												
JCA=John E. Chance & Associates, Inc.												
OOS= Odom Offshore Surveys												
IRC=Intersea Research Corporation												
ST=Sea Tales												
CGI=Comap Geosurveys, Inc.												

AREA	GREEN CANYON											
BLOCK	41	52	52	53	53	54	59	60	61	68	72	73
CONTRACTOR	JCA	ME	RGI	ME	RGI	RGI	RGI	JCA	JCA	RGI	JCA	JCA
COMPANY	Texaco	Conoco	Conoco	Conoco	Conoco	Conoco	Conoco	Sohio	Chevron	Gulf	Mobil	Shell
HAZARD REPORT	X							X			X	X
ENGINEERING REPORT	X	X	X	X	X	X	X			X	X	X
BATHYMETRIC MAP	X	X	X	X	X	X	X	X		X	X	X
DEEP TOW												
SURFACE TOW												
3.5 kHz	X	X	X	X	X	X	X	X	X	X	X	X
Boomer												
Sparker	X		X		X	X	X		X		X	X
Minisleeve		X		X					X			
Air-Gun												
Water-Gun												
Side-Scan		X	X	X	X	X	X				X	
3D-SEISMIC SURFACE AMPLITUDES												
WATER DEPTH (m)	625-823	110-235	79-274	110-235	79-274	79-274	214-303	232-348		343-625	511-635	530-799
CORES		X		X								
SUBMERSIBLE OBSERVATIONS												
FM=Fugro-McClelland												
ME=McClelland Engineers, Inc.												
JCA=John E. Chance & Associates, Inc.												
OOS= Odom Offshore Surveys												
IRC=Intersea Research Corporation												
ST=Sea Tales												
CGI=Comap Geosurveys, Inc.												
RDS=Racal-Decca Survey, Inc.												

AREA	GREEN CANYON										
BLOCK	75	79	80	81	89	91	97	98	102	103	104
CONTRACTOR	GSI	GSI	JCA	JCA	CGI	CGI	CGI	RDS/CAGC	CI	JCA	CCS
COMPANY	Amoco	Amoco	Texaco	Texaco	Exxon	Eddon	Arco	Conoco	Mobil	Sohio	Marathon
HAZARD REPORT	X	X	X	X			X			X	X
ENGINEERING REPORT	X	X	X	X	X	X		X	X	X	X
BATHYMETRIC MAP	X	X	X	X	X	X	X	X	X	X	X
DEEP TOW											
SURFACE TOW											
3.5 kHz	X	X	X	X	X	X	X		X	X	X
Boomer											
Sparker	X	X	X	X				X			
Minisleeve					X					X	
Air-Gun											
Water-Gun											
Side-Scan					X	X	X	X		X	X
3D-SEISMIC SURFACE AMPLITUDES											
WATER DEPTH (m)	577-681	567-703	549-923	549-923	110-238	98-262	170-320	243-564	284-363	273-360	305-392
SUBMERSIBLE OBSERVATIONS											
FM=Fugro-McClelland											
ME=McClelland Engineers, Inc.											
JCA=John E. Chance & Associates, Inc.											
OOS= Odom Offshore Surveys											
IRC=Intersea Research Corporation											
ST=Sea Tales											
CGI=Comap Geosurveys, Inc.											
RDS=Racal-Decca Survey, Inc.											

AREA	GREEN CANYON									
BLOCK	105	110	111	112	116	117	133	134	138	140
CONTRACTOR	CCS	RGI	RGI	RGI	JCA	JCA	IRC	RDS	CGI	CI
COMPANY	Marathon	Marathon	Gulf	Gulf	Shell	Shell	Gulf	Exxon	Exxon	CAGC
HAZARD REPORT	X				X	X	X			
ENGINEERING REPORT	X		X	X	X	X	X	X	X	X
BATHYMETRIC MAP	X	X	X	X	X	X	X	X	X	X
DEEP TOW		X								
SURFACE TOW										
3.5 kHz	X	X	X	X	X	X	X	X	X	X
Boomer										
Sparker		X			X	X		X		X
Minisleeve									X	
Air-Gun		X	X	X						
Water-Gun							X			
Side-Scan	X	X					X		X	X
3D-SEISMIC SURFACE AMPLITUDES									X	
WATER DEPTH (m)										
CORES										
SUBMERSIBLE OBSERVATIONS										
FM=Fugro-McClelland										
ME=McClelland Engineers, Inc.										
JCA=John E. Chance & Associates, Inc										
OOS= Odom Offshore Surveys										
IRC=Intersea Research Corporation										
ST=Sea Tales										
CGI=Comap Geosurveys, Inc.										
RDS=Racal-Decca Survey, Inc.										

AREA	GREEN CANYON										
BLOCK	141	142	143	144	146	147	148	152	153	154	158
CONTRACTOR	RGI	RDS/CAGC	AGO	JCA	JCA	JCA	OOS	OOS	RGI	RGI	M E
COMPANY	Conoco	Conoco	Arco	Mobil	Sohio	Texaco	Marathon	Marathon	Marathon	Marathon	Shell
HAZARD REPORT				X	X	X	X	X			
ENGINEERING REPORT	X	X	X	X	X	X	X	X	X	X	X
BATHYMETRIC MAP	X	X	X	X	X	X	X	X	X	X	X
DEEP TOW											X
SURFACE TOW											
3.5 kHz	X	X	X	X	X	X	X		X	X	X
Boomer											
Sparker	X	X		X		X					X
Minisleeve					X		X				
Air-Gun											
Water-Gun			X					X	X	X	X
Side-Scan		X		X	X		X				X
3D-SEISMIC SURFACE AMPLITUDES											
WATER DEPTH (m)	320-823	243-564	131-564	307-492	349-574	348-412	357-488	441-549	396-762	396-762	671-1055
CORES											
SUBMERSIBLE OBSERVATIONS											

RGI-Racal Geophysics Inc.
ME=McClelland Engineers, Inc.
JCA=John E. Chance & Associates, Inc.
OOS= Odom Offshore Surveys
AGO- Arco Geoscience Operations
CAGC-C.A.G.C. Marine Region

AREA		GREEN CANYON									
BLOCK	179	180	181	180	181	182	184	184	184 (Boring 1)	184 (Boring 2)	184 (Boring 3)
CONTRACTOR	CGI			JCA	JCA	OI	ME	RDS/CAGC	ME	ME	ME
COMPANY	Exxon	Shell	Shell	Shell	Shell	CAGC	Conoco	Conoco	Conoco	Conoco	Conoco
HAZARD REPORT				X	X		X				
ENG NEERING REPORT	X		X	X	X	X	X	X	X	X	X
BATHYMETRIC MAP	X		X	X	X	X	X				
DEEP TOW				X	X						X
SURFACE TOW											
3.5 kHz	X			X	X	X	X	X			
Boomer											
Sparker						X		X			X
Minisleeve	X						X				
Air-Gun											X
Water-Gun											
Side-Scan	X			X	X	X					
3D-SEISMIC SURFACE AMPLITUDES				X	X						
WATER DEPTH (m)	262-543			280-883	280-805	335-732	274-640	243-762			
CORES							X				X
SUBMERSIBLE OBSERVATIONS											

CGI=Comap Geosurveys, Inc.
ME=McClelland Engineers, Inc.
JCA=John E. Chance & Associates, Inc.
RDS-Racal-Decca Survey, Inc.
IRC=Intersea Research Corporation
CAGC-C.A.G.C. Marine Region
RDS=Racal-Decca Survey, Inc.

AREA	GREEN CANYON												
BLOCK	185	190	191	193	196	197	198	202	204	228	232	233	237
CONTRACTOR	RGI	JCA	JCA	JCA	FM	FM	CCS	ME	JCA	RGI	IRC	IRC	JCA
COMPANY	Conoco	Sohio	Sohio	BHP	Shell	Shell	Marathon	Shell	Texaco	Conoco	Placid	Placid	BHP
HAZARD REPORT		X	X	X			X		X				X
ENGINEERING REPORT	X	X	X		X	X	X	X	X	X	X	X	
BATHYMETRIC MAP	X	X	X	X	X	X	X	X	X	X	X	X	X
DEEP TOW				X	X	X		X				X	X
SURFACE TOW													
3.5 kHz	X	X	X	X	X			X	X	X	X	X	X
Boomer													
Sparker	X				X	X		X	X	X		X	
Minisleeve													
Air-Gun													
Water-Gun							X				X	X	
Side-Scan		X	X	X	X	X		X					X
3D-SEISMIC SURFACE AMPLITUDES				X									X
WATER DEPTH (m)	320-823	383-574	394-531		457-963	457-963	498-914	671-1055	766-1008	450-823	476-914	475-914	560
CORES													
SUBMERSIBLE OBSERVATIONS				X									X

FM=Fugro-McClelland
ME=McClelland Engineers, Inc.
JCA=John E. Chance & Associates, Inc.
RGI- Racal Geophysics, Inc.
IRC=Intersea Research Corporation

AREA	GREEN CANYON							
BLOCK	234	235	241	509	863	864	907	908
CONTRACTOR	IRC	RGI	FM	FM/JCA	FM	FM	FM	FM
COMPANY	Placid	Conoco	Shell	Taxaco	Shell	Shell	Shell	Shell
HAZARD REPORT								
ENGINEERING REPORT	X	X	X	X	X	X	X	X
BATHYMETRIC MAP	X	X	X	X	X	X	X	X
DEEP TOW			X	X	X	X	X	X
SURFACE TOW				X				X
3.5 kHz	X	X	X	X	X	X	X	X
Boomer								
Sparker		X	X		X	X	X	XX
Minisleeve								
Air-Gun				X				X
Water-Gun	X			X				X
Side-Scan			X	X	X	X	X	X
3D-SEISMIC SURFACE AMPLITUDES								
WATER DEPTH (m)	476-914	495-884	457-963	1158-1359	1347-1719	1347-1719	1469-1719	1469-1719
CORES								
SUBMERSIBLE OBSERVATIONS								

FM=Fugro-McClelland
JCA=John E. Chance & Associates, Inc.
RGI-Racal Geophysics, Inc.
IRC=Intersea Research Corporation

AREA	GARDEN BANKS									
BLOCK	21	65	84	104	135	147	148	152	161	189
CONTRACTOR	JCA	JCA	GSI	JCA	GSI	JCA	JCS	JCA	CGI	FM
COMPANY	Chevron	Chevron	Amoco	Chevron	Amoco	Chevron	Chevron	Sohio	Pennzoil	Texaco
HAZARD REPORT	X	X	X	X		X	X	X		X
ENGINEERING REPORT	X	X	X	X		X	X	X	X	
BATHYMETRIC MAP	X	X	X	X	X	X	X	X	X	X
DEEP TOW										
SURFACE TOW										
3.5 kHz	X	X	X	X	X	X	X	X		
Boomer										
Sparker	X	X		X	X	X	X		X	X
Minisleeve										
Air-Gun										
Water-Gun								X		
Side-Scan	X	X	X	X	X	X	X	X	X	
3D-SEISMIC SURFACE AMPLITUDES										
WATER DEPTH (m)	131-187	131-187	107-192	152-234	23-125	152-234	152-234	134-226	198-413	171-238
CORES										
SUBMERSIBLE OBSERVATIONS										

FM=Fugro-McClelland
GSI-Gardline Surveys, Inc.
JCA=John E. Chance & Associates, Inc.
OOS= Odom Offshore Surveys
CGI=Comap Geosurveys, Inc.

AREA	GARDEN BANKS											
BLOCK	189	191	192	193	195	196	201	215	236	237	240	241
CONTRACTOR	JCA	JCA	JCA	JCA	JCA	JCA	JCA	JCA	JCA	JCA	JCA	JCA
COMPANY	Texaco	Chevron	Chevron	Chevron	Sohio	Sohio	Chevron	Hess	Chevon	Chevron	Sohio	Sohio
HAZARD REPORT	X	X	X	X	X	X	X	X	X	X	X	X
ENGINEERING REPORT	X	X			X	X					X	X
BATHYMETRIC MAP	X	X	X	X	X	X	X	X	X	X	X	X
DEEP TOW								X				
SURFACE TOW												
3.5 kHz	X	X			X	X	X	X			X	X
Boomer												
Sparker												
Minisleeve						X					X	X
Air-Gun												
Water-Gun					X		X	X				
Side-Scan		X	X	X	X	X	X	X	X	X	X	X
3D-SEISMIC SURFACE AMPLITUDES												
WATER DEPTH (m)	165-258	152-234	126-219	126-219	134-226	148-498	304-615	350-545	126-219	126-219	248-498	248-498
CORES												
SUBMERSIBLE OBSERVATIONS												

JCA=John E. Chance & Associates, Inc.

A-6

AREA	GARDEN BANKS											
BLOCK	244	255	256	257	260	298	300	304	343	359	368	369
CONTRACTOR	FM	JCA	JCA	JCA	JCA	GSI	GSI	JCA	GSI	OOS	AOSS	AOSS
COMPANY	Shell	Shell	Shell	Shell	Hess	Amoco	Amoco	Hess	Amoco	Amoco	Conoco	Conoco
HAZARD REPORT		X	X	X	X	X	X	X	X	X		
ENGINEERING REPORT		X	X	X			X	X	X	X	X	X
BATHYMETRIC MAP	X	X	X	X	X	X	X	X	X	X	X	X
DEEP TOW												
SURFACE TOW												
3.5 kHz	X	X	X	X	X	X	X	X	X		X	X
Boomer												
Sparker	X	X	X	X					X			X
Minisleeve												
Air-Gun												
Water-Gun		X	X	X	X					X	X	X
Side-Scan	X	X	X	X								
3D-SEISMIC SURFACE AMPLITUDES												
WATER DEPTH (m)	239-689	442-561	430-586	421-696	412-518	341-555	383-668	400-670	337-637	344-498	230-425	230-425
CORES												
SUBMERSIBLE OBSERVATIONS												
FM=Fugro-McClelland												
AOSS-Alpine Ocean Seismic Surveys, Inc.												
JCA=John E. Chance & Associates, Inc.												
OOS= Odom Offshore Surveys												
GSI-Gardline Surveys, Inc.												

AREA	GARDEN BANKS									
BLOCK	413	426	427	470	471	499	500	543	544	545
CONTRACTOR	JCA	FM	FM	FM	FM	CGI	CGI	CGI	CGI	CGI
COMPANY	Chevron	Shell	Shell	Shell	Shell	Exxon	Exxon	Exxon	Exxon	Exxon
HAZARD REPORT	X							X		
ENGINEERING REPORT	X	X	X	X	X	X	X		X	X
BATHYMETRIC MAP	X	X	X	X	X		X	X	X	X
DEEP TOW		X	X	X	X					
SURFACE TOW		X	X	X	X					
3.5 kHz	X	X	X	X	X	X	X	X	X	X
Boomer										
Sparker	X									
Minisleeve						X	X		X	X
Air-Gun										
Water-Gun										
Side-Scan		X	X	X	X	X	X	X	X	X
3D-SEISMIC SURFACE AMPLITUDES										
WATER DEPTH (m)	396-601	472-1005	472-1005	472-1005	472-1005	506-601	518-853	536-793	536-853	655-893
CORES										
SUBMERSIBLE OBSERVATIONS										
FM=Fugro-McClelland										
JCA=John E. Chance & Associates, Inc.										
CGI=Comap Geosurveys, Inc.										

AREA	MISSISSIPPI CANYON										
BLOCK	20	538	539	582	583	709	713	714	757	758	762
CONTRACTOR	WCO	ME	ME	ME	ME	ME	KCO	KCO	KCO	KCO	FM
COMPANY	Sohio	Shell	Shell	Shell	Shell	Arco	Texaco	Texaco	Texaco	Texaco	Shell
HAZARD REPORT						X	X	X	X	X	
ENGINEERING REPORT	X	X	X	X	X		X	X	X	X	
BATHYMETRIC MAP	X	X	X	X	X	X	X	X	X	X	X
DEEP TOW		X	X	X	X						X
SURFACE TOW						X					
3.5 kHz	X	X	X	X	X	X	X	X	X	X	X
Boomer											
Sparker		X	X	X	X	X					X
Minisleeve											
Air-Gun										X	
Water-Gun											
Side-Scan	X	X	X	X	X						
3D-SEISMIC SURFACE AMPLITUDES						X					
WATER DEPTH (m)	49-168	482-945	482-945	482-945	482-945	685	943-1066	943-1066	943-1066	943-1066	884-1036
CORES	X					X					
SUBMERSIBLE OBSERVATIONS						X					

FM=Fugro-McClelland

ME=McClelland Engineers, Inc.

WCO-Woodward Clyde Oceaneering

KCO-KC Offshore, L.L.C.

AREA	MISSISSIPPI CANYON						
BLOCK	736	806	807	810	854	885	929
CONTRACTOR	FM	FM	FM	SCI	SCI		KCO
COMPANY	Shell	Shell	Shell	Shell	Shell	Texaco	BHP
HAZARD REPORT						X	X
ENGINEERING REPORT				X	X		
BATHYMETRIC MAP	X	X	X	X	X	X	X
DEEP TOW	X	X	X				
SURFACE TOW				X	X	X	X
3.5 kHz	X	X	X	X	X	X	X
Boomer							
Sparker	X	X	X	X	X	X	X
Minisleeve							
Air-Gun							
Water-Gun						X	X
Side-Scan	X	X	X	X	X		
3D-SEISMIC SURFACE AMPLITUDES						X	X
WATER DEPTH (m)	884-1036	884-1036	884-1036	994-1331	994-1331	580	640
CORES						X	X
SUBMERSIBLE OBSERVATIONS						X	X

FM=Fugro-McClelland

SCI-Shell Offshore, Inc.

KCO-K.C. Offshore, L.L.C.

AREA	VIOSCA KNOLL		
BLOCK	786	786	864 (Boring 1)
CONTRACTOR	FM	KCA	ME
COMPANY	Taxaco	Texaco	Conoco
HAZARD REPORT	X	X	
ENGINEERING REPORT	X	X	X
BATHYMETRIC MAP	X	X	
DEEP TOW	X		
SURFACE TOW			
3.5 kHz	X	X	
Boomer			
Sparker	X		
Minisleeve			
Air-Gun			
Water-Gun			
Side-Scan			
3D-SEISMIC SURFACE AMPLITUDES	X		
WATER DEPTH (m)		378-908	
CORES	X		
SUBMERSIBLE OBSERVATIONS			
FM=Fugro-McClelland			
ME=McClelland Engineers, Inc.			
KC-K.C. Offshore, L.L. C.			

AREA	EWING BANKS				
BLOCK	305 (Plat. A)	305 (Boring a1)	305 (Boring a2)	305 (Boring a2)	305 (Boring 1)
CONTRACTOR	ME	WWC	WWC	WWC	ME
COMPANY	Conoco	Conoco	Arco	Conoco	Conoco
HAZARD REPORT					
ENGINEERING REPORT					X
BATHYMETRIC MAP	X				
DEEP TOW					
SURFACE TOW					
3.5 kHz					
Boomer					
Sparker					
Minisleeve					
Air-Gun					
Water-Gun					
Side-Scan	X				
3D-SEISMIC SURFACE AMPLITUDES					
WATER DEPTH (m)	81-87				
CORES					
SUBMERSIBLE OBSERVATIONS					
WWC-Woodward Clyde Oceaneering					
ME=McClelland Engineers, Inc.					

AREA	EWING BANKS						
BLOCK	305 (Boring 2	302 (Boring 3	(305 (Boring 4)	500	543	544	545
CONTRACTOR	ME	ME	ME	CGI	CGI	CGI	CGI
COMPANY	Conoco	Conoco	Conoco	Exxon	Exxon	Exxon	Exxon
HAZARD REPORT							
ENGINEERING REPORT	X	X	X	X	X	X	X
BATHYMETRIC MAP				X	X	X	X
DEEP TOW							
SURFACE TOW							
3.5 kHz				X	X	X	X
Boomer							
Sparker							
Minisleeve							
Air-Gun							
Water-Gun							
Side-Scan				X	X	X	X
3D-SEISMIC SURFACE AMPLITUDES							
WATER DEPTH (m)				518-853	536-793	537-853	655-893
CORES							
SUBMERSIBLE OBSERVATIONS							
ME=McClelland Engineers, Inc.							
CGI=Comap Geosurveys, Inc.							

AREA	EWING BANKS										
BLOCK	869	870	871	875	909	910	912	913	914	915	916
CONTRACTOR	JCA		JCA	JCA	ME	ME	JCA	JCA	JCA	JCA	JCA
COMPANY	Sohio		Mobil	Sohio	Exxon	Exxon	Sohio	Sohio	Mobil	Mobil	Mobil
HAZARD REPORT				X	X	X					
ENGINEERING REPORT				X	X	X					
BATHYMETRIC MAP				X	X	X					
DEEP TOW											
SURFACE TOW											
3.5 kHz	X		X	X	X	X	X	X	X	X	X
Boomer											
Sparker	X		X	X			X	X	X	X	X
Minisleeve					X	X					
Air-Gun											
Water-Gun											
Side-Scan				X	X	X					
3D-SEISMIC SURFACE AMPLITUDES											
WATER DEPTH (m)				297-360	146-311	146-311					
CORES											
SUBMERSIBLE OBSERVATIONS											
ME=McClelland Engineers, Inc.											
JCA=John E. Chance & Associates, Inc.											

A-11

AREA	EWING BANKS									
BLOCK	932	933	937	938	953	958	959	966	991	994
CONTRACTOR	JCA	JCA	ME	ME	ME	JCA	JCA	JCA	ME	
COMPANY	Sohio	Sohio	Exxon	Exxon	Exxon	Sohio	Sohio	Texaco	Exxon	
HAZARD REPORT	X	X	X	X	X			X	X	
ENGINEERING REPORT	X	X	X	X	X			X	X	
BATHYMETRIC MAP	X	X	X	X	X			X	X	
DEEP TOW										
SURFACE TOW										
3.5 kHz	X	X	X	X	X	X	X	X	X	
Boomer										
Sparker						X	X	X		
Minisleeve	X	X	X	X	X				X	
Air-Gun										
Water-Gun										
Side-Scan	X	X	X	X	X	X			X	
3D-SEISMIC SURFACE AMPLITUDES										
WATER DEPTH (m)	114-169	14-169	128-183	128-183	146-311			518-579	155-430	
CORES										
SUBMERSIBLE OBSERVATIONS										
ME=McClelland Engineers, Inc.										
JCA=John E. Chance & Associates, Inc										

AREA	EWING BANKS				
BLOCK	1003	1005	1006	1010	1011
CONTRACTOR	JCA	JCA	JCA	JCA	JCA
COMPANY	Sohio	Mobil	Mobil	Texaco	Texaco
HAZARD REPORT	X	X	X	X	X
ENGINEERING REPORT	X	X	X	X	X
BATHYMETRIC MAP	X	X	X	X	X
DEEP TOW					
SURFACE TOW					
3.5 kHz	X	X	X	X	X
Boomer					
Sparker		X	X	X	X
Minisleeve	X				
Air-Gun					
Water-Gun					
Side-Scan	X	X	X		
3D-SEISMIC SURFACE AMPLITUDES					
WATER DEPTH (m)	421-610	480-606	480-606	488-625	518-655
CORES					
SUBMERSIBLE OBSERVATIONS					
JCA=John E. Chance & Associates, Inc.					

AREA	EAST BREAKS									
BLOCK	118	120	122	165	165	166	170	206	207	208
CONTRACTOR	CGI	CGI	JCA	ME	JCA	JCA	CCS	JCA	JCA	JCA
COMPANY	Gulf	Gulf	Texaco	Sohio	Sohio	Texaco	Amoco	Sohio	Sohio	Sohio
HAZARD REPORT	X	X	X	X	X	X	X	X	X	X
ENGINEERING REPORT			X	X	X	X	X	X	X	X
BATHYMETRIC MAP	X		X		X	X	X	X	X	X
DEEP TOW										
SURFACE TOW										
3.5 kHz	X	X	X	X	X	X	X	X	X	X
Boomer										
Sparker			X			X				X
Minisleeve				X	X					
Air-Gun										
Water-Gun										
Side-Scan	X	X	X			X	X	X	X	X
3D-SEISMIC SURFACE AMPLITUDES										
WATER DEPTH (m)	128-177		85-378	146-351	146-351	85-378	180-446	264-434	264-434	258-439
CORES										
SUBMERSIBLE OBSERVATIONS				X						

ME=McClelland Engineers, Inc.

JCA=John E. Chance & Associates, Inc.

CGI=Comap Geosurveys, Inc.

AREA	EAST BREAKS									
BLOCK	211	244	245	247	248	250	251	288	289	302
CONTRACTOR	IRC	ST	ST	RDS	RDS	JCA	JCA	ST	ST	JCA
COMPANY	Texaco	Exxon	Exxon	Tenneco	Tenneco	Sohio	Sohio	Exxon	Exxon	Texaco
HAZARD REPORT						X	X			X
ENGINEERING REPORT	X	X	X	X	X	X	X	X	X	X
BATHYMETRIC MAP	X	X	X	X	X	X	X	X	X	X
DEEP TOW										
SURFACE TOW										
3.5 kHz	X	X	X	X	X	X	X	X	X	X
Boomer										
Sparker	X			X	X					X
Minisleeve		X	X					X	X	
Air-Gun										
Water-Gun	X					X	X			
Side-Scan	X	X	X	X	X	X	X	X	X	X
3D-SEISMIC SURFACE AMPLITUDES										
WATER DEPTH (m)	234-449	366-488	366-488	372-463	372-463	264-434	264-434	366-488	366-488	320-625
CORES										
SUBMERSIBLE OBSERVATIONS										

JCA=John E. Chance & Associates, Inc.

IRC=Intersea Research Corporation

ST=Sea Tales

RDS=Racal-Decca Survey, Inc.

AREA	EAST BREAKS									
BLOCK	303	339	340	341	342	383	384	386	425	428
CONTRACTOR	CGI	CGI	CGI	CGI	CGI	FM	FM	CGI	IRC	FM
COMPANY	Exxon	Pennzoil	Pennzoil	Pennzoil	Shell	Shell	Shell	Shell	Conoco	Shell
HAZARD REPORT										
ENGINEERING REPORT	X	X	X	X	X	X	X	X	X	X
BATHYMETRIC MAP	X	X	X	X	X	X	X	X	X	X
DEEP TOW						X	X			X
SURFACE TOW										
3.5 kHz	X	X	X	X	X	X	X	X	X	X
Boomer										
Sparker						X	X			X
Minisleeve	X									X
Air-Gun									X	X
Water-Gun										
Side-Scan	X	X	X	X	X	X	X	X	X	X
3D-SEISMIC SURFACE AMPLITUDES										
WATER DEPTH (m)	305-526	321-626	302-610	463-617	281-732	402-853	402-853	281-732	654-910	402-853
CORES										
SUBMERSIBLE OBSERVATIONS										
FM=Fugro-McClelland										
IRC=Intersea Research Corporation										
CGI=Comap Geosurveys, Inc.										

AREA	EAST BREAKS								
BLOCK	469	684	685	728	729	920	921	964	965
CONTRACTOR	IRC	FM	FM	FM	FM	FM	FM	FM	FM
COMPANY	Conoco	Shell	Shell	Shell	Shell	Shell	Shell	Shell	Shell
HAZARD REPORT									
ENGINEERING REPORT	X	X	X	X	X	X	X	X	X
BATHYMETRIC MAP	X	X	X	X	X	X	X	X	X
DEEP TOW						X	X	X	X
SURFACE TOW									
3.5 kHz	X					X	X	X	X
Boomer									
Sparker						X	X	X	X
Minisleeve									X
Air-Gun									
Water-Gun	X								X
Side-Scan	X					X	X	X	X
3D-SEISMIC SURFACE AMPLITUDES	654-910	975-1280	975-1280	975-1280	975-1280	305-610	305-610	305-610	305-610
WATER DEPTH (m)									
CORES									
SUBMERSIBLE OBSERVATIONS									
FM=Fugro-McClelland									
IRC=Intersea Research Corporation									

APPENDIX B
Equipment Used On MMS/CMI Project

A. Field Data Collection Phase

1. *Navigation*

The navigation control program, "M4200DT", is designed to acquire data from the Magnavox MX4200d differential GPS, provide steering information to a user-designated way point, and output fix marks with annotation to several survey instruments. Way point annotation is currently supporting the EG&G Model 260 side scan sonar, the DELPH 2 seismic system and the Raytheon (Ocean Data System) DSF-6000 precision depth recorder.

A provision has been made to allow the user to input a table of way points that can be incremented or decremented as necessary during a survey. The user can also manually input way point coordinates. The software will provide the user with navigation information updates at a one second interval. Fix marks and associated fix mark data are output at 1-, 2-, 4-, 6-, or 10-minute intervals at the user's preference. The fix mark data can be written to a disk file as ASCII text. Steering information is provided at one second intervals reporting course over ground, speed over ground, distance to way point, bearing to way point, distance from survey line in meters, and which side of the vessel the survey line is located (i.e., to port or starboard).

This system requires an IBM 80386 or 80486 compatible computer with MS-DOS operating system, 640K memory, hard disk, floppy disk, at least one serial port, and a least one 8-printer port. Up to four serial ports and two printer ports are supported. An interface was designed and built to work with this system. It provides an analog output (0-5 volts DC) for a steering meter, a digital event mark out, and a switch closure event mark out for up to four recorders. This interface will connect to an IBM PC or compatible computer with a serial port and a printer port.

2. *Seismic*

a. ORE GeoPulse Boomer This resilient high resolution acoustic system employs an electro-mechanical sound source that delivers increased energy over a broader frequency spectrum than other similar conventional systems. It provides increased penetration and resolution over a wide range of sub-bottom features in deep water and in high noise environments. The out-going pulse is short, powerful, and damps rapidly to provide unusually high resolution (< 1 m bed resolution). A CSI-built surf board towing arrangement was found to produce less noise on the records than the conventional catamaran sold with the GeoPulse system. A convenient acoustic receiver unit provided gain controls filter combinations, hydrophone preamp power, and other necessary programming for collection of excellent seismic profiles. We consistently acquired mappable data to subsurface depths of 100-200 ms. Both the GeoPulse and water gun data were acquired by a newly designed hydrophone produced by Innovative Transducers/Source Technology of Houston, Texas. This hydrophone was found to be extremely efficient with regard to eliminating extraneous sea surface and water column noise. The GeoPulse system worked well throughout the survey till a power supply problem was encountered near the end of the project. An EG&G power supply was substituted and worked well until Phase 1 was complete. In general, the GeoPulse records were of outstanding quality.

b. Water Gun Maximum subsurface penetration in our survey was provided by an S-15 (15 in^3) water gun acoustic source manufactured by Seismic Systems, Inc. of Houston, Texas. This water gun is a pneumatic seismic source that uses compressed air (2000 psi-operating pressure) as air guns do. A Hamworthy seismic compressor capable of delivering 50 cfm at 3000 psi during 1 second shots was used for the survey. The water gun is an implosive source creating an acoustic pulse which is free of bubble oscillations and has a broad spectrum extending to high frequencies. Another important characteristic of this acoustic source is the repeatability of both shape and amplitude of the outgoing signal. The water gun was used primarily for the deep water parts of our survey where GeoPulse penetration was minimal. Bed resolution for the water gun is slightly over 1 m and subsurface penetration was routinely over 500 ms. Water gun profiles have been run to water depths of about 1000 m with good success.

c. Air Gun A seismic System 50 in^3 (GI Gun) will be used during the Phase 2 "fill-in" seismic acquisition program. It operates with the same compressor as the water gun but is a more powerful and lower frequency source. Bed resolution has been estimated at ~ 2m from previous field data collection programs. It will be used to penetrate hard bottom areas where the high resolution sources may suffer from signal attenuation.

3. *Side-Scan Sonar*

The EG&G Model 260 sea floor imaging system was used in conjunction with an electric winch containing nearly 800 m of cable. The basic Model 260 unit is coupled to a digital recorder module (Model 380) so that in addition to analog copies, side-scan data can be archived on Exabyte tape. A 100 kHz fish is used to image the sea floor and navigation fixes are written into the records directly from our GPS positioning system. Side-scan sonar data were used to help interpret bottom features observed on seismic profiles especially these related to fluid and gas vents/seeps. Both data sets are calibrated in real-time with bottom sediments using an underway sampler designed to take short surface cores while in survey mode. In general, side-scan data are of high quality at the depth to be used.

4. *Digital Data Acquisition System (DELPH 2)*

Both GeoPulse boomer and water gun data are acquired in analog as well as digital format. The analog data are printed on EPC recorders while the digital data are acquired using the dual channel DELPH 2 high resolution seismic data acquisition/processing system. The DELPH 2 program provides synchronization of both seismic channels to avoid interference, dual channel triggering, and independent sampling frequency on each channel. The DELPH 2 system is configured to enable quality control of data and monitoring of source characteristics while data are being acquired. Data can also be processed in real time. The processing consists of filtering (low pass and high pass linear phase filter), automatic gain control, time variable gain, swell filter, horizontal stacking, predictive deconvolution, time variant filtering, and spectral analysis. The DELPH 2 program is loaded on a dedicated 486 DX computer and a Goulton plotter is used to print out the seismic data. Two Exabyte tape drives are used to transcribe the data from the disk to an 8 mm tape format. A dedicated computer program converts the Elics format data produced by the DELPH 2 system to SEG-Y.

B. Technical Capability

1. *The CSI Field Support Facility and Personnel*

Coastal Studies Institute maintains a field support facility staffed by experienced, professional research associates. This seven-man team of support personnel has a combined sixty-nine years of experience in conducting the Institute's research studies. Their professional training, skills, and experience span a wide range of expertise, i.e., electronic and mechanical engineering and fabrication, seamanship, instrument deployment and recovery techniques, data collection and diving. Unique to this team is that, although each member is specialized in at least one of these disciplines, each member has a practical working ability in all of them.

The Field Support Group (FSG) is located at LSU in the CSI Field Support Building. This is a dedicated 8000 ft^2 building housing separate office space for each team member, maintenance and calibration laboratories, fabrication and machine shops, and equipment storage areas. The design, fabrication, and calibration of the instrument systems described in this proposal will be fabricated and tested within this facility. Specific FSG capabilities relative to this task are as follows:

a. Electronics
- a laboratory for design, prototype testing and printed circuit layout.
- a laboratory for general electronic maintenance.
- a shop for printed circuit etching, fabrication, assembly and testing.
- a shop for fabrication of underwater cables.

b. Electronic test equipment on hand
- dual trace storage scope
- two general purpose dual trace scopes
- two precision voltage standards
- numerous digital and analog mulitmeters
- two frequency counters
- two frequency generators
- numerous other electronic support instruments

c. Calibration
- dual temperature controlled salinity baths
- pressure calibration to 0.015 % accuracy up to 100 psi. and 0.1% up to 1500 psi
- temperature calibration to 0.02 deg. C. accuracy
- salinity calibration to 0.003 ppt accuracy

d. Calibration instruments on hand
- Guildline Autosal
- Hewlett/Packard Quartz thermometer
- Amtek precision dead weight tester
- Amtek hydraulic dead weight tester

e. Mechanical

- a complete machine shop for precision machine work and large scale fabrication
- gas, rear gas and electrical welding
- plastic composite fabrication
- mooring wire fabrication

f. Machine tools on hand

- two Bridgeport mills
- two laths, 40" x 10" dia. capacity and 50" x 16" capacity
- electric welder and rare gas welder
- gas welder
- two drill presses
- band saw
- two grinders
- two pressure test vessels:
- 10" diameter by 60" length at 1500 psi.
- 24" diameter by 38" length at 100 psi.
- Fenn rotary swedger
- numerous other small machine tools

g. Inventory of Field Equipment Relevant to this Proposal

- 4 each Aanderra RCM7 Solid state, vector averaging recording current meters (copy of specifications attached)

APPENDIX C

A Summary of Sites Surveyed under MMS/CMI Support
and Types of Data Collected

High resolution geophysical data were collected in support of this project on two cruises, one in July 1995 and the other in May 1997. A May 1996 cruise was aborted because of problems with a seismic air compressor. The 1995 cruise was conducted from the M/V *Sea Gull* rented from LaSalle Marine, Inc. of Lockport, Louisiana. Data were collected on a 24-hour schedule for five days. The 1997 cruise was conducted from the R/V *Pelican* of Louisiana Universitites Marine Consortium (LUMCON). This ship proved to be an extremely quiet vessel, which promoted a favorable signal-to-noise ratio on our records, a factor that improved our record quality as compared to records collected during the 1995 cruise. Sea state was excellent for both cruises and in general, data quality was exceptional. The tables and plots that follow summarize the sites where data were collected, general characteristics of the features being investigated, and the survey tracts associated with each feature. All data collection was spatially controlled with differential GPS navigation through a software program written and implemented by Mr. Walker Winans of the Coastal Studies Institute Field Support Group. All data were stored on 8 mm magnetic tape while on board ship and then transferred to CD ROM in the laboratory at Coastal Studies Institute as a means of permanently archiving the data.

CMI/MMS Cruise 1

Ships Track, Target 1
Ship Shoal 286

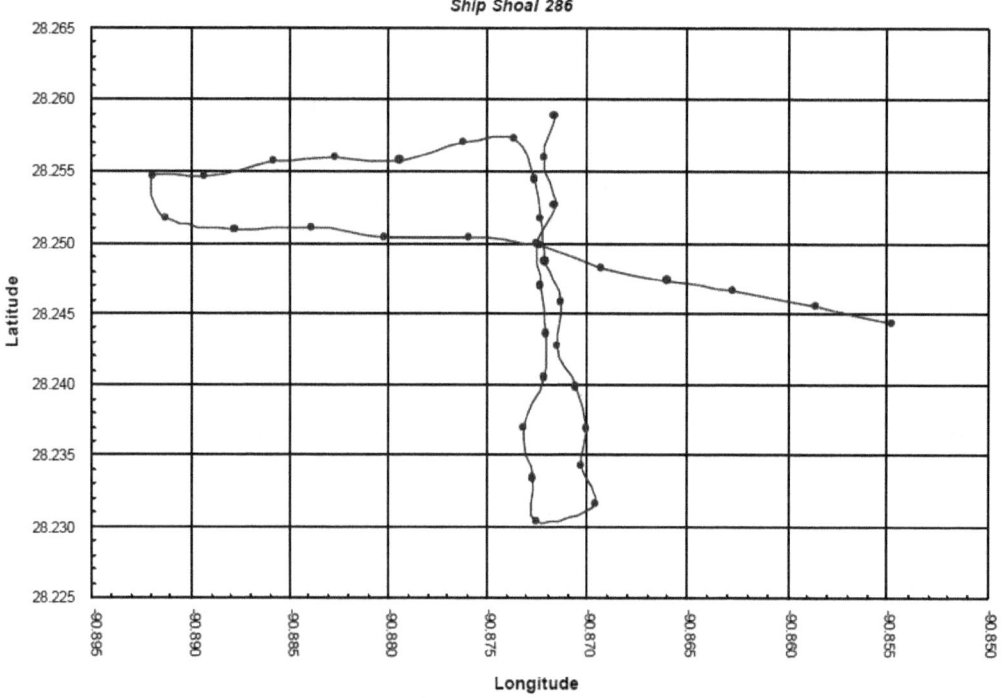

CMI/MMS Cruise 1

Ships Track, Target 2
Mud Vent NE GC 53

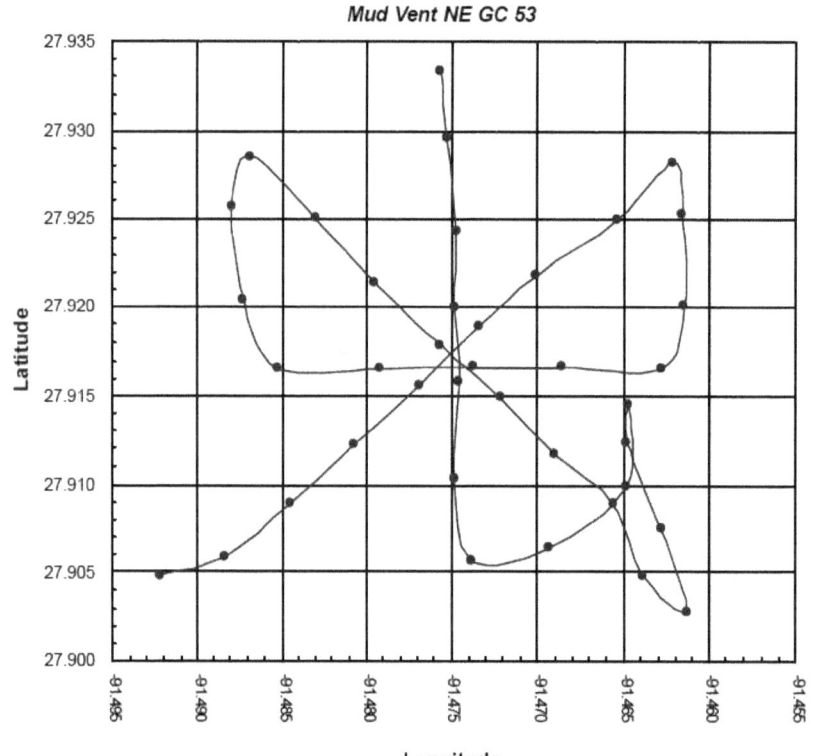

CMI/MMS Cruise 1
Ships Track, Target 3
Mounded Area GC 53

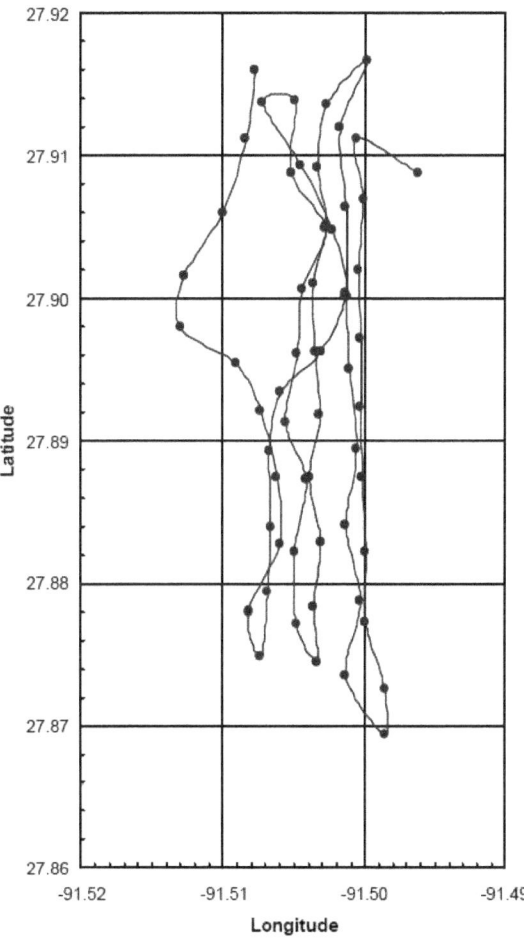

CMI/MMS Cruise 1

Ships Track, Target 4
Collapsed Depression GC 53

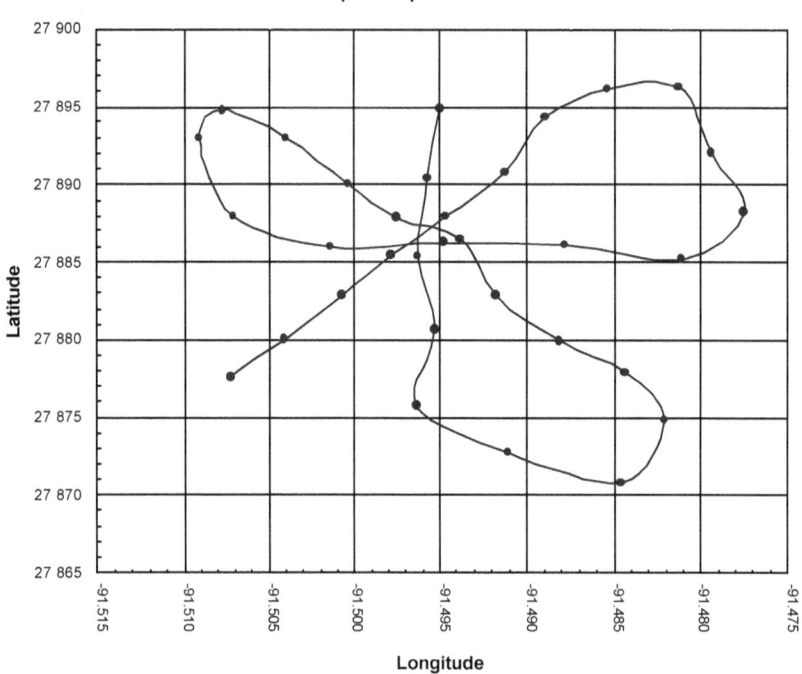

Ships Track, Target 5
Mud Volcano GC 143

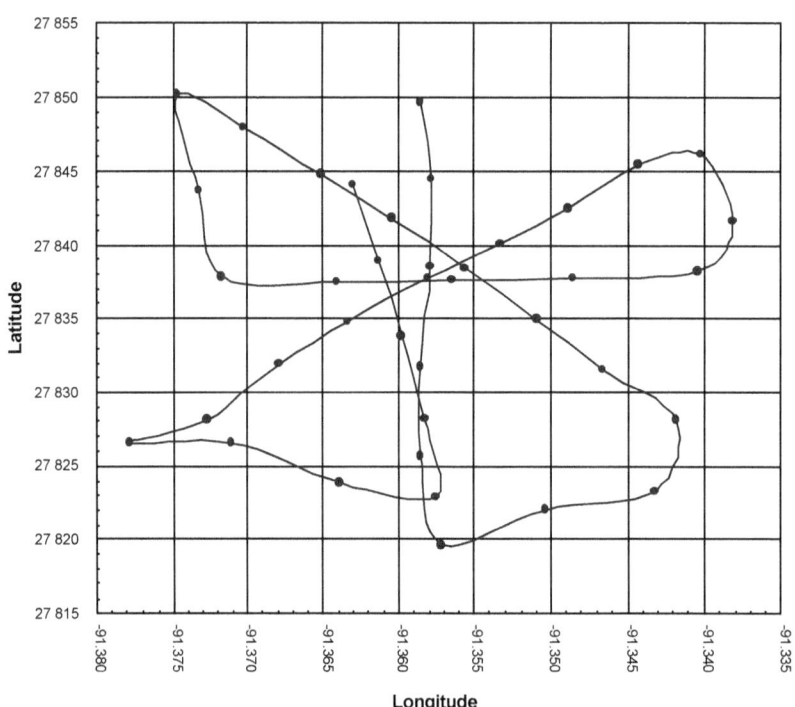

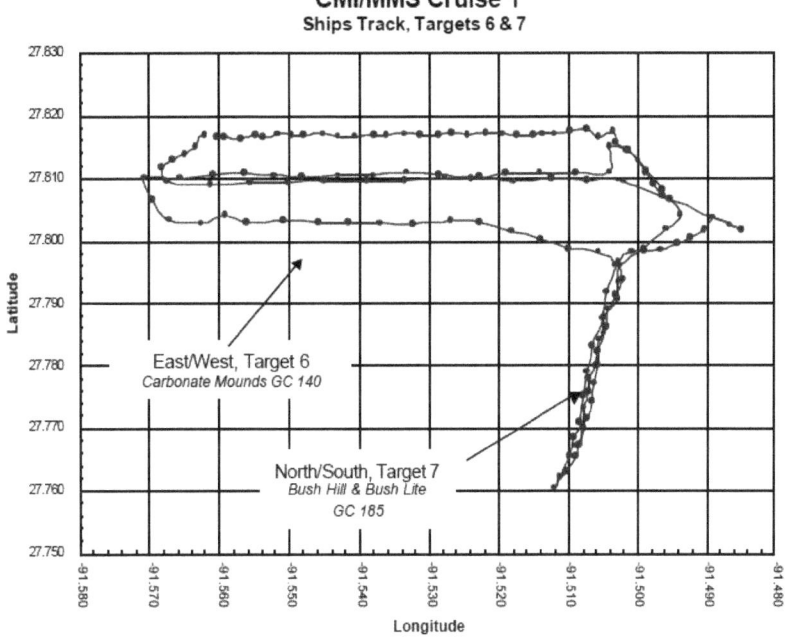

CMI/MMS Cruise 1
Ships Track, Targets 6 & 7

East/West, Target 6
Carbonate Mounds GC 140

North/South, Target 7
Bush Hill & Bush Lite
GC 185

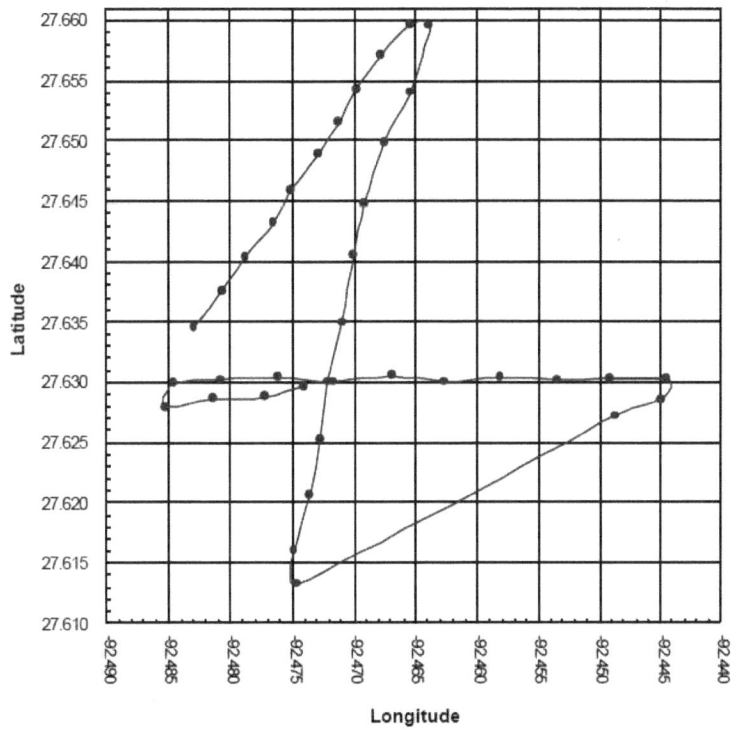

CMI/MMS Cruise 1
Ships Track, Target 10
Garden Banks 382

CMI/MMS Cruise 1
Ships Track, Last Line
GC 234

CMI/MMS Cruise 2
Mobile Delta Survey

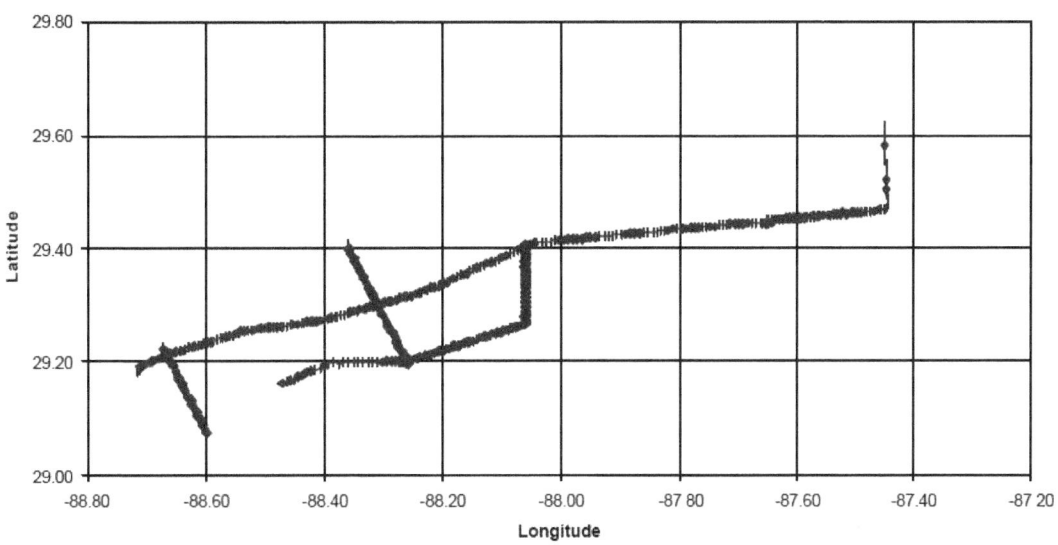

CMI/MMS Cruise 2
Mississippi Canyon Blocks 929, 931

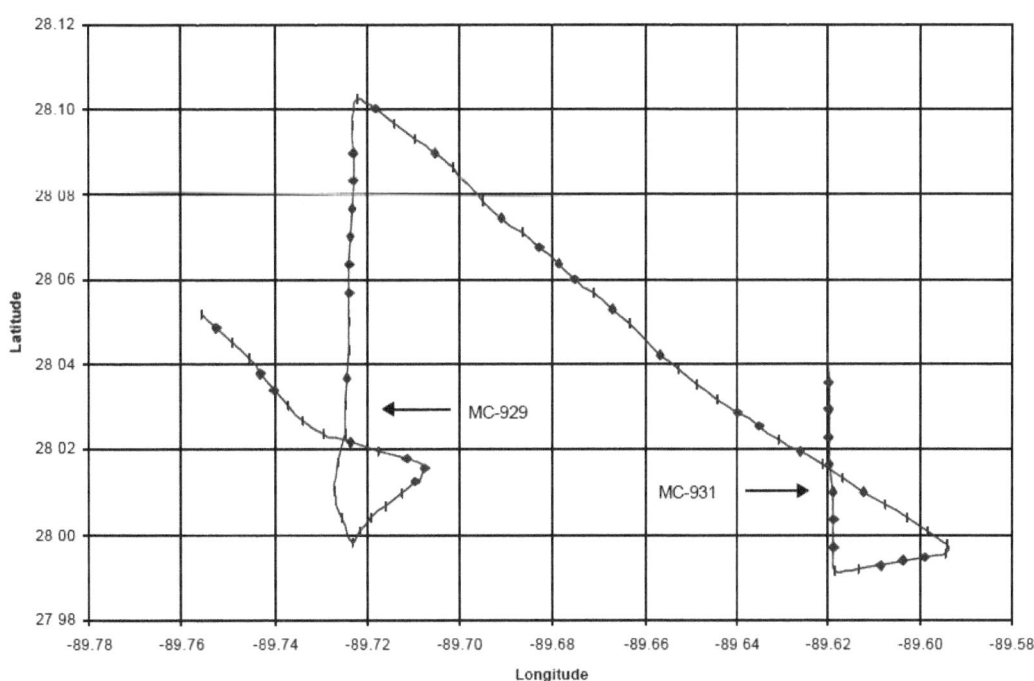

CMI/MMS Cruise 2
Mississippi Canyaon Block 843

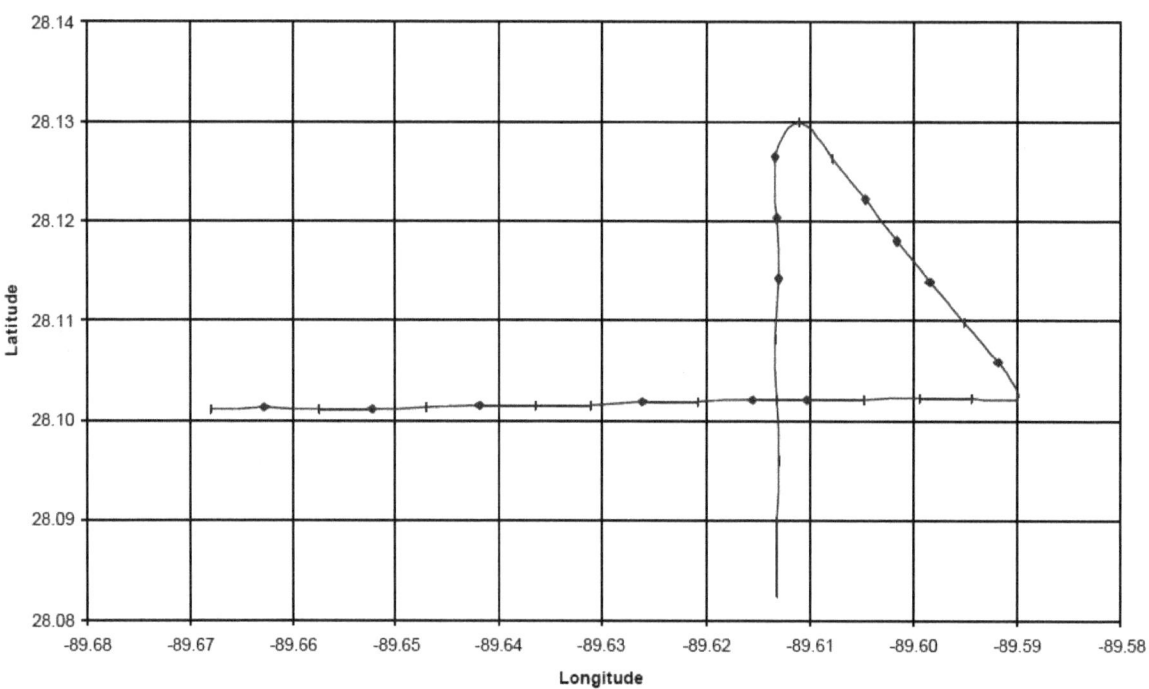

CMI/MMS Cruise 2
Mississippi Canyon Block 709

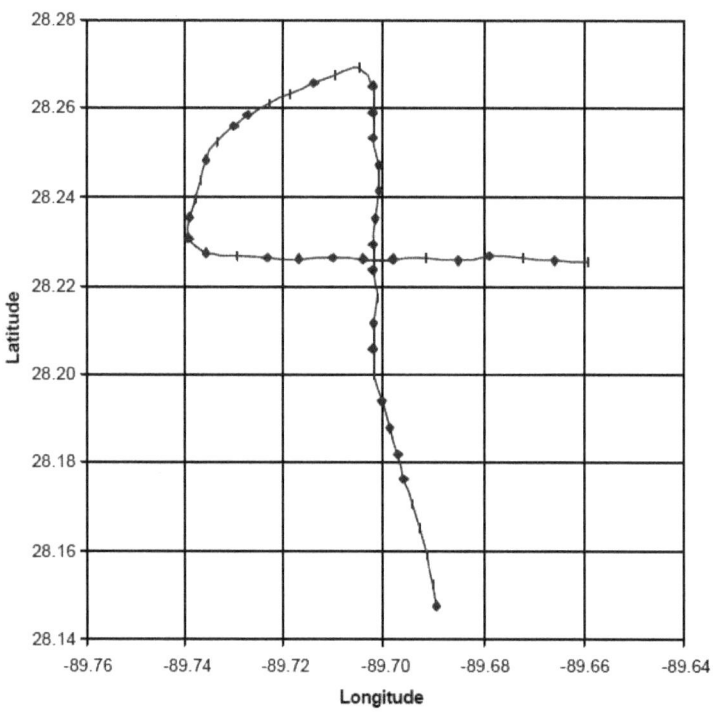

C-8

CMI/MMS Cruise 2
Mississippi Canyon Block 709

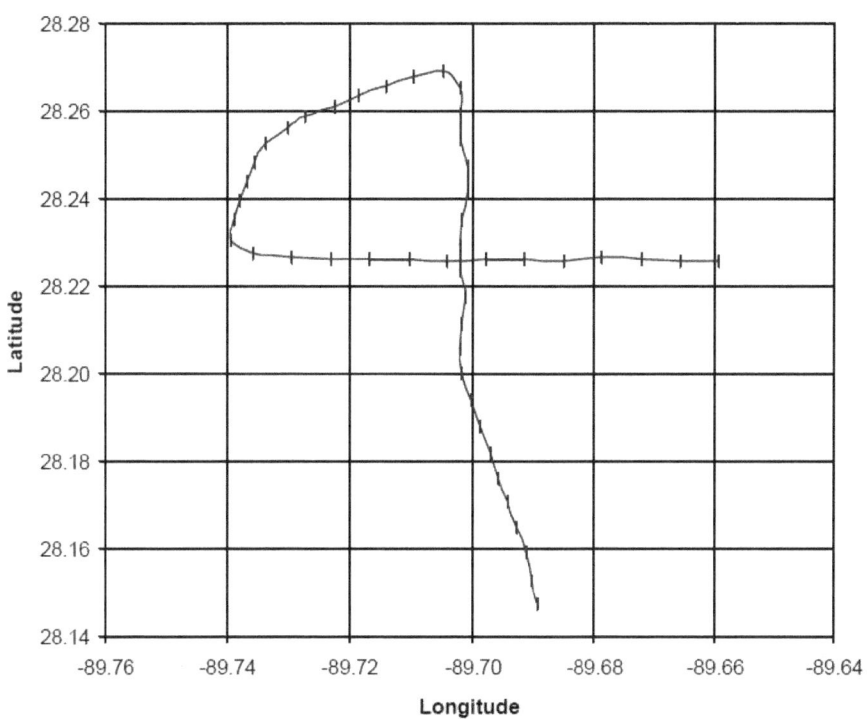

CMI/MMS Cruise 2
Mississippi Canyon Block 539

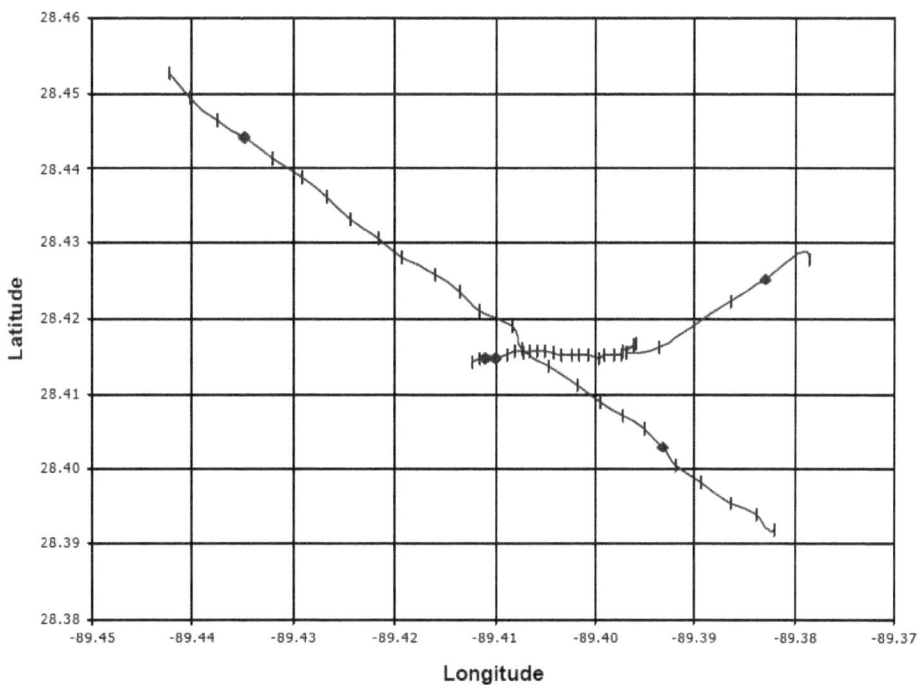

CMI/MMS Cruise 2
Green Canyon Blocks 180, 181

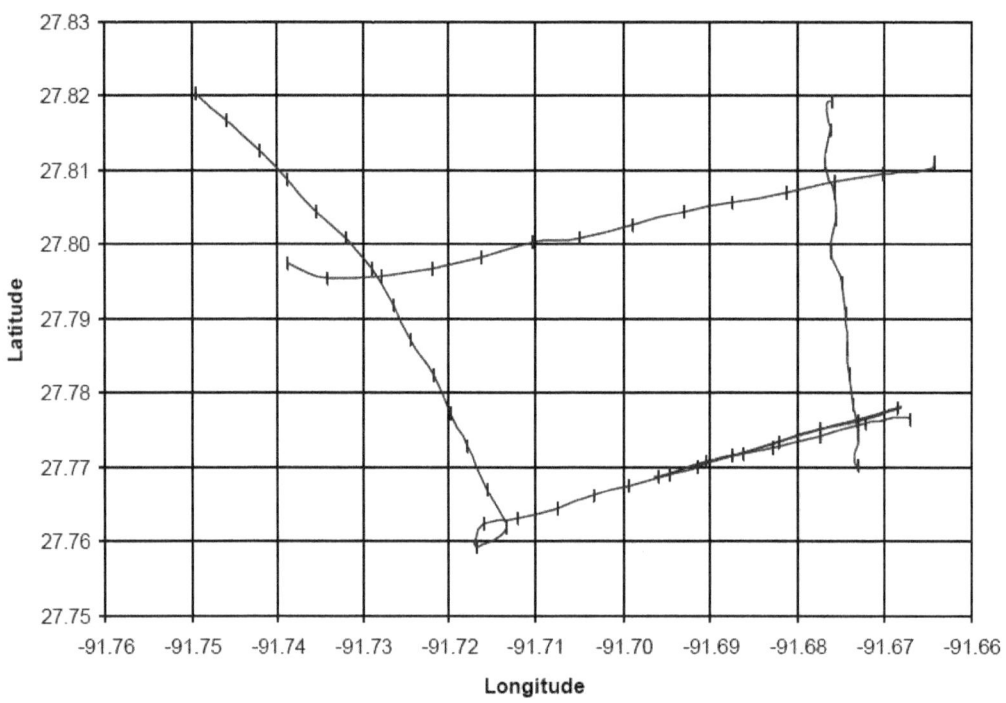

CMI/MMS Cruise 2
Green Canyon Block 18

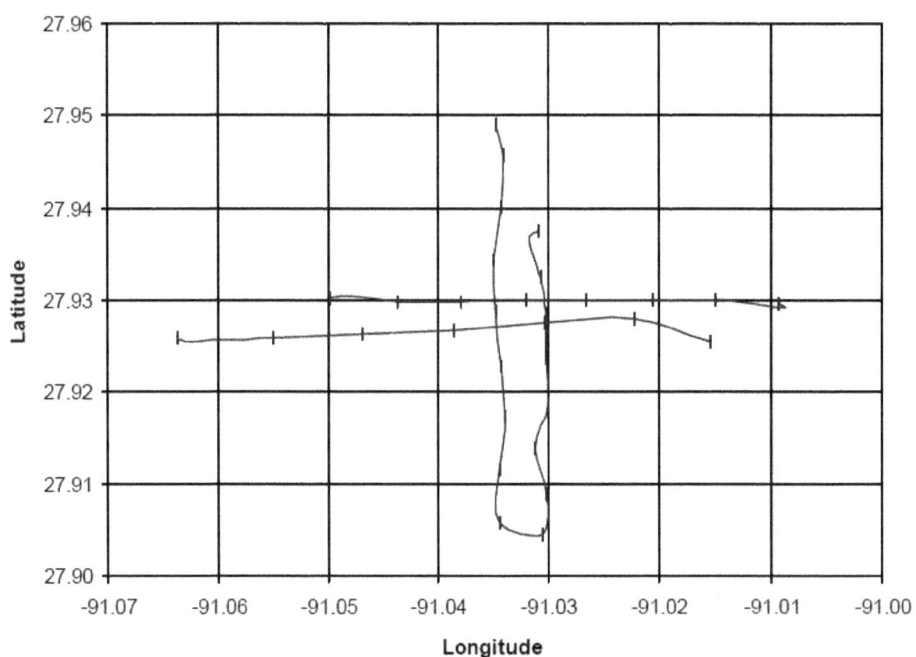

C-10

CMI/MMS Cruise 2
Green Canyon Block152

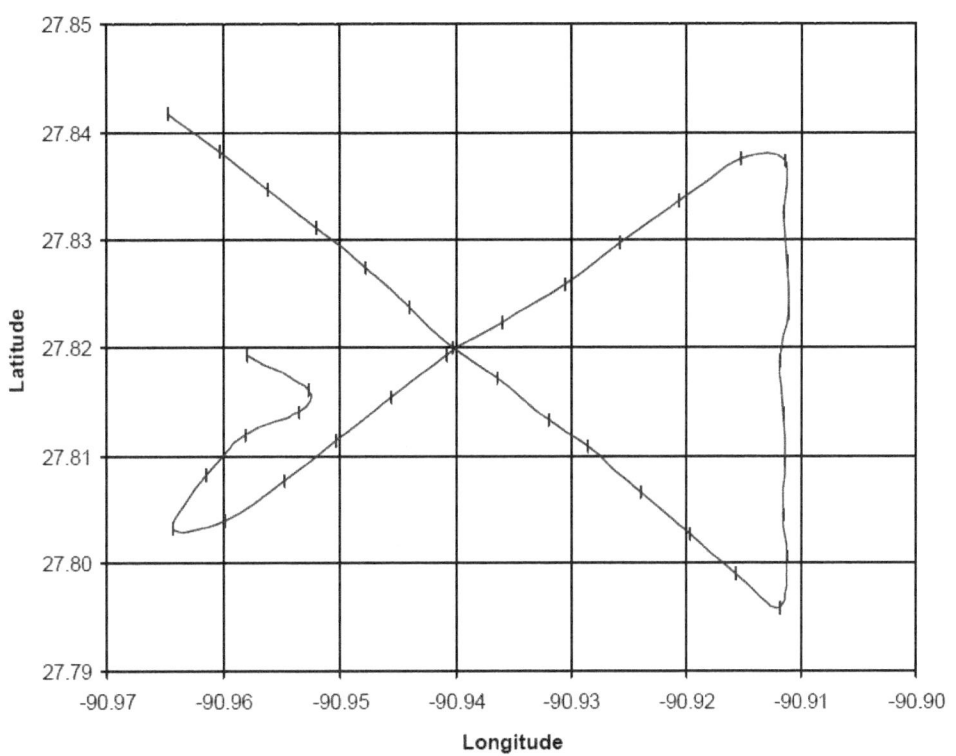

CMI/MMS Cruise 2
Garden Banks Blocks 260, 304
Area 4

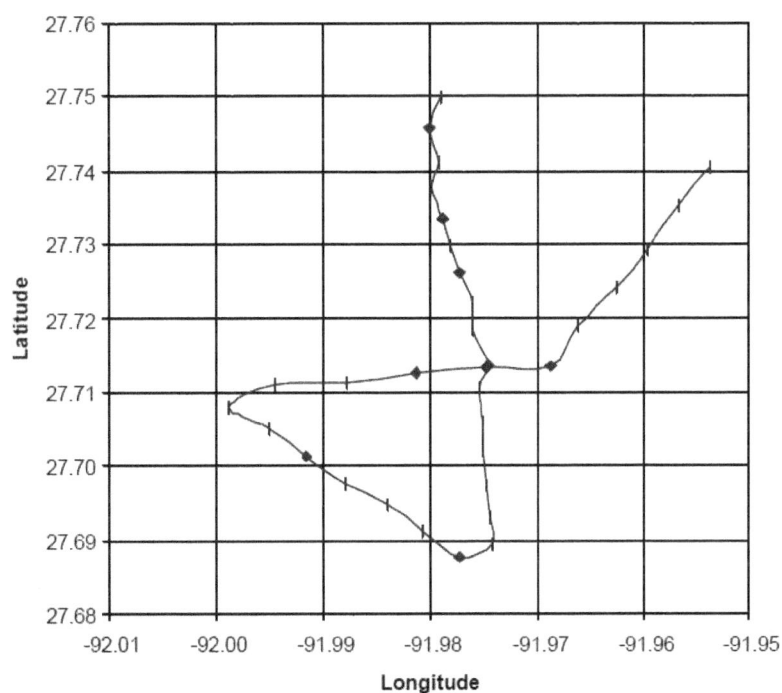

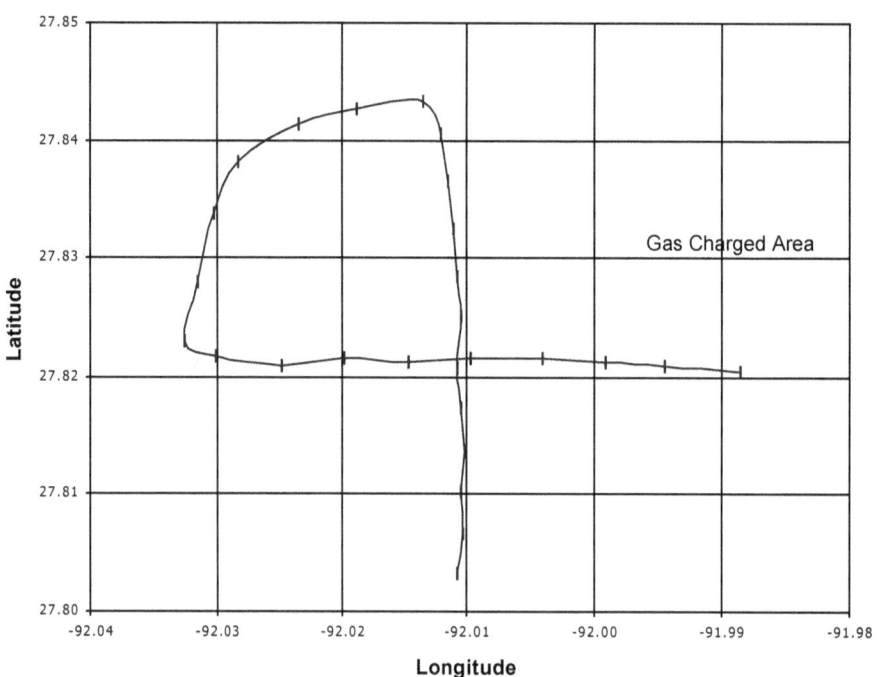

CMI/MMS Cruise 2
Garden Banks Blocks 260, 304
Area 3

Gas Charged Area

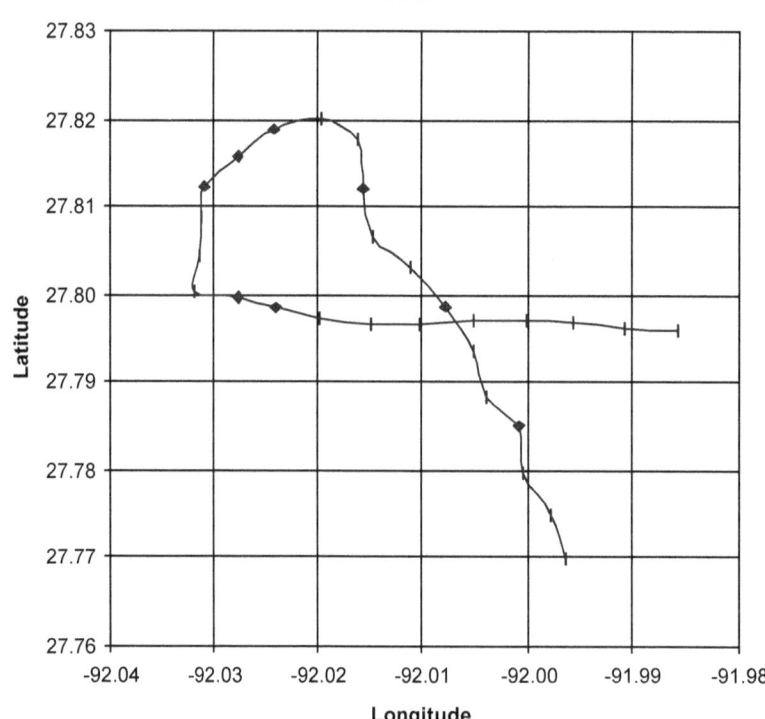

CMI/MMS Cruise 2
Garden Banks Block 260, 304
Area 2

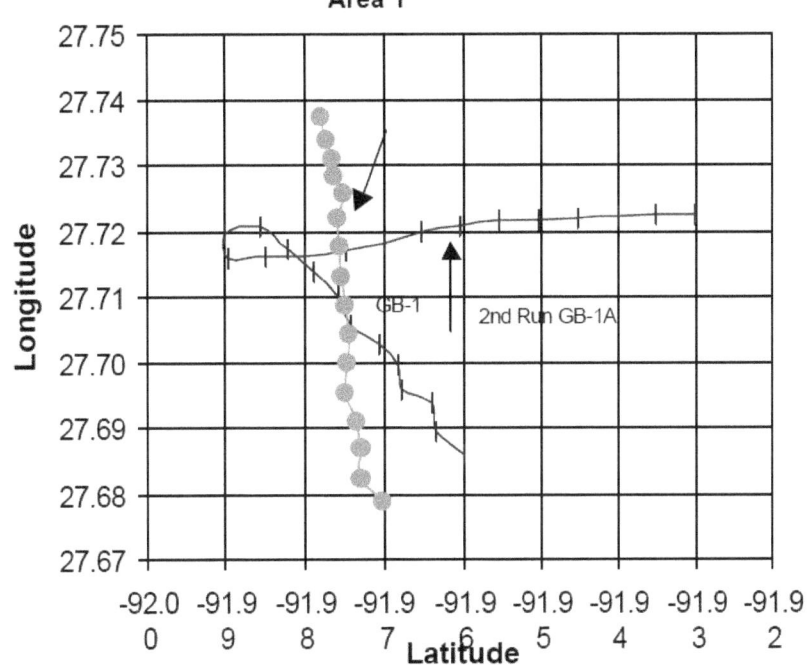

CMI/MMS Cruise 2
Garden Banks Blocks 260, 304
Area 1

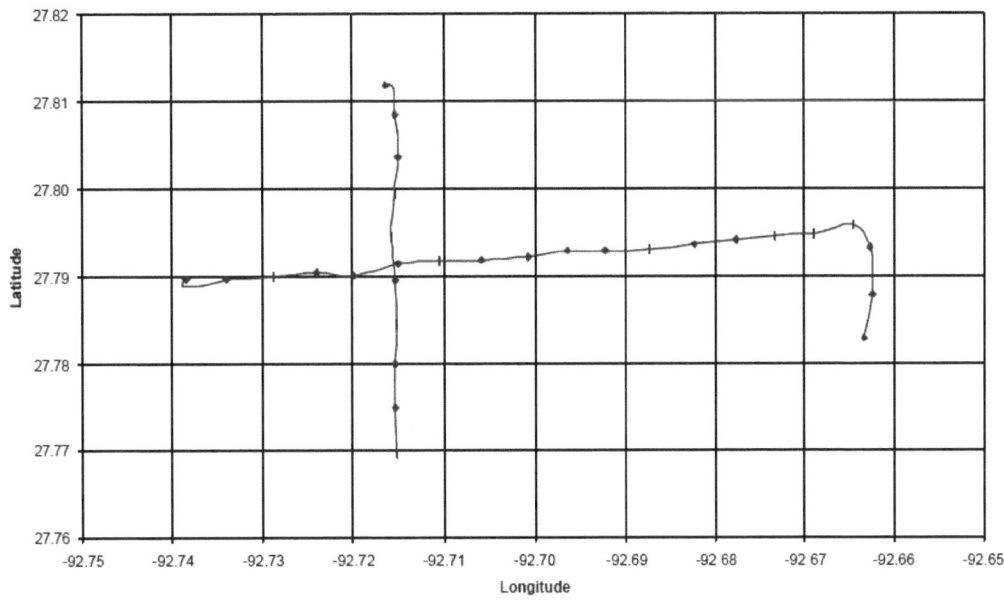

CMI/MMS Cruise 2
Garden Banks Block 201

CMI/MMS Cruise 2

Tuning Run in Garden Banks Blocks 260, 304
Using Air Gun Model GI-90

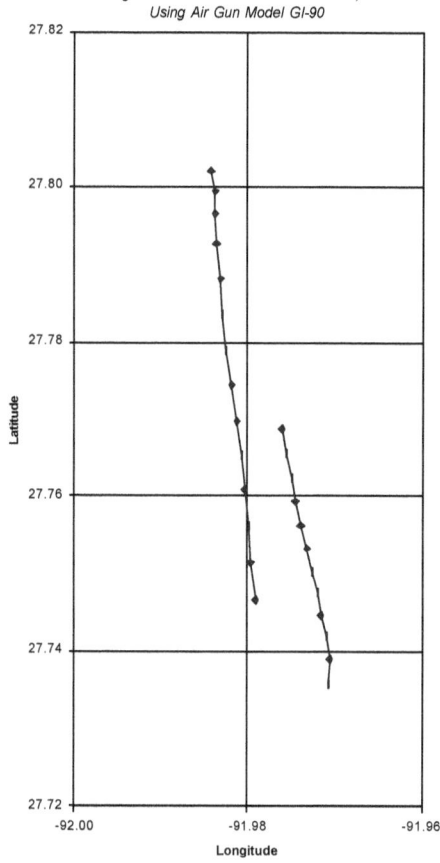

CMI/MMS Cruise 2

All Sites with Recorded Digital Data

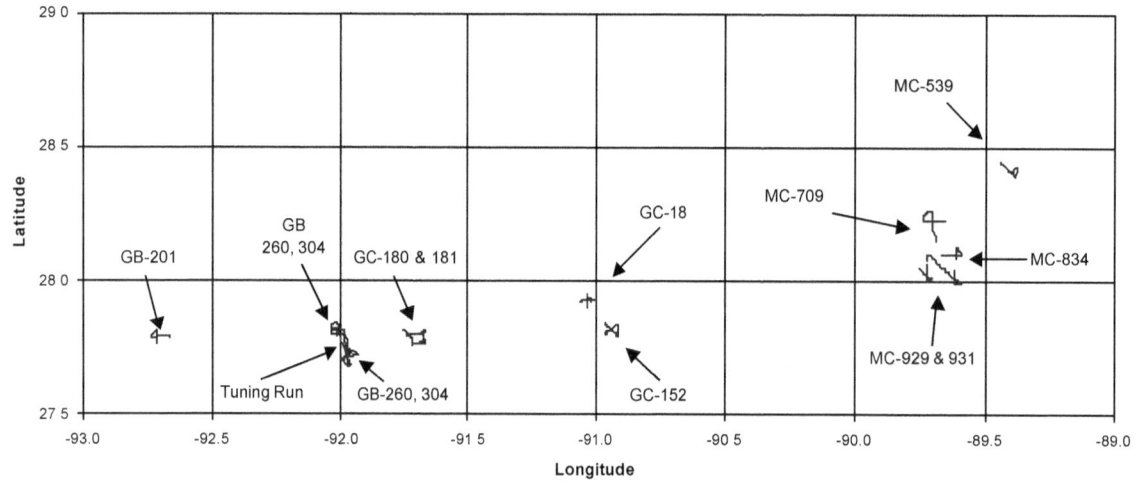

CMI/MMS Cruise 2

All Sites with Recorded Digital Data

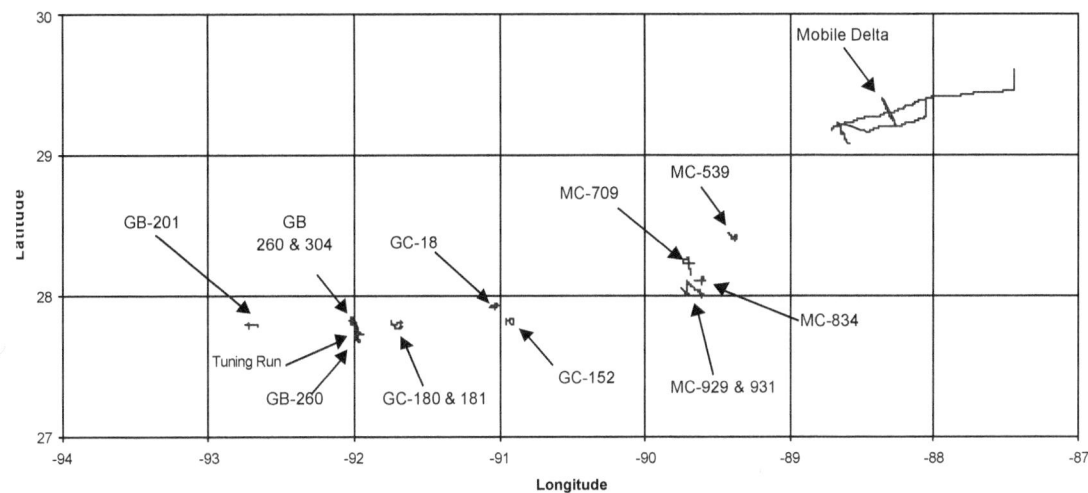

CMI/MMS Cruise 1

Sites Surveyed

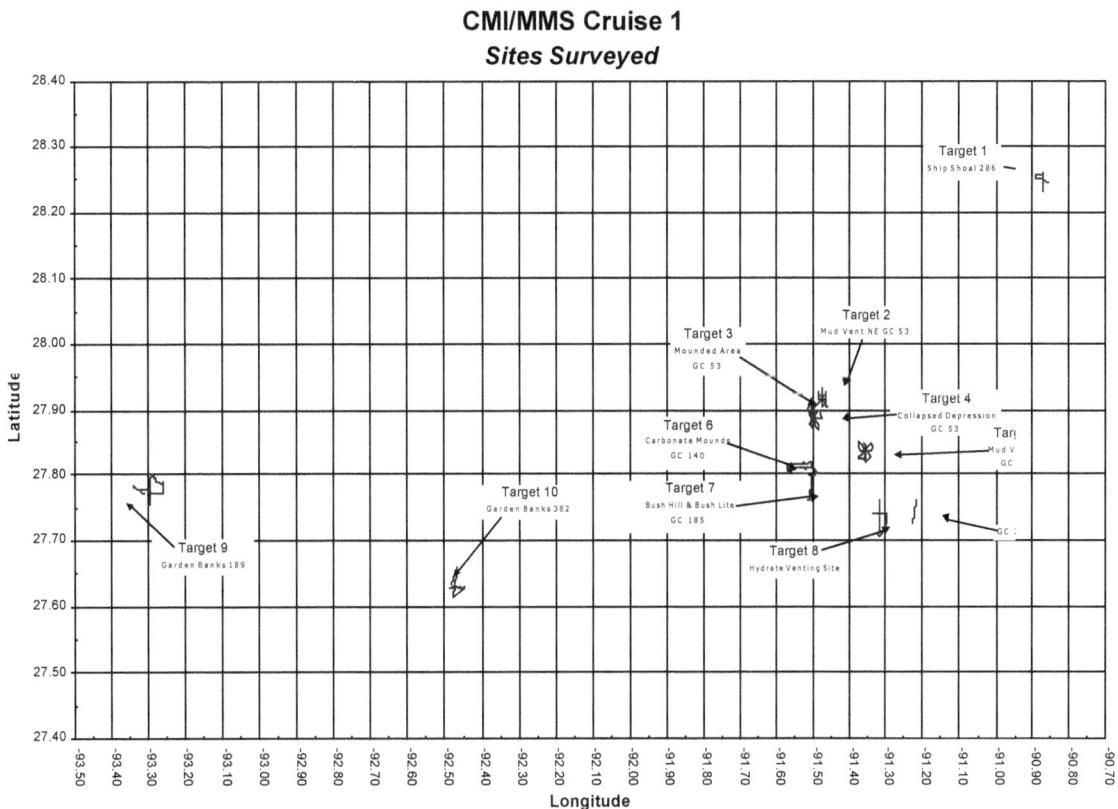

Appendix D: Glossary

acoustic impedance: The product of seismic velocity and density. At normal incidence, the reflection coefficient depends on changes in acoustic impedance.

acoustic transparency: This condition results from a sedimentary medium that has constant acoustic impendance so that no reflectors appear within it. A thick and remolded submarine landslide deposit has these properties.

acoustic turbidity: Chaotic seismic reflections caused by the presence of something (commonly gas) within the sediments that scatters and/or absorbs the acoustic energy. Commonly used as a synonym for acoustic wipeout.

acoustic wipeout: A term used for describing zones on a seismic record that have little or no reflector character. This lack of reflectors is commonly attributed to the presence of bubble phase gas that settles and/or absorbs the acoustic energy.

airgun: An energy source extensively used in marine seismic surveys. Air under high pressure is abruptly released into the water to generate a seismic wave. Air guns are also used in boreholes, and in modified form on the land surface. Arrays of airguns of different sizes are often used in marine surveys so that a broad frequency spectrum will be generated.

ALVIN: a manned submersible operated by the Woods Hole Oceanographic Institute (Massachusetts, USA). This vehicle has been used for most of the deep ocean surveys during which major scientific discoveries, such as hydrothermal vents, black and white smokers and the associated ecosystems, have been discovered.

amplitude: The maximum deviation of a wave from the average value. Commonly used to describe reflection strength.

amplitude anomaly: A local increase or decrease of seismic reflection amplitude. Amplitude anomalies may be caused by geometric focusing, velocity focusing, interference, processing errors, etc. Amplitude analysis is commonly used to locate hydrocarbons at the seafloor as well as in the subsurface.

amplitude mapping: A methodology used primarily in conjunction with 3D-seismic data sets where amplitudes are mapped in plan-view on a given stratigraphic horizon, e.g., amplitude mapping of the seafloor to identify areas of hydrocarbon venting/seepage.

amplitude variation with offset (AVO): The variation in the amplitude of a seismic reflection with source-geophone distance. This technique is used as a hydrocarbon indicator for gas.

anomaly: A deviation from uniformity in physical or acoustic properties. As used in acoustic surveys, this term may apply to unusual shapes or reflection characteristics of targets on side-scan sonar records or features on seismic profiles.

anoxia: A state of having no free oxygen in the system, e.g. in anxoic sediments.

apparent polarity: A convention that relates a peak or trough of a seismic reflection to the sign of the reflection coefficient, assuming the reflecting interface is an isolated one.

assemblage density: The count per unit area of all fauna in a particular assemblage of organisms.

authigenic carbonates: Carbonates that have formed or been generated in place. As applied to hydrocarbon seep/vent-related carbonates, these are carbonate minerals (ususally Mg-calcite, aragonite, or dolomite) that have formed as a by-product of microbial utilization of hydrocarbons (both crude oil and gas) and are therefore C^3-depleted.

autonomous underwater vehicle (AUV): a non-tethered self-propelled vehicle used for collecting data on the sea floor, shall subsurface, and water column. These vehicles are currently replacing deep-tow technologies for high resolution acoustic data collection used for geohazards assessment.

backscatter: the scattering of radiant energy into the hemisphere bounded by a plane normal to the direction of the incident radiation and lying on the same side as the incident ray; the opposite of a *forward scatter*. Atmospheric back scatter depletes 6 to 9 percent of the incident solar energy before it reaches the Earth's surface. In radar usage, backscatter generally refers to the microwave radiation scattered back toward the antenna.

bacteria mats: As applied to hydrocarbon seep/vent areas, these are filamentous accumulations of the large bacterium *Beggiatoa* sp. that live at the sediment-water interface in areas where hydrocarbonds have permeated the near-surface sediments.

bandwidth: the range of frequencies over which a given devise is designed to operate within certain limits

barite: A white, yellow, or colorless orthorhombic mineral: $BaSO$. Strontium and calcium are often present. Barite occurs in tabular crystals, in granular form, or in compact masses resembling marble, and it has a specific gravity of 4.5. It is used in paint, drilling mud, and as a filler for paper and textiles, and is the principal ore of barium. Cores and chimneys of barite form on the Gulf of Mexico slope as a product of the flux of barium-rich fluids to the modern seafloor.

bedded: [ore dep]: Formed, arranged, or deposited in layers or beds, or made up of or occurring in the form of *beds;* especially said of a layered sedimentary rock, deposit, or formation. The term has also been applied to nonsedimentary material that exhibits depositional layering, such as the "bedded deposits" of volcanic tuff alternating with lava in the mantle of a stratovolcano.

Beggiatoa: The generic name for a large (to 0.2 mm in diameter and several cm in length) white or pigmented filamentous bacterium that commonly forms mats on the seafloor over areas of hydrocarbon seepage. *Beggiatoa* is an H_2S oxidizing bacteria in the sulfur cycle of marine sediments.

bioherm: Mound-like buildups that contain the remains of a limited variety of calcareous organisms that are not frame-builders like the corals in a coral reef. Bioherms have no latitudinal restrictions like true coral reefs.

benthic assemblage: A multi-species group of organisms found in a restricted location on the ocean bottom, with no assumptions being made about the cause of the grouping or functional interactions. Incorrectly as a synonym of community.

benthic community: A multi-species group of organisms found in a restricted location on the ocean bottom. It is assumed that the group has been caused to exists due to a common set of factors, and the organisms in the community interact in ways that regulate the community. Discovery of the causal factors and the interactions is often the main purpose of community research. Incorrectly used as a synonym of assemblage.

biogenic gas: gas produced by the biological degradation of organic matter within shallowly buried sediments. The principal biogenic hydrocarbons are methane, ethane and propane.

biogenic veneer: As used in reference to seep/vent-related geology, a biogenc veneer is a non-chemo-synthetic biologic community that now covers a once active seep/vent-related feature, such as a hard substrate community covering an outcrop of C^{13}-depleted authigenic carbonate.

blow-out: In the context of deep marine settings, a low-out is a general term used to describe sauver-, cup-, or trough-shaped depressions in the seafloor usually related to the winnowing effects of gas and/or fluid expulsion. This class of features can be small, less that 1 meter in diameter, to features tens of meters in diameter. Pockmarks, gas craters, and other terms have been used to describe these features.

boomer: A type of high resolution seismic profiler that produces a very clean out-going pulse that can achieve penetration in most marine sediments of a few 10s of meters with a bed resolution of <1 m. The boomer acoustic source consists of capaitors that are charged to high voltage and then discharged through a transducer in the water (charged plates sealed with a rubber diaphram).

bottom simulating reflector (BSR): high amplitude reflection event on a seismic profile that may cut across normal stratigraphy. This relector originates from the high acoustic impedance at the phase boundary between gas hydrates and free gas at the base of the hydrate stability zone.

box corer: a type of corer that retrieves relatively undisturbed and quantitative sediment samples in a block rather than in a cylinder.

bright spot: A local increase of amplitude on a seismic section. A hydrocarbon accumulation is one way a bright spot can be generated.

bubble effect: The result of bubble oscillations (bubble noise) on a seismic record. This effect commonly manifests itself as a repeat of the first arrivals and all other source-generated events.

bubble train (plume): A verticaly iriented set of reflectors in the water column portion of a high resolution seismic record resulting from venting of gas from the seafloor to the water column.

calcareous: containing a substantial proportion of calcium carbonate minerals, especially calcite (or aragonite).

cap rock: A dense limestone, anhydrite, and gypsum rock that occurs above a salt diapir that results from a variety of processes that include leaching of soluble minerals in the salt body and re-precipitation, as well as precipitation of C^{13}-depleted carbonates as a by-product of bacterial degradation of hydrocarbons.

chaotic facies: as applied to slope geology, a chaotic facies has not organized internal reflection horizons or seismic profiles and is generally the product of sediment remolding associated with mass transport processes.

character: When applied to seismic data, character refers to the recognizable aspect of a seismic event, usually a frequency or phasing effect. When used in conjunction with side-scan sonar data, character refers to the recognizable aspect of a target or field of targets.

chemoherm: a mound-shaped feature composed primarily of Ca-Mg carbonates that have been precipitated at a hydrocarbon seep site as a product of microbial utilization of hydrocarbons

chemosynthesis: The synthesis of carbohydrates via fixation of inorganic carbon (carboxylation) through a pathway which derives energy from a chemical oxidation rather than light.

chemosynthetic: An organism with carries out chemosynthesis; limited to prokaryotes. The term is also applied to host metazoans which harbor symbiotic chemosynthetic organisms.

chemotrophic: An prokaryote organism which derives it primary nutrition from chemosynthesis, or a metazoan host deriving primary nutrition from chemosynthetic symbiotes.

chimney: a columnar mass of rock formed by precipitation of minerals as miner-charged fluids are expelled at the seafloor. Various carbonates and barite comprise most chimneys on the northern Gulf of Mexico slope.

chirp: a signal of continuously varying frequency (a linear change of frequency with time). Broad frequency subbottom profilers (chirp sonars utilize this technology.

chirp sonar: a very high resolution subbottom profiling instrument that utilizes a broad frequency range

clathrate: a hydrate of natural gas (biogenic, thermogenic or mixed origin). A frozen gas and water mixture found in permafrost regions and in continental margins below water depths of about 500 m.

coherent reflectors: These are responses on a seismic record that are produced when seismic reflections line up to represent a seismic reflector.

collapse depression: A seabed depression morphologically similar to a pockmark, but formed by the collapse of the sediment as a result of dewatering or degassing, and not by the erosion of the sediment material.

columnar disturbance: A vertical column seen on seismic reflection profiles in which the seismic layering is absent. Migrating fluids are considered to be responsible for them.

cone: [geomorph] A depositional form shaped like a cone, having relatively steep slopes and a pointed top. In context of expulsion topography, the term cone is generally applied to mud volcanoes of various sizes.

diagenesis: The chemical, physical and biological changes, modifications or transformations undergone by a sediment after its initial deposition, during and after its lithification.

diapir: A geological structure formed when a sediment of low density which is overlain by a denser sediment flows upwards, bending or piercing the overlying layers. These are most commonly produced by salt (halite) to produce "salt domes," but diapirs may also be produced by mud. In the Gulf of Mexico, both types occur.

dome: A positive relief feature characterized by bowing-upwayrd of the seafloor as seen in cross section on seismic records. This process can result from gas pressure or diapiric intrusions of salt or shale.

drape deposit: hemipelagic sediments that drape topography of the Gulf of Mexico continental slope. This unit varies in thickness between about 1-5 m and is eroded from many positive relief features of the upper slope. Sediments of these drape deposits are highly calcarious because of a high perentage of pelagic foraminifera tests. Drape deposits appear "transparent" or only weakly stratified on high resolution seismic profiles largely because they are highly bioturbated.

echo-sounder: a high frequency seismic instrument for determining water depth and profile configuration of the water bottom

e e l: an array of hydrophones enclosed in tub to be towed behind a vessel when acquiring high resolution seismic profiles

effective permeability: this property of fluids depends on their relative saturations; that is, the presence of one fluid effectively changes the permeability to another fluid

electric log: the general term used for all electical borehole logs (e.g, SP, normal, induction, microsensitivity logs)

endobenthos: Animals dwelling within the bottom. Contrasted with epibenthos, animals on the surface of the bottom.

epicenter: the location of the earth's surface below which the first motion is an earthquake occurs

eustacy: this term refers to worldwide sea level change. In stratigraphy the interplay of eustatic changes with sediment supply, isostatic subsidence, and thermal uplift produces sequence boundaries

eustatic cycle: the time interval over which a global rise and fall of sea level occurs

exosystem: Lying outside a restricted system.

exploration: in the Gulf of Mexico, this term is generally applied to the search for commercial deposits of hydrocarbons

exploration geophysics: the application of geophysics and the equipment associated with this discipline for exploration pruposes

exploration 3D: a widely spaced form of 3D-seismic acquisition that relies on interpolation to give the data sampling required for migration

exploratory well: a well drilled to an objective not previously known to be productive

facies: the aspect, appearance, and characteristic of a rock or sedimentary unit, usually reflecting its origin

facies change: a lateral or vertical variation in lithologic or paleontologic characteristics of contemporaneous sedimentary deposits

facies map: a general term for a map sowing the gross areas variation in observable attributes of different sedimentary units within a given stratigraphic interval

fairway: the region within which effort is concentrated (e.g. drilling fairway) or a trend of hydrocarbon accumulations

fathometer: a device for measuring water depth by timing sonic reflections from the water bottom

fault: a fracture or a zone of fractures along which there has been displacement of the sides relative to one another parallel to the fracture. Faults are known to be avenues for fluid and gas migration.

fault scarp: (a) a steep slope formed directly by movement along a fault and representing the exposed surface of the fault before modification by erosion

filter: the part of a seismic data acquisition system that discriminates against some of the information entering it, usually frequency

fish: with regard to side-scan sonar, the fish is the sensor towed in the water

fluidization: the mixing process sediment and fluid so that there is a breakdown of sediment structure so that grains become entrained in moving pore fluids

fluid mud: highly fluidized sediment of clay and silt sized particles

fluid expulsion: in the context of the Gulf of Mexico continental slope geology, fluid expulsion refers to the release of formation fluids and fluidized sediment at the seafloor. This release usually occurs in association with faults.

fluid expulsion feature: in the process of fluid expulsion, features such as mud vents, mud volcanoes, mud flows, brine pools, etc., are created. These are fluid expulsion features.

foraminifera: any single-celled organizm belonging to the subclass Sarcodina, order Foraminifera. They are characterized by calcareous tests that contribute greatly to the calcareous nature of hemipelagic deposits (drape deposits as the are commonly called in the deep Gulf)

formation: a lithologic unit with characteristics that allow it to be distinguished from other lithologic units

frequency: the repetition rate of a periodic wave form measured in cycles per second or hertz

gain: an increase (or change) in signal amplitude (or power) from one point in a circuit to another. Gas in used to compensate for variations in input signal strength (i.e., in seismic or side-scan sonar data acquisition)

gas chimney: on seismic profiles, this is a vertical region of poor-to-no-data assocaited with bubble phase gas in the sediments. Often there

gas front: the upper or lateral limit of gas-charged sediments as indicated by acoustic blanking and/or acoustic turbidity on shallow seismic profiles.

gas hydrates (or clathrates): crystalline, ice-like compounds composed of water and natural gas (most commonly methane but other gases can also be involved)

gas seep: an area on the seafloor where gas is escaping at a slow rate compared to a gas vent. Gas seeps and vents can be sometimes be identified on acoustic profiler data s vertical or near-vertical "plumes" in the water column. Acoustic wipe-out zones in the subsurface usually accompany gas seeps.

gas vent: a location on the seafloor where gas is released at a vigorous rate as opposed to a gas seep which exhibits a relatively slow rate of gas release

geophone: an instrument used transform seismic energy into an electrical voltage

geophysical exploration: making and interpreting physical property measurements of the earth to determine subsurface conditions, usually for economic purposes such as the serach for hydrocarbons

geophysics: the study of the earth by quantitative physical methods, especially seismic refelection and refraction as well as other methods such as gravity and magnetics

geopressure: subsurface formation pressure that differs significantly from normal hydrostatic pressure

geothermal gradient: the rate of change of temperature with depth in the earth (average is about 30°C/km at shallow depths)

geothermal heat flow: heat flow from the earth's interior per unit area per unit time (the product of thermal conductivity and thermal gradient)

giant gas mounds: large mud mound seabed features, up to 2km across and 100m high, reported from the Gulf of Mexico that some have attributed to diapiric processes. Another interpretation is that these large features are actually the product of accretionary processes are actually mud volcanoes

global positioning system (GPS): a U.S. government system of 24 satellites that permit determination of latitude, longitude and elevation by trilateration

grab sampler: an ocean-bottom sampler that commonly operates by enclosing material from the seafloor between two jaws upon contact with the bottom.

graben: as used in a marine setting, a down-dropped block of seafloor bounded by normal faults, often long and narrow. Grabens are tensional features that commonly form over vertically migrating salt masses

gravity corer: a device for obtaining a solid sediment core of seafloor solely under its own weight

ground truth: as applied to marine studies, ground truth refers to data acquired directly from the seafloor (cores, direct measurements, etc.) as compared to indirect data like acoustic data (seismic, side-scan sonar, echo sounder, etc.). Ground truth data are commonly used to "calibrate" remotely sensed data sets to real seafloor conditions

hard target: a highly reflective target as identified on side-scan sonar imagery or other type of sonar images

hemipelagic: sediments formed by the slow accumulation on the sea floor of biogenic and fine terrigenous particles deposited through the water column to the seabed

hertz (Hz): the unit of frequency that is equivalent to cycles per second (cps)

hiatus: an interval of time that is not represented the sedimentary record (sediments were removed by erosion or never deposited)

high resolution seismic: seismic frequencies above the normal, lower frequency exploration range. Frequency ranges for this type of seismic is commonly 500 Hz or higher and it is used to improve resolution of the near-sruface sediment column for geohazards assessments, engineering purposes, and basic science. Penetration is highly dependent on power of the system used and sediment type, but most systems used in the Gulf of Mexico will penetrate well over 100 m in clay-rich soils

horst: a structural term used in marine settings to identify a block of seafloor raised, by normal faulting, above neighboring blocks of seafloor

hot spot: in conjunction with hydrocarbon exploration and seep research, a region on a seismic profile or 30-amplitude slice that records an abnormal amplitude that probably represents hydrocarbons

hydrocarbon indicator: a response in seismic data (bright spot, dim spot, phase change, flat spot, shadow zone, or velocity sag) that may indicate the presence of hydrocarbons

hydrocarbon seep: the slow seepage of hydrocarbons, a diverse group of chemical compounds of hydrogen and baron that may occur in gas or liquid (crude oil) form, to the seafloor

hydrocarbon vent: as opposed to a hydrocarbon seep, a hydrocarbon vent displays a very vigorous delivery of hydrocarbons (as well as formation fluid and sometimes fine-grained sediment) to the seafloor and into the water column

hydrothermal: pertaining to hot water; especially with respect to the process whereby water is circulated through hot rocks and during which it may leach metals from the rocks. These metals are precipitated when the water is returned to the seawater and cooled.

hypoxia: A state of having little free oxygen.

impedance: the product of density and velocity as applied to accoustics

incident angle: the angle which a raypath makes with a perpendicilar to an interface

interslope basin: as applied to the Gulf of Mexico, this term refers to small sedimentary basins formed on the continental slope by rapid sedimentation is a setting of salt deformation

isobath: a line of equal water depth

isopod: Any malacostracan crustacean belonging to the order Isopoda, characterized by absence of a carapace, serial segmentation, a single podia type (iso-poda), and dorsoventral flattening.

Johnson Sea-Link: a manned submersible with a maximum diving depth of 1000 m, owned by Harbor Branch Oceanographic Institution of Fort Pierce, Florida

Jurassic salt: a regional salt unit, the Louzanne Salt, deposited in the early stages of formation of the Gulf of Mexico. the Jurassic is a period of geologic time ranging between 190-136 million years ago.

kerogen: organix matter disseminated throughout many sedimentary rocks from which hydrocarbons (cruise oil and gas) are formed

layered: terminology referring to the sedimentary configuration of the seafloor, consisting of a number of horizontal to subhorizontal sedimentary units

liquid limit: the water-content boundary between the semiliquid and the plastic states of a sediment, e.g. a soil. It is one of the *Atterberg limits*.

liquifaction: the abrupt breakdown of grain-to-grain contacts in a sedimetn so that the grains become temporarily suspended in the pore fluid until grain structure is re-established

lithification: the conversion of a newly deposited, unconsolidated sediment into a coherent and solid rock.

lithoherm: a deep-water mound (can be up to several hundred meters long by 50 m high) of limestone, apparently formed by submarine lithification of carbonate mud, sand, and skeletal debris; e.g., in the Florida Straits.

lithologic log: a log illustrating lithology as a function of depth

lithostatic pressure: the pressure produced by the weight of overlying sediment or rock

low velocity layer: a layer whose velocity is lower than units above and below. This term can also be appleid to a surface layer that has a lower velocity signature than deeper units

lowstand system tract: the earlies (lowermost) systems tract within a sequence with a lower boundary defined as a Type-1 sequence boundary where sea level falls below the pre-existing shelf edge. A lowstand systems tract is deposited during a rapid eustatic sea level fall. It can be separated into units by downlap surfaces: lowstand fan, slope fan, and lowstand wedge

lucinids: Bivalve molluscs of the family lucinidae. Common in anoxic and hypoxic muds at all depths and known to be sulfide detoxifying and possibly chemosynthetic.

magnetometer: an instrument for measuring magnetic field strength

marine flooding surface: a surface above which sediments were deposited in appreciably greater water depth than those below

mass movement: a unit movement of a portion of the seabed; specifically *mass wasting* or the gravitative transfer of material down a slope. These processes are especially important in the Gulf of Mexico because they produce potential geohazards.

meiofauna: Organisms passing through a 0.63 micrometer seive; size class between macrofauna and microfauna.

microbial mats: Filamentous mats of the large bacterium *Beggiatoa* sp. that occur on the seafloor in areas of hydrocarbon seepage or venting.

migration (seismic): an inversion operation involving re-arrangement of seismic information elements so that reflections and diffractions are plotted at their true locations

millisecond (ms): a thousandth of a second

mixed assemblage: an assemblage composed of some specimens representing a fossil community, plus others representing one or more transported asssemblages brought into the locality where found

mosaic (side-scan sonar): an assemblage of side-scan swath images whose edges have been matched or overlapped to form a continuous presentation

mud clasts: semilithified or compacted angular-to-rounded fragments of fine-grained sediment (mud) created by mass movement or expulsionof sediment at the seafloor cometimes along with formation fluids, hdrocarbons, and fine-grained sediment

mudflow: a term applied to a mass-movement geomorphic form and process characterized by a gravity-driven flowing mass of fine-grained sediment with a high degree of fluidity. In the context of fluid and gas expulsion at the seafloor, mudflows are highly fluidized fine-grained sediments extruded from a localized vent and transported down-slope under the influence of gravity

mud volcano: a volcano-shaped structure composed of mud that has been forced above the normal surface of the sediment, creating a positive relief feature

multiple (seismic): seismic energy that has been reflected more than once. Multiples may obscure or "overprint" primary reflection information (i.g., stratigraphy)

mussel: Any of the common marine bivalves belonging to the family Mytilidae. Not to be confused with fresh water "mussels", the clam superfamily Unionacea.

natural gas: a highly compressible mixture of hydrocarbons occurring naturally in gaseous form. The most common components are methane (usually over 80%) ethane, propane, isobutane, butane, pentane, and others.

neritic: relating to water depths between low tide and 200 m

nose: a plunging anticline with structural closure in three out of four directions

onlap: successive landward termination of strata at the base of a depositional unit. In seismic terms onlap refers to a reflection termination at the base of a unit where the reflection is flat or dips away from the termination.

outcrop (marine): formations, rocks or structures that appear at the seafloor

overburden (seismic): the sedimentary section above a given reflector

penetration (seismic): the greatest depth from which seismic refletors can be picked with reasonable certainty

permeability: a measure of the ease with which a fluid can pass through the pore spaces of a sediment or rock

petroleum: natural gas, crude oil and related substances, such as asphalt, formed by the thermal cracking of plant and animal remains (kerogens).

phase (seismic): the angle of lag or lead of a sine wave with respect to a reference

phase velocity (seismic): the velocity of any given phase (such as a trough) or a wave of single frequency. It may differ from group velocity because of dispersion.

phytoplankton: planktonic plants (usually microscopic)

pinger: A transponder or device that emits an acoustic signal, ususally used for marking sites or equipment on the seafloor. A type of shallow seismic profiling system producing a high frequency acoustic signal, achieving a penetration of a few tens of metres and very good (<1m) resolution.

piston core: sediment sample obtained by dropping a dart-like corer (a hollow metal tube topped by a heavy weight) into the seabed. As the corer penetrates, sediment is forced into a plastic liner inside the metal barrel. An internal piston moves up the core tube as sediment intrudes. The piston reduces distortion of the sedments both during the coring process and during post-coring handling.

Pleistocene: an epoch of geologic time immediately preceding the Holocene (e.g., 1.8 million years before present)

Pliocene: an epoch of geologic time within the Tertiary period (7-1.8 million years before present)

pockmark: shallow seabed depression typically a few meters to
several tens of meters across and up to a few metres deep; generally formed in soft, fine-grained seabed sediments by the winnowing effects of escaping fluids and gases of fluids into the water column.

pogonophora: A phylum of tube-dwelling marine worms distinguished by a crown of tentacles and the lack of a gut and now generally regarded as chemosynthetic. The status as a phylum separate from the Annelida Is now under debate.

porosity: pore volume per unit gross volume

positioning (marine): determining the location of a ship, data points, samples, etc., using reference beacons whose geodetic locations may not be exactly known or by the Global Positioning System (GPS), which can provide extremely accurate estimates of positions expressed in latitude and longitude

primary reflection (seismic): energy that has been reflected only once and hence is not a multiple

profiler: a high frequency marine seismic refelction system usually involving a low power source. this class of seismic tools is used for geohazards and engineering studies (e.g., 3.5 kHz profiler)

prograding: deposition of sediment that builds progressively into deeper and deeper water

pull-apart structure: an extensional feature usually accomodated by normal faulting. In the Gulf of Mexico pull-apart features are common to sediments over rising salt structures.

push core: a short sediment core taken by forcing a tube into surface sediments. Most push cores have a vlave assembly that allows water to be forced out of the tube as sediment enters. The valve closes, creating a vacuum, as the core tube is extracted from the bottom.

Quaternary: a period of geologic time incorporating the Pleistocene and Holocene epochs

radar: a system in which short electromagnetic waves are transmitted and the energy scattered back by reflecting surfaes is received and imaged to detect objects. In the marine environment radar is ued by ships to detect and range other ships, coasts, and buoys, etc.

Recent: in geologic time, the Holocene epoch, the last 10,000 years to present

reef: a carbonate buildup that contains the remains of both framework and cementing organisms, e.g., a coral reef. In general nautical terms, a reef can be any positive relief feature than can be a hazard to navigation.

reflection configuration (seismic): the pattern is which relfections group

reflection event (seismic): a well-defined reflector or set of reflectors on a seismic record

reflection strength: amplitude of the envelope of a seismic wave

reflector: a contrast in acoustic impendance that gives rise to a seismic reflection

refraction: the change in direction of a seismic ray upon passing into a medium with a different velocity

relief (marine): the difference between the highest and lowest elevation of a feature above or below the surrounding seafloor

reservoir geophysics: the use of geophysical methods to assist in delineating, describing or monitoring a hydrocarbon reservoir

reverse polarity: having polarity opposite to normal convention. Seismic sections are often plotted with both normal and reverse polarity.

rim syncline: a ring of depressed sediments surrounding a salt diapir caused by subsidence following salt withdrawal

ROV (remotely operated vehicle): unmanned submersible (submarine) commonly equipped with video and stills cameras, manipulator arm, etc.; extensively used for the inspection of and maintenance work on offshore structures.

salt diapir (dome): a salt mass that intrudes on the sedimentary column at a high angle

scarp: (a) a line of cliffs produced by faulting or by erosion. The term is an abbreviated form of *escarpment*, and the two terms commonly have the same meaning, although "scarp" is more often applied to cliffs formed by faulting. (b) a relatively straight, cliff like face or slope of considerable linear extent, breaking the general continuity of the land by separating surfaces lying at different levels, as along the margin of a plateau or mesa. A scarp may be of any height. The term should not be used for a slope of highly irregular outline.

scattering: the irregular and diffuse dispersion of energy caused by inhomogeneities in the medium through which the energy is traveling

secondary porosity: additional porosity in a sediment or rock created by subsequent diagenetic (geochemical) changes/solution rugs, porosity caused by a mineralogical change like calcite to dolomite, fractures, etc.)

sedimentary basin: a confined area of thick sediment acumulation as compared to surrounding areas. In the continental slope province of the northern Gulf of Mexico these basins are found by salt withdrawal related to sedimentary loading.

sedimentary facies: a term used by Moore for a stratigraphic *facies* representing any areally restricted part of a designated stratigraphic unit (or of any genetically related body of sedimentary deposits) which exhibits lithologic and paleontologic characters significantly different from those of another part or parts of the same unit. It comprises "one of any two or more different sorts of deposits which are partly or wholly equivalent in age and which occur side by side or in somewhat close neighborhood".

seepage: escape of fluids (gas or liquids) from the seabed (or the land surface). Seabed seepages take the form of macro-seepages where gas bubbles are large enough to be visible to the naked eye, and micro-seepages, where individual bubbles are of microscopic size, or the seeping fluid is in liquid form (e.g. gases and solids dissolved in pore water).

seep lithoherm: a deepwater mound that has been formed by precipitation of dominantly Ca-Mg carbonates as a by-product of microbial utilization of hydrocarbons.

seismic: having to do with elastic waves. Energy may be transmitted thorugh the body of an elastic solid by body waves of two types: P-waves (compressional waves) or S-waves (shear waves).

seismic exploration: the use of seismic techniques to map subsurface geology with the focus on finding economically viable products, particularly hydrocarbons

seismic profiler: geophysical instrument akin to an echo-sounder but emitting an acoustic signal of lower frequency in order to penetrate the seabed. Seismic profiles show the configuration of sediment layers beneath the seabed.

seismic reflection: acoustic signal reflected from a boundary (seismic reflector) between sediments of different physical properties, most particularly density and elasticity. The greater the difference between the sediments, the stronger (darker) the reflection. Coherent seismic reflections make up a seismic reflector.

seismic reflector: a sediment boundary which causes a seismic reflection. Differences in physical properties, most particularly density and elasticity (demonstrated by a difference in seismic velocity), are required for a seismic reflection to occur. These differences are not necessarily represented by a change in lithology or the visual appearance of the sediment.

seismic section: a plot of seismic data long a line

seismic stratigraphy: methods of determining the nature and geologic history of sedimentary rocks and their depositional environment from seismic evidence

seismic (or acoustic) velocity, Vp: the speed of propagation of an acoustic signal (or other pressure wave); dependent upon the physical properties of the medium, most particularly density and elasticity.

sequence analysis: the procedure of picking unconformities and correlative conformaties or seismic sections so as to separate out the packages involved with different time depositional units

sequence stratigraphy: the study of genetically related strata bounded by unconformities or their correlative conformities

sessile: living attached to the sub-strate.

shallow gas: bubble-phase gas within unlithified sediments. Pockets of shallow gas under high pressure present a hazard to drilling.

shear strength: resistance of a sediment (or soil) to failure by shear; normally measured in kPa (kilopascals: 1 kPa = $1kN/m^2$).

side-scan sonar: geophysical instrument designed to acoustically image the surface topography and roughness of the seafloor. this instrument is typically towed behind a ship or smaller boat. It pulses energy in the 100-500 kHz range to produce a swath of data rather than a profile like seismic systems.

sideswipe: evidence or a seismic record of a feature which lies off the side of the seismic profile

slant range (side-scan sonar): a distance measurement that involves both horizontal and vertical components (e.g., distance from the side-scan fish to an object on the bottom)

slump: (a) a landslide characterized by a shearing and rotary movement of a generally independent mass of rock or earth along a curved slip surface (concave upward) and about an axis parallel to the slope from which it descends, and by backward tilting of the mass with respect to that slope so that the slump surface often exhibits a reversed slope facing uphill. (b) the sliding-down of a mass of sediment shortly after its deposition on an underwater slope; especially the downslope flowage of soft, unconsolidated marine sediments, as at the head or along the side of a submarine canyon. (c) the mass of material slipped down during, or produced by, a slump.

slump deposits: a depositional unit caused by flope failure (slumping)

smokers (black and white): hydrothermal vents at ocean spreading centers from which high temperature mineralized water (black smokers) and lower temperature water believed to contain abundant bacteria (white smokers) is exhaled. In both cases chimneys of precipitated minerals may form on the seabed around the vent.

sniffer: a geochemical survey tool for measuring the concentration of hydrocarbon compounds in seawater. ('Sniffer' is a trademark of the Interocean Corporation.)

sonogram (side-scan sonar): an acoustic image btained by side-scan sonar

sparker: a type of seismic profiling system. Conventional sparkers achieve a penetration of over 100 m, while deep-towed sparkers, which operate at a higher frequency, do not penetrate so far, but achieve better resolution.

species diversity: A statistically and mathematically complex means of expressing the variety of species found in an assemblage or community. The simplest form is species richness, the number of species present. The utility of species diversity is severely limited by sample-size effects and the quality of taxonomic identification.

streamer: a marine cable incorporating pressure hydrophones designed for towing through water while acquiring seismic data

sub-bottom profiler: an instrument that produces a cross-sectional view of the near-surface sediment column. The 3.5 kHz subbottom profiler is commonly used in the Gulf of Mexico for geohazards and engineering studies.

subsurface: n. (a) the zone below the surface, whose geologic features, principally stratigraphic and structural, are interpreted on the basis of drill records and various kinds of geophysical evidence. (b) rock and soil materials lying beneath the Earth's surface. —adj. Formed or occurring beneath a surface, especially beneath the Earth's surface.

surficial sediments: sediments exposed at or very near the modern seafloor

systems tract: a subdivision within a sequence: lowstand or shelf-margin, transgressive, and highstand. System tracts are characterized by geometry and facies associations

target (side-scan sonar): an object that creates a well-defined reflectance pattern on a side-scan sonogram

thermocline: a discontinuity in water temperature and density in the ocean. Many thermoclines may be encountered as one descends from the surface to depth in the ocean.

thermogenic (or petrogenic) gas: petroleum gas produced by the thermal cracking of organic material within deeply buried sedimentary rocks.

three-dimensional (3D) seismic: seismic data collected over an area with the objective of determining spatial relationships in three dimensions, as opposed to determining components along separated data acquisition lines. Three-dimensional (3D) seismic data collection is structured on a grid so that data are uniformly distributed overn an area.

timing lines (seismic): marks at precise intervals of time such as used on seismic profiles

tube worms: A general term for tube-dwelling worms of the phylum Vestimentifera. These worms are chemotrophic and have affinities with the annelids and pogonophorans which challenge the validity of a separate phylum. Many types of worms are tube-dwelling, and the term is easily misleading.

turbidity current: a bottom-flowing current resulting from a fluid that has higher density because it contains suspended sediment

unit pockmarks: small (<5 m diameter), shallow pockmarks.

vent: site of escape of seeping fluids; most particularly used in describing the source of hydrothermal fluids, for example at ocean spreading centers.

vent communities: faunal and micro-faunal communities found at vents, particularly the hydrothermal vents of, for example, ocean spreading centers.

vented gas column: a stream of gas bubble above the seafloor (in the water column) that is the product of expulsion of gas from the subsurface

vesycomiyids: Clam-like bivalves of the family Vesycomyidae. These are known to be chemotrophic.

water gun: a seismic source that propels a slug of water into the water mass, producing an explosive effect

wavelet: a seismic pulse usually consisting of only a few cycles

wipe-out zone: a region on a seismic record without internal reflections, commonly representing grassy sediments or zones of thoroughly remolded sediments

The Department of the Interior Mission

As the Nation's principal conservation agency, the Department of the Interior has responsibility for most of our nationally owned public lands and natural resources. This includes fostering sound use of our land and water resources; protecting our fish, wildlife, and biological diversity; preserving the environmental and cultural values of our national parks and historical places; and providing for the enjoyment of life through outdoor recreation. The Department assesses our energy and mineral resources and works to ensure that their development is in the best interests of all our people by encouraging stewardship and citizen participation in their care. The Department also has a major responsibility for American Indian reservation communities and for people who live in island territories under U.S. administration.

The Minerals Management Service Mission

As a bureau of the Department of the Interior, the Minerals Management Service's (MMS) primary responsibilities are to manage the mineral resources located on the Nation's Outer Continental Shelf (OCS), collect revenue from the Federal OCS and onshore Federal and Indian lands, and distribute those revenues.

Moreover, in working to meet its responsibilities, the **Offshore Minerals Management Program** administers the OCS competitive leasing program and oversees the safe and environmentally sound exploration and production of our Nation's offshore natural gas, oil and other mineral resources. The MMS **Minerals Revenue Management** meets its responsibilities by ensuring the efficient, timely and accurate collection and disbursement of revenue from mineral leasing and production due to Indian tribes and allottees, States and the U.S. Treasury.

The MMS strives to fulfill its responsibilities through the general guiding principles of: (1) being responsive to the public's concerns and interests by maintaining a dialogue with all potentially affected parties and (2) carrying out its programs with an emphasis on working to enhance the quality of life for all Americans by lending MMS assistance and expertise to economic development and environmental protection.